THE ALIGNMENT OF POLITICAL GROUPS IN CANADA
1841-1867

CANADIAN STUDIES IN HISTORY AND GOVERNMENT

A series of studies edited by Kenneth McNaught, sponsored by the Social Science Research Council of Canada, and published with financial assistance from the Canada Council.

THE
ALIGNMENT OF
POLITICAL
GROUPS
IN CANADA
1841-1867

By Paul G. Cornell

UNIVERSITY OF WATERLOO

UNIVERSITY OF TORONTO PRESS

Reprinted in paperback 2015
ISBN 978-1-4426-3938-6

For Peggy

PREFACE

HISTORICAL RESEARCH into the political life of the Province of Canada began very soon after Confederation with the appearance of several narrative political histories in both English and French. Thereafter, collections of biographies of public men were popular, and since 1900 more and more insight into the political activity of the Union period has been gained from scholarly monographs, biographies, and articles in learned journals. The last generation of historians was concerned in part with discovering the stages by which Canada achieved responsible government and with seeking the sources of the Confederation movement. At the same time, enquiries into the many fields of Canadian economic history uncovered new, related aspects in the political history of the United Province. At present, further researches are being pursued which throw light on the political traditions that stem from the period of the Union, and on the part played by organized religion in this era. In all this work, the political press, private correspondence, and state papers have provided the principal source materials.

Although the main landmarks in the public life of the United Province have thus been identified, and the contributions of many leaders analysed, it is still possible to ask a number of general questions about the nature of political parties during the period for which no answers have yet been found. Were the parties of the time really organic entities which preserved their identity from one stage of growth to another, or were they simply *ad hoc* groupings of public men, assembled from time to time to deal with the current situation? No enquiry has undertaken so far to deal with the "rank and file" members of the Legislative Assembly, seeking to discover their normal habits of alignment in the day-by-day business of the House. Such terms as "Hincksite Reformer," "Compact Tory," "Rouge," or "Clear Grit" are often used in historical works, and are well understood as expressing political viewpoints; but the reader is left as frequently with the uneasy feeling that there is no real indication of the numerical strength of the groups denominated; nor are the names of more than a few leading members of a group usually known. And without some measurement of the extent of the political forces available to them, any estimate of the stature of outstanding political leaders is incomplete.

It is apparent from their writings that nearly all historians who have dealt seriously with the Union period have at one time or another gone to the *Journals of the Legislative Assembly* in order to define the lines drawn between members as they divided on crucial questions. But any piecemeal sampling of the division lists leaves the enquirer still eager for a broader view over a longer period, in order to confirm the impressions gained from a few periods. It would seem, in fact, that an investigation of the voting in the Assembly through more than two decades of parliamentary sessions would furnish a sufficient perspective to enable fairly definite conclusions to be reached about the party affiliations of the members in general.

As a basis for a study of this kind, the *Journals of the Legislative Assembly of the Province of Canada* have been examined for all sessions from 1841 to 1866 and records made of the votes of each member in all divisions that involved important public questions, the confidence of the House in the executive, or a number of special issues which seemed to illustrate characteristic behaviour on the part of Reformers, Tories, Rouges, French-Canadian Conservatives, and certain regional political groups. In this way some 727 divisions were chosen as useful for study. At first glance it might be anticipated that a purely mechanical technique would be evolved and that the party affiliation of members of the legislature could be read out automatically as the end product of the whole process. But in practice, while many members were found to be consistent in their voting, complex problems presented themselves for interpretation. At certain periods, moreover, the very basis of party alignment was undergoing change, and on these occasions the members took different courses at different times in seeking out their new alignments.

The concentration upon divisions in the Legislative Assembly for the basic source material of this study posed special problems. Whereas most historical source material presents human viewpoints in sentence form, complete with modifying adjectives, adverbs, and clauses, the members of the Legislative Assembly, in dividing, were in fact emitting a whole series of single words, "yes" and "no," quite without modification, and in certain circumstances the research worker could be led far astray. Thus for example, in the sessions of 1841, 1850, 1851, 1854 and to some extent 1866, the executive branch of the government enjoyed the confidence of moderate members, but was opposed by men of more extreme view, both on the "left" wing and on the "right" wing of politics. The voting of the "left" wing radical L. J. Papineau might thus appear identical at some periods with that of the "right" wing tory William Badgley, simply because they shared the one common sentiment of distrusting the moderate administration. The sampling of votes over a longer period provided the means of obviating errors of this sort.

The workings of parliamentary government presented other complications. At every stage of the investigation, there was felt the desire to account for all members of the House—and hence a wish to bring all enumerations of the representatives to the full complement of 84, down to 1854, and 130 in the enlarged Assembly thereafter. But disputed elections, resignations, by-elections, and simple absences constantly required attention, since they affected the basic pattern of the alignment of members at virtually every division. On many occasions, besides, the crucial divisions of the House did not take place on the factual question at issue, but on a procedural motion to adjourn or to divide "this day six months," or on amendments to the original question which in themselves were not very meaningful. Thus the divisions which were recorded in the Journals with names appended had always to be interpreted in the context of parliamentary convention and political manœuvre. It is quite true, therefore, that the technique of investigation used here was not simply mechanical in its operation, but posed many problems requiring subjective interpretation.

Some aspects of association or disassociation within political groups which are known to us through other evidence did not show up in the division lists of the Legislative Assembly. For example, it has been claimed that J. E. Cauchon had a large following of members at his command, at one stage, in furthering the project for a North Shore Railway. Again, the private papers of the protagonists indicate that the "Clear Grit" and other advanced Reformers of the early 1850's were divided among themselves into a number of differing viewpoints. Yet neither of these circumstances appeared clearly in the division lists of the House.

This work, accordingly, does not attempt to supply a new general political history of the Province of Canada. Instead, by a careful and extensive examination of voting records, it seeks to make definite statements about the alignment of members and groups in the Assembly of the United Province; and as a result it has been possible to fill in many of the gaps in knowledge of the political battles of the era. In one sense, the study tries to provide evidence in terms of specific names and reasonably clear numbers to accompany the generally accepted analysis of the political struggles of the period. In another sense, it may serve as a companion reference authority to J. O. Coté, *Political Appointments and Elections in the Province of Canada,* providing the dynamic element of political partisanship which is not presented in that compilation. It is essentially to satisfy this latter purpose as a reference work that much detail is provided and on occasion is repeated in two or more forms.

Although some attention was also given in preparatory examination to the activities of the Legislative Council, it soon appeared that the additional and quite extensive expenditure of time required for a full and consistent investigation of the Council's votes would not be very rewarding, for on no occasion did the actions of the "Upper House" seem to impinge decisively upon the course of political conflict. The Legislative Assembly of the United Province sought to acquire as many attributes of sovereignty as possible, and indeed behaved at all times as if it were a Canadian image of the House of Commons at Westminster. The ultimate goal of the activities of political groups was to "capture" the Legislative Assembly. It does not seem unrealistic then to deal chiefly with this body.

The mid-nineteenth century politician, his press, his biographer, and his historian were all thinking in terms of party. But in the present undertaking, it was felt that institutional studies of political parties in the period, speculations about the franchise, and estimates of the actual popular support of certain political groups lying beyond the qualified electorate were all foreign to purposes of the study and were avoided. All the protagonists that appear herein were autonomous individuals; and though their habits of action led usually to concerted political activity, care has been taken not to marshal them in "files" and "platoons" under some facile label. Again, a purely statistical approach has been avoided, both in the sampling of division lists and in interpreting the behaviour of individual members, for the members of the Legislative Assembly were individual human beings, not automatons responding predictably on all occasions. The opinion of the research worker at times must necessarily obtrude itself, since many members are missing from some of the telling divisions, and on occasion vital questions were decided without a formal division of the House that recorded names. In such cases, where doubt could not be resolved, no opinion has been expressed about a member's outlook; but where prior and subsequent evidence is available as a guide, it has been assumed that members would vote and behave consistently.

The period from 1841 to 1867 has special aspects of its own in Canadian political history since the constitutional arrangements of the union of the two Canadas imposed peculiar problems for parliamentary tacticians. But a number of men entered the first Union parliament in 1841 in the middle of their public careers, and many who sat in the parliaments of the early 1860's went on to sit in the federal House of Commons and participate in the course of Dominion political life. The collective life of the Canadian community flowed through this era without being conscious of its terminals as "opening" and "closing" dates. There is no attempt here, in consequence, to isolate the period of the Union.

CONTENTS

ILLUSTRATIONS AND TABLES

THE ALIGNMENT OF POLITICAL GROUPS IN CANADA
1841-1867

CHAPTER ONE

REDEAL, SHUFFLE, AND REDEAL

THE POLITICAL GROUPS that participated in the first election of United Canada, that of 1841, did not start *de novo,* but conformed in many respects to the well-developed traditions established in both Upper and Lower Canada during the 1820's and 1830's. But there was much that was new in the political situation in the spring of 1841. The proclamation of the Union on February 5 inauguarted a new era in Canadian constitutional life. Existing political groups in both Upper and Lower Canada were forced to re-examine their position in the new enlarged field of a united province and seek new policies and tactics which would be appropriate. Could tories from the two late provinces combine forces? Would the French-Canadian members find themselves isolated in the new House? Where would Upper Canadian reformers fit? Would, in fact, the old political groupings have a meaning in the new parliament, or would they be superseded by new ones? In any case, the old groupings are recognizable in the election campaign of 1841, and the fact of the Act of Union was the major issue over which they fought.

I

The idea of uniting the two Canadian provinces was not new, but its implementation in the year 1841 was a matter of Colonial Office policy, brought about, in the final analysis, by strong executive action on the part of governor-general Poulett Thomson, become Lord Sydenham. It was not the result of political pressure from large groups within Canada. Prior to implementing the union, the governor had consulted the Special Council in Lower Canada, the appointed body that had replaced the Lower Canadian legislature after the outbreak of rebellion, and had manœuvered with the legislature of Upper Canada, the Assembly of which had been elected in 1836 before the troubles erupted; but neither body had been recruited at a time when union was a public issue. The general election in 1841 was thus the first electoral testing of the policy of union and followed its accomplishment.

While the practical effects of the new union appealed to some Canadian groups, it was equally unpalatable to others. The political press of the day tagged candidates as "unionists," that is, supporters of the governor and the policy of union, and "anti-unionists," chiefly the French-Canadian representatives organized by John Neilson. The Tories of the Family Compact were only grudgingly acquiescent in the union, though moderate men in Upper Canada, now Canada West, could see advantages particularly in the transfer of the Upper Canadian debt to the consolidated revenue of the new United Province, the imperial guarantee for new loans to finish major public works, and the elimination of haggling over the revenues of the St. Lawrence seaports. The British party of Lower Canada, now Canada East, by tradition looked to the governor as a benevolent patron, and identified itself with the union project as the solution to the decades-old racial controversy.

While the office of governor in the two Canadas had been strong before 1837, a number of new permanent factors, and several transient ones, emphasized it in 1841 as the centre of governmental life. The question of a civil list was dealt with in the Act of Union and preserved the governor's independent control of the essential offices of government. The new consolidated province doubled the scope of the governor's authority, while Lord Stanley's dispatch of October 16, 1839, gave him complete control of the composition of his Executive Council, and rendered him free of the thraldom of permanent councillors. In addition to these considerations, Sydenham was personally a most able and energetic man, clothed with the special influence of a dynamic leader in an amorphous situation. Moreover, his most bitter potential opponents had been eliminated from public life by the action taken against the leaders of 1837, and his possession of power to implement the Imperial guarantee of an enormous new public loan rendered him and his policy most acceptable to many. Lord Sydenham's influence over the election of 1841 and the course of business in parliament was thus exceptionally strong.

On February 13, 1841, the governor-general had appointed his Executive Council for the United Province. It included three English-speaking Lower Canadians —professional men—and five Upper Canadians representing both tory and reform opinions in the upper section of the province.[1] They were, as a group, fairly able administrators, well able to carry out Sydenham's policy, but several active and important political groups in the province, including the French Canadians and Compact Tories, were not represented. Yet the new Council might have been expected to inspire the confidence of the moderate people of the land, whom Sydenham was wooing.

Few men envisaged a large-scale political strategy for the whole province. The governor held the initiative and his main hopes were pinned upon securing the return of supporters from urban and English-speaking rural areas of Canada East, and the strong support of sympathetic moderates in Canada West. The inclusion of Robert Baldwin in his Council was a coup to secure confidence among more advanced reformers. The Compact Tories were the one extreme group that most probably might oppose him in Canada West. There was little that could be done to win over the solidly French-Canadian ridings, but the distribution of seats was so arranged that their population was not represented proportionately.

In the more localized areas, the French Canadians and the Upper Canadian reformers worked out their own separate strategies. John Neilson and A. N. Morin led a movement against the union and aimed at consolidating French-Canadian conservative opinion. In Upper Canada there was energetic correspondence between Baldwin and his followers in lining up "dependable" men in an effort to return to parliament a homogeneous group of reformers. Francis Hincks' scheme for cementing a working confidence between French Canada and Upper Canadian reformers was based upon one of the few sound general appreciations of the political scene.

II

It becomes clear, as soon as the facts of the 1841 general election are tabulated, that this was no simple contest between neatly regimented "parties." Although the two former sections of Canada were now united in one province, the election was still fought in two arenas corresponding to the old divisions.

In Canada East there was no contest in eighteen ridings, which returned thirteen anti-unionists and five supporters of the governor's policy:

Bellechasse	A. G. Ruel (A.U.)	Montreal (2 seats)	G. Moffatt (U.)
Drummond	R. N. Watts (U.)		B. Holmes (U.)
Gaspé	R. Christie (A.U.)	Nicolet	A. N. Morin (A.U.)
Kamouraska	A. Berthelot (A.U.)	Portneuf	T. C. Aylwin (A.U.)
Leinster	J. M. Raymond (A.U.)	Quebec County	J. Neilson (A.U.)
L'Islet	E. P. Taché (A.U.)	Rimouski	M. Borne (A.U.)
Lotbinière	Dr. J. B. J. Noel (A.U.)	Sherbrooke County	J. Moore (U.)
Megantic	D. Daly (U.)	St. Hyacinthe	Dr. T. Boutillier (A.U.)
Montmorency	F. A. Quesnel (A.U.)	Verchères	H. Desriviers (A.U.)

In eleven further ridings, there was clearly a contest between an anti-unionist and a unionist, and in six of these the governor's unionist candidate was returned:

Beauharnois	J. W. Dunscomb (U.), J. DeWitt (A.U.)
Chambly	J. Yule (U.), L. M. Viger (A.U.)
Champlain	Dr. R. J. Kimber (A.U.), Sheriff Ogden (U.)
Huntingdon	A. Cuvillier (A.U.), Walker (U.)
Montreal County	A. M. Delisle (U.), J. Leslie (A.U.)
Richelieu	D. B. Viger (A.U.), Edmund Peel (U.)
Rouville	M. A. DeSalaberry (U.), T. Franchère (A.U.)
Saguenay	E. Parent (A.U.), John Nairne (U.)
St. Maurice	J. E. Turcotte (A.U.). B. C. A. Gugy (U.)
Terrebonne	Dr. M. McCulloch (U.), L. H. Lafontaine (A.U.)
Vaudreuil	J. Simpson (U.), A. Jobin (A.U.)

Three-sided contests in Three Rivers and Yamaska included in each case a unionist and an anti-unionist, and although the viewpoint of the unsuccessful candidates in Bonaventure and Ottawa County are not known, it is likely that these contests were in the same pattern:

Bonaventure	J. R. Hamilton (A.U.), McDonald (?)
Ottawa County	C. D. Day (U.), Thos. McGoey (?)
Three Rivers	C. R. Ogden (U.), Alex. T. Hart (?), J. E. Turcotte (A.U.)
Yamaska	J. G. Barthe (A.U.), J. Wurtele (U.), Ignace Gill (?)

In Berthier and four of the "English-speaking" ridings, the opposing candidates appear to have had substantially the same views about the Act of Union and the governor's policy:

Berthier	D. M. Armstrong (A.U.), W. Berczy (A.U.)
Missisquoi	R. Jones (U.), S. H. Moore (U.)
Sherbrooke Town	E. Hale (U.), B. C. A. Gugy (U.)
Stanstead	M. Child (U.), Dr. Colby (U.)
Two Mountains	C. Robertson (U.), C. J. Forbes (U.)

The elections in the remaining four ridings of Canada East present special problems of interpretation. In Quebec City, contesting two seats, David Burnet, an independent, and the Honourable Henry Black, a governor's candidate, defeated Louis Massue, an anti-unionist, and James Gibb, the second official candidate. At Dorchester A. Charles Taschereau, an anti-unionist, campaigned against his nephew André Taschereau whose views are not known. The political complexion of Alphonse Wells, the unsuccessful opponent of S. S. Foster, the unionist candidate in Shefford, is also unknown.

In Canada West the general election was contested in thirty-eight of the forty-two ridings, and in most of these it is possible to identify one candidate as reformer, and one as tory. But "reformer" must be recognized as a broad term, including many shades of opinion from Ultra Reformers like Caleb Hopkins, to Moderate Reformers, men of affairs like Isaac Buchanan. And at the other pole of politics, the word "tory" includes Compact Tories in the tradition of George Sherwood and also more moderate men of the ilk of W. H. Draper.

The contests for twenty-six seats lay between two candidates, a reformer and a tory, and in nineteen of these a reformer was returned:

Brockville	G. Sherwood (T.), John Bogert (R.)
Cornwall	S. Y. Chesley (T.), Rolland Macdonald (R.)
Dundas	J. Cook (R.), Peter Shaver (T.)
Durham	J. T. Williams (R.), Geo. S. Boulton (T.)
Grenville	S. Crane (R.), H. D. Jessup (T.)
Halton East	C. Hopkins (R.), Chisholm (T.)
Hamilton	A. N. MacNab (T.), S. B. Harrison (R.)
Hastings	R. Baldwin (R.), E. Murney (T.)
Huron	J. M. Strachan (R.), W. Dunlop (T.)
Kent	J. Woods (T.), S. B. Harrison (R.)
Kingston	A. Manahan (R.), Forsythe (T.)
Lanark	M. Cameron (R.), John A. H. Powell (T.)
Leeds	J. Morris (R.), O. R. Gowan (T.)
Lennox & Addington	J. S. Cartwright (T.), Benjamin Ham (R.)
London	H. H. Killaly (R.), Douglas (T.)
Niagara	E. C. Campbell (T.), H. J. Boulton (R.)
Northumberland South	G. M. Boswell (R.), Meyers (T.)
Oxford	F. Hincks (R.), Caroll (T.)
Prescott	D. McDonald (R.), McIntosh (T.)
Prince Edward	J. P. Roblin (R.), Bockus (T.)
Stormont	A. McLean (T.), D. A. Macdonell (R.)
Toronto (2 seats)	J. H. Dunn (R.), H. Sherwood (T.)
	I. Buchanan (R.), Geo. Monroe (T.)
Wentworth	Dr. Hermanus Smith (R.), John Willson (T.)
York 1 (South)2	J. H. Price (R.), Gamble (T.)
York 3 (East)	J. E. Small (R.), J. S. Macauley (T.)

Four constituencies returned members by acclamation:

Bytown	S. Derbishire (R.)	Russell	W. H. Draper (T.)
Carleton	J. Johnston (T.)	York 4 (North)	R. Baldwin (R.)

In a further five ridings, where three or more candidates were nominated, the same general pattern of reformer opposed to tory is discernible:

Glengarry   J. S. Macdonald (R.), Dr. Jas. Grant (T.), D. McDonell
(of Greenfield)
Lincoln South (Welland)   D. Thorburn (R.), Dr. Lefferty (T.),
G. McMicken (R.)
Middlesex   T. Parke (R.), E. Ermatinger (T.), Clench (?), Burwell (?)
Northumberland North (Peterborough)   J. Gilchrist (R.), Alex. McDonald
(T.), Fred. Ferguson (T.)
(a special return was made to the election writ *not* naming a member from Northumberland North)

York 2 (West)   G. Duggan (T.), Connell J. Baldwin (R.), Wm. Thompson
(?), Ed. Thomson (R.), John Carey (?)

In Halton West (later called Waterloo) and Lincoln North, the contest appears to have lain between two reformers:

Lincoln North   W. H. Merritt (R.), George Rykert (?R.)
Halton West (Waterloo)   J. Durand (R.), Robt. Christie (R.)

In the remaining five ridings, unknown candidates or independent candidates make it impossible to interpret the contest:

Essex	J. Prince (Indep.), Caldwell (?)
Frontenac	Henry Smith (T.), Jas. Mathewson (?)
Haldimand	D. Thompson (R.), Fitch (?), Evans (?)
Norfolk	I. W. Powell (R.), Wilson (?)
Simcoe	Capt. Elmes Steele (?), W. B. Robinson (T.)

On the morrow of the general election of 1841 it might have appeared that twenty-two anti-unionist, nineteen unionist, and the independent Burnet had been returned from Canada East; while the successful candidates of Canada West were twenty-seven reformers, eleven tories, and the two independents, Prince and Steele. (The special return from Northumberland North, and Baldwin's double return from both York 4 and Hastings, account for the remaining two of the eighty-four seats.)

Lord Sydenham is reported[3] to have "formed the judgment" in April that the election had returned twenty-four government members, twenty French members, twenty Moderate Reformers, five Ultra-Reformers, seven Compact party, six doubtful, one special return, and one double return. Because these figures represent an official, contemporary, and very shrewd estimate of the results of the election before divisions in the legislature began to exert a polarizing tendency upon members, and because they do not fit exactly into the foregoing analysis, they deserve comment at this point.

Those members from Canada East who most consistently opposed the union and Sydenham's major policies, were twenty in number as specified by the governor, and all from "French" ridings:

D. M. Armstrong (Berthier)	J. Neilson (Quebec County)
T. C. Aylwin (Portneuf)	J. B. J. Noel (Lotbinière)
J. G. Barthe (Yamaska)	E. Parent (Saguenay)
A. Berthelot (Kamouraska)	F. A. Quesnel (Montmorency)
M. Borne (Rimouski—much absent)	J. M. Raymond (Leinster)
T. Boutillier (St. Hyacinthe)	A. G. Ruel (Bellechasse—much absent)
A. Cuvillier (Huntingdon)	E. P. Taché (L'Islet)
H. Desriviers (Verchères)	A. C. Taschereau (Dorchester)
R. J. Kimber (Champlain—much absent)	J. E. Turcotte (St. Maurice)
A. N. Morin (Nicolet)	D. B. Viger (Richelieu)

The five Ultra-Reformers were most probably: J. Cook (Dundas), J. Durand (Halton West), Caleb Hopkins (Halton East), F. Hincks (Oxford), and J. H. Price (York 1). Six members of tory complexion generally opposed the governor's measures in the Legislative Assembly: J. S. Cartwright (Lennox & Addington), S. Y. Chesley (Cornwall), J. Johnston (Carleton), A. N. MacNab (Hamilton), G. Sherwood (Brockville), and J. Woods (Kent). The seventh Compact Tory is probably G. Duggan (York 2) rather than Henry Smith or A. McLean from along the St. Lawrence, though none of the three were as consistent in opposing Sydenham as the previously named six. There is no basis for determining precisely which six members the governor labelled as "doubtful," but judged by their voting in the Legislative Assembly, Prince (Essex), Steele (Simcoe), Christie (Gaspé), Hamilton (Bonaventure), and Burnet (Quebec) would have been of this number. The two remaining large groups "twenty Moderate Reformers" and "twenty-four government members" can be arrived at by eliminating these smaller groups. Of the twenty-seven "reform" candidates returned from Canada West, five have been identified as "ultras," and Robert Baldwin was in the Executive Council. The remaining reformers number twenty-one (and not twenty as specified by the governor). It is to be noted that Sydenham mentioned first the largest group of twenty-four "government members"—the backbone of his anticipated support in the Legislative Assembly. This grouping included men from both sections of the province and probably was made up of the nineteen unionists from Canada East, and the four moderate tories, Campbell (Niagara), Draper (Russell), A. McLean (Stormont), and Henry Smith (Frontenac). It is not clear who the twenty-fourth government member was. In Canada East, this group represented the "official" class, English seigniors, and some minor office holders: R. N. Watts of Drummond was an "Assistant Governor's Secretary"; A. M. Delisle of Montreal County was "Clerk of the Crown in the Criminal Court of the Montreal District"; J. Simpson of Vaudreuil was "Collector, Coteau du Lac"; D. Daly (Megantic), C. D. Day (Ottawa County), and C. R. Ogden (Three Rivers) were executive councillors; J. Yule (Chambly) was a seignior and flour mill owner, while Jonathan Wurtele, defeated at Yamaska, was the Seignior of St. David; DeSalaberry (Rouville) represented the aristocratic-military, French-Canadian tradition. In Canada West, the group of four represented a middle view, willing to support the governor, yet opposed to reform principles in general.

The true affiliation of members was demonstrated on the ninth day of the first session when on June 23 a series of three divisions,[4] a motion by Neilson and Morin concerning the Act of Union, with amendments by Hincks and Price, and by Cameron and Merritt, tested confidence in the governor's administration. Thirty-three Upper Canadians and twenty Lower Canadians supported the Union while six Upper Canadian Ultra-Reformers and nineteen Lower Canadians opposed it in principle. Six seats were accounted for by the speaker, absences, and vacancies (Table 1). This was a most significant support for the opening of the governor's projects.

The members who supported the Union in principle were not, of course, a homogeneous party, but were made up of various elements. As soon as the Legislative Assembly began to consider the whole range of detailed business, the initial simple alignment of members began to appear in its true complexity.

Perhaps a fair indication of its general composition is disclosed in divisions concerning Sydenham's major items of legislation. Seven divisions[5] have been chosen as a basis for generalization, because all measures did not come to a recorded vote on the principle involved. Four Ultra-Reformers and three Compact Tories from Canada West, and thirteen members of the anti-unionist group from Canada East consistently opposed the governor's policies in these divisions. On the other hand, nine Moderate Reformers, one member with tory leanings, and nine "British Party" members from Canada East consistently supported his policies. Table 2 has attempted to place all members of the House on a basis of their voting on Sydenham's favourite measures.

In general, except for the consistent voting of the Ultra-Reformers and the French-Canadian group, there was a great measure of independence in the behaviour of the other members in the first session. In this session the alignment of political groups that was evident in dealing with the major items of Sydenham's policy was not reflected in divisions concerning the location of the head offices of the Banks of Upper Canada and Montreal, the disputed Bonaventure election, the remuneration of members of the Legislative Assembly, the abolition of feudal tenure, a small debts bill, a mill-dam bill, the use of the Bible as a text in common schools, tavern licences, paper currency, the taxation of imported produce, and the law of usury. It was a testing time in which the governor's influence tended in a direction contrary to many of the traditional relationships between politicians and groups of politicians. But at no time, in this first session, did Sydenham fail to secure a majority for any important division.[6]

III

In the interval between the first and second sessions of the first parliament Lord Sydenham died and his successor, Sir Charles Bagot, arrived to assume the reins of power. The contrasts in their habits of mind and experience have been examined elsewhere, in detail. During the same interval, a number of changes had occurred in the personnel of the Legislative Assembly. In four cases, followers of Lafontaine were replaced by members of the same view:

December 28, 1841, Verchères: J. Leslie vice H. Desriviers
February 15, 1842, Nicolet: L. M. Viger vice A. N. Morin
June 9, 1842, Bellechasse: A. Turgeon vice A. G. Ruel
August 8, 1842, Leinster: J. DeWitt vice J. M. Raymond

while in a further two cases, government members replaced government members:

April 18, 1842, Two Mountains: C. J. Forbes vice C. Robertson
July 7, 1842, Rouville: W. Walker vice M. A. DeSalaberry

On August 17, 1842, in Ottawa County, D. B. Papineau replaced C. D. Day. It was at this time too that Lafontaine found a seat in the Fourth Riding of York, released when Baldwin elected to sit for Hastings. Finally, H. J. Boulton, a firm reformer, was declared elected in Niagara, unseating Campbell, a supporter of Sydenham. The net result of these changes was the gain of two new French-Canadian members and an added supporter for the Ultra-Reformers—a gain of three seats by the opposition and corresponding losses for the governor.

In the same interval, C. D. Day had been dropped from the Executive Council and Henry Sherwood, a Tory, and F. Hincks, an Ultra-Reformer, were sworn in. In forecasting the mood of the second session before its opening, there was great uncertainty as to whether the Executive Council would enjoy the confidence of the House. The changes in personnel in by-elections and by resignation do not in themselves account for this change. Those intimately acquainted with the behaviour of members must have sensed the attraction of some Moderate Reformers into opposition with the Ultra-Reformers, and perhaps a similar uneasiness in the ranks of the Moderate Tories, who had supported Sydenham, inclining them toward the Compact Tory group.

There is no recorded division early in the second session that could identify exactly the position of each member before the admission of Lafontaine and Baldwin to the Council. Table 3 is an attempt to reconstruct the alignment of the Legislative Assembly at this time. The governor's supporters had lost the initiative in ordering the business of the House, however, and Bagot carried out his premeditated reconstruction of the Executive Council. He sought to gain the support of the French-Canadian group of members for his government by inducing Lafontaine to join the Executive Council. But the latter made it a condition of his taking office that Baldwin would also be added to the Council. Thus as the changes in the Council were worked out, Ogden, Draper, and H. Sherwood resigned, and Lafontaine, Baldwin, and subsequently T. C. Aylwin, J. E. Small, and A. N. Morin were brought in. Although R. B. Sullivan, J. H. Dunn, D. Daly, S. B. Harrison, F. Hincks, and H. H. Killaly remained in the Council, the reconstruction had the desired effect of securing the support of a much larger portion of the House.

The views of the Legislative Assembly were quickly tested on September 19, 1842, when Dunscombe (Beauharnois) and Simpson (Vaudreuil), two government supporters from the days of Sydenham, offered a motion expressing entire satisfaction with the new Council and stating that "it was absolutely necessary to invite that large portion of our fellow subjects who are of French origin to share in the government of this country." Unfortunately for our purposes of analysis, this motion did not come to a division unamended, and the ultimate division on a long and flowery amendment by J. Morris and Merritt was passed by the overwhelming majority of 55-5[7] and is almost meaningless in identifying political groups. The amendment sponsored by MacNab and Cartwright, including the terms that "in order to place government on a firm and permanent basis, it is necessary and proper to invite that large portion of our fellow subjects who are of French origin to share in the Government of their country... carrying into effect the wise and just designs of the Imperial Authority," may well serve to identify the main critics of the new Council. These critics were: Cartwright (Lennox & Addington), Chesley (Cornwall), Dunlop (Huron), Johnston (Carleton), MacNab (Hamilton), Henry Smith (Frontenac), Williams (Durham), Woods (Kent), from Canada West, and Burnet (Quebec), Forbes (Two Mountains), Foster (Shefford), Hale (Sherbrooke Town), Moffatt (Montreal City), Moore (Sherbrooke County), and Watts (Drummond); but Duggan, McLean, G. Sherwood, Daly, Jones, McCulloch, Ogden, Walker, and Yule, who might have included themselves in opposition, do not appear on the division rolls.

The work of the second session in 1842 was little in volume and almost without significance. The principal new executive councillors were out of the House throughout the session seeking re-election and the absence of their leadership was felt in the Assembly. It is thus not possible to identify any division in this session as having the value of a vote of confidence in the new Council and the executive policy.

Before the third session met, in late September 1843, there was again a considerable change in government personnel. Sir Charles Bagot had died and Sir Charles Metcalfe took the helm, his policy and attitude proving to be a new alternative to those of his two predecessors. In the by-elections that occurred at this period three new Tory members were returned, two of these gaining seats from Reformers:

March 6, 1843, Toronto: H. Sherwood vice I. Buchanan (Tory gain)
September 14, 1843, Russell: W. Stuart vice W. H. Draper (Tory, no change)
November 4, 1843, Hastings: E. Murney vice R. Baldwin (Tory gain)

In Lower Canada, the trend was in the other direction as two English-speaking Reformers and five French Canadians were returned, in four cases winning seats from former Sydenham supporters:

November 9, 1842, Beauharnois: E. G. Wakefield vice J. W. Dunscombe (Reform gain? Supported

the policies of the Council till late 1843, when he supported Metcalfe and opposed the late coun-
cillors)
November 28, 1842, Saguenay: A. N. Morin vice E. Parent (no change)
January 30, 1843, Rimouski: R. Baldwin vice M. Borne (Reform, no change)
September 18, 1843, Quebec City: J. Chabot vice D. Burnet (French gain)
September 22, 1843, Champlain: H. Judah vice R. J. Kimber (no change)
September 25, 1843, Rouville: T. Franchère vice W. Walker (French gain)
October 23, 1843, Chambley: L. Lacoste vice J. Yule (French gain)

The strength of Tory successes in Canada West was undoubtedly a reaction to the
new policies apparent in the remaking of the Executive Council in 1842. The
trend toward strengthening the French group in the Assembly was not new, but
was to continue steadily through by-elections and general elections till virtually
no "government party," in Sydenham's sense, was left. Two further by-elections
occurred before the climax at the close of the third session and witnessed the
return of two more French members in place of English:

October 26, 1843, Montreal County: A. Jobin vice A. M. Delisle
November 22, 1843, Montreal City: P. Beaubien vice G. Moffatt

In spite of the uneasy undercurrents now known to have been growing between
Metcalfe and his Council, the third session seemed to embark with energy on a
firm legislative and administrative programme. Two divisions on the Secret
Societies Bill and one division on the second reading of the Assessment Bill,[8] taken
together, seem to provide a fairly consistent picture of party affiliation in the midst
of the 1843 session (see Table 4). Although Bagot had passed from the scene, the
Executive Council supported largely by Reformers and French members was in
reality his creation as inaugurated in September 1842. It is possible to appraise
the effects of his new policy upon political alignment by examining divisions in
the House only thirteen months later.

While the Ultra-Reformers and French group had been the principal opponents
of the government down to September 1842, they had since that time formed the
very core of its support. A great body of the Moderate Reformers of Canada West
found no difficulty in supporting the new executive. A first obvious result of
Bagot's adjustments in the Executive Council was to remove the distinction between "ultra" and "moderate" reformers, all of whom could now support official
measures. But these same changes placed a new burden for decision upon the
members from both Canada East and Canada West who stood at the extreme right
of political opinion. In Canada East the English-speaking members, who had for
decades formed a British-Tory-Official party in alliance with the governors, now
found that the more numerous French group had become the largest element in
support of the governor and Council. In one blow they had lost the exclusiveness
of their position and thereafter had to choose a path either in coalition with the
French group or in opposition to the governor and all that his office implied. The
immediate result was a division of the "British" group, some to support the
Lafontaine-Baldwin–dominated Council, and some to cross into the opposition.
The ultimate result, probably inevitable in a predominantly French-Canadian
section, was the extinction of this Lower Canadian Tory group as an effective
unit in the Legislative Assembly. In Canada West the Compact Tories now stood
out in clear opposition to the new Executive Council, and they drew to their
support growing numbers of moderates. These new recruits to the "right" position
were the "charter members" of the Conservative party, as distinguished from

Compact Tories who continued on from the pre-1837 era (see Tables 4 and 5).[9]

Sir Charles Bagot's decision, under the pressure of circumstance, to include the French group in support of his government had amounted to the adopting of quite a different basis of support in the House from that employed by Sydenham. Sydenham had sought support from the considerable middle-of-the-road, moderate opinion in Canada West, and, in the absence of a "middle" in Lower Canada, had patronized the British-Tory-Commercial group. By contrast, as it appeared in 1843, the new bases of governmental power were elements of the left, from both sections of the province, and to these was added as much of the moderate centre as possible. Sydenham had taken advantage of the weakened state of party affiliation whenever possible. By late 1842, however, party discipline was sufficient to compel Bagot to choose between groups.

IV

But almost on the heels of the erection of the "Bagot" system as a working arrangement a loss of confidence and understanding between Metcalfe and his Council thrust all these considerations into the balance again. On November 27, 1843, all the executive councillors except Daly resigned over the principle that the governor had not acted upon their tendered advice, and had not consulted the councillors on all matters of domestic government business. It was a sufficiently confusing issue because the governor-general was not, in himself, a constitutional monarch but a servant of the British government, and the executive councillors represented the majority will of a colonial assembly, not a sovereign parliament. Long and detailed debate, at that time and since, has explored the ramifications of the issues involved. For the purposes of this study the plain fact was that the executive councillors did enjoy the confidence of a majority of the members of the Legislative Assembly, and when they resigned it remained for the governor-general to take what measures he might on a basis of his very large powers and influence, supported by the British government.

On December 1, Price (York 1) and Holmes (Montreal City) offered a motion that an address be presented to the governor voicing the "regret of the House at the retirement of the members of the Provincial Administration," and going on to assure His Excellency that their advocacy of principle "entitles them to the confidence of this House, being in strict accordance with the principles embraced in the Resolutions adopted by this House on the 3rd of September 1741 [sic]" (the Harrison Resolutions). The alignment of members in adopting this resolution on December 2, is given in Table 5. It is likely that the absent members were carefully paired, so that they would not have changed the picture materially. The blocks of Reform and French votes together account for one-half of the full membership of the House. The two independent members, Prince (Essex) and Christie (Gaspé), supported the Executive Council, as did Child (Stanstead) and J. Moore (Sherbrooke County) from the Eastern Townships. The hard core of Tory members, thirteen from Canada West and four from Canada East, who supported the governor stand out clearly. The inclusion in the governor's following of J. Neilson, J. B. J. Noel, and D. B. Viger, who were up to this crisis staunch members of the French group, is the most striking item in the alignment. It was at this time, too that Hamilton (Bonaventure), Simpson (Vaudreuil), and Wakefield (Beauharnois) left their association with the Reform-French group and stood by the governor. It was Metcalfe's hope, later in 1844, that he might build upon these symptoms of larger Lower Canadian support and erect a new official party in that section.

The session continued to sit for a dozen days after the resignation of the Executive Council. Some regular business was dealt with, but attention was focused upon the desirability of addressing the governor further, and a long series of resolutions was passed attacking the civil list and the vestiges of non-parliamentary revenue of the Crown. The Tory members from both sections of the province continued to fight a rearguard action in these ensuing divisions. The session was prorogued on December 9, 1843, with the question of a new Executive Council still unresolved and with the temper of the large majority of the House unfaltering in their support of the late Council.

From the proroguing of parliament until the calling of a general election in the late fall of 1844, all official governmental activity emanated from the governor personally. In the country at large there was much political activity, in theoretical debate and in practical negotiations, to reinforce old party alignments and to build a new alternative system.

The Baldwin Reformers and Lafontaine's supporters in Canada East contended that the late Council had acted strictly in accordance with the rules of responsible government as agreed upon by all parties in the Harrison Resolutions of September 3, 1841. They had quite properly resigned, they claimed, when the governor had declined to act exclusively on their advice in transacting domestic governmental business. The governor was free, they implied, to name any alternative advisers to his Council so long as these alternative councillors had the support of a majority of the members of the Legislative Assembly. But the governor had refused their advice, excluded them from his confidence, and was yet carrying on government by policies and through officers not acceptable to a majority of the Legislative Assembly.

The partisans of the governor took issue with the late councillors but approached the question obliquely. The central core of their argument revolved around an analysis of "royal prerogative" as exercised in the colony by the governor-general. The functioning of governor, Council, and Assembly in the Colony of Canada could not be an exact copy of the conventions governing Queen, "cabinet," and parliament in England, for the colonial status of Canada implied that complete sovereignty in Canadian affairs did not lie to the west of the Atlantic Ocean. A portion of the sovereignty in Canada lay in the British government and was exercised in Canada through the governor-general. The governor-general was less than a viceroy and was the channel for communicating and executing the policy of the British government in Canada. In practice, the late Council had failed to recognize the true nature of the governor's office, and had subjected him to demands impossible to accept. Nor was the fact neglected that the controversy with Metcalfe had arisen over a matter of the distribution of patronage. Beyond the arguments on theory dealing with quite fundamental principles, an emotional issue which concerned the whole British connection and Canada's status was raised, and at times overshadowed other questions in debate.

On the level of party politics, however, the conflict had yet another face. The large design of Hincks, Baldwin, and Lafontaine, first worked out in 1841, had come to realization in the alliance of the French group and Reformers that controlled the administration from September 16, 1842, until November 27, 1843. Great headway had been made in maintaining a disciplined political party organization, quite at variance with the scheme devised by Sydenham for avoiding party consolidation. Now the governor had withdrawn his confidence and the control of patronage from their hands, and might well revert to a policy of building non-partisan administrations based as broadly as possible upon moderates from all corners of the political scene. Beyond the question of "responsible government," the future of the Baldwin-Lafontaine alliance was in the balance. The partisans of the late Council took to feverish activity to hold their majority together.

Meanwhile the governor-general, knowing well that the combination of opponents in the 1843 crisis did not form a homogeneous party and feeling conscientiously that his non-partisan policy was legal, fair, and acceptable to all men not infected by parochial partisanship, strove to solve the crisis by seeking councillors who were themselves moderates, and who might hope to enlist the support of moderate men in general. From the late Council Metcalfe retained the services of Daly (Megantic), a career civil servant from England, who acted as provincial secretary. Daly felt himself to be a non-political figure, but no follower of Lafontaine or Baldwin would join the Council while Daly remained a member, since, as a professional servant, he could not be a "minister" responsible to parliament. Immediately after the close of the 1843 session, D. B. Viger (Richelieu), once a respected "Patriot" leader, and W. H. Draper (Russell), a moderate conservative but without a personal following, were sworn in to the Council. In themselves these men were moderates with a non-partisan flavour, but in the heat of the political situation they did little to draw support away from the Baldwin-Lafontaine group. Viger, far from attracting support, found that his acceptance of office seemed to the great majority of French Canadians an inexplicable apostasy.

The debate continued throughout the spring and summer within the governor's circle, but the passing of time did not provide the hoped-for cooling of partisan enthusiasm; the members of the first parliament had committed themselves too decisively to feel able, even if they had desired, to change their political allegiance.[10] By early September 1844 the governor's negotiations had not decisively broken the circle of the Baldwin-Lafontaine group, but three more executive councillors of reasonably moderate opinions were appointed. William Morris, a legislative councillor and moderate reformer, D. B. Papineau, a brother of Louis Joseph Papineau and a French-Canadian member of some apparent influence, and James Smith, a Montreal lawyer without previous governmental experience, constituted the group. Seemingly there was still some hope of securing an Upper Canadian reformer to be inspector-general.[11] The hope was disappointed.

A further consideration was constantly dwelt upon: was there any chance of resolving the deadlock in a fourth session of the first parliament, or should a new election be called? The prospect of a general election was hazardous, but in the end preferable to the known dangers of the late House. The dissolution of the first parliament was proclaimed on September 23.

The issues at stake in the general election in the late fall of 1844 were those remaining from the third session prorogued in December 1843: the contest was between the principles of the late executive councillors and those of the governor. Egerton Ryerson, a prime mover in the Wesleyan Methodist community in Canada West, had espoused the governor's cause and had written and advised potently in his favour: "loyalty" to the Governor and the British connection were strong factors in his advice.

In September, early in the campaign, the Baldwin and Lafontaine interests held two great dinner meetings, in Toronto on the twenty-third and in Montreal on the twenty-seventh. The leading associates of the movement assembled, spoke, and no doubt cemented their campaign policies. The report of the guests present is virtually a directory of the Reform party leadership in the two sections of the province. At the Toronto meeting:

Hon. H. J. Boulton was in the chair. On his right the guest [Hon. Wm. Young of N.S.], William Notman, Esq., Barrister, Dundas; and Andrew Jeffrey Esq., of Coburg. On his left were Hon. Adam Fergusson of Woodhill, John Wetenhall Esq., Warden of the Gore District, James Smith Esq., of Port Hope and the Hon. R. B. Sullivan. The Hon. Robert Baldwin acted as Croupier . . . E [*sic?*] Perry Esq., of Cobourg, . . . Caleb Hopkins Esq., MPP for East Halton, John Ross, Esq., Barrister, Belleville, . . . J. H. Price, J. C. Morrison, Wm. A. Baldwin, . . . John Shuter Smith, . . . Jas. Leslie, . . . Angus Morrison. . . .12

And concerning the Montreal gathering:

After the opening speech of the Chairman James Leslie, Esq., the meeting was addressed by the Hon. Mr. Lafontaine, Doctor Neilson, Hon. Mr. Morin, L. T. Drummond, Dr. Beaubien, G. E. Cartier, Esq., A. Jobin Esq., J. DeWitt Esq., and J. E. Mills Esq.13

Among the signatures of the meeting's statement were Wolfred Nelson, H. Judah, Ovide LeBlanc, Alexis Laframboise, J. E. Turcotee (*sic*), Norbert Dumas, L. H. Holton, A. Prevost, L. Duverney, F. X. Brazeau, L. Groulx, M. Laframboise, J. A. Berthelot, Leon Doutre, L. S. Gauvreau, and T. Leflamme. It is interesting to see this fellowship of "liberals" who in a few years, in both sections of the province, were to break into antagonistic moderate and radical political groups.

In both sections of the province the general election of 1844 was a political duel between "supporters of the late Council" and "supporters of the governor." From any general scanning of the contests in ridings it is impossible to make a distinction between "high tories" and moderate governor's men. And for once it seems quite realistic to label the opponents of the governor as "reformers" whatever their geographic or racial origin. At the same time, the large number of ridings of Canada East which returned French-Canadian reformers unopposed are signal proof that there was no second political viewpont, generally, throughout rural French Canada. In the following tabulations, the asterisk indicates the sitting member at the close of the first parliament, while "G." and "R." indicate governor's men and reformers.

Bellechasse	A. N. Morin (R.)	Portneuf	L. T. Drummond (R.)
Berthier	D. M. Armstrong* (R.)	Quebec City (2 seats)	T. C. Aylwin (R.)
Bonaventure	J. LeBoutillier (G.)		J. Chabot* (R.)
Chambly	L. Lacoste* (R.)	Rimouski	L. Bertrand (R.)
Dorchester	P. Elzéar Taschereau (R.)	Rouville	T. Franchère* (R.)
Gaspé	R. Christie* (Indep.)	Saguenay	A. N. Morin* (R.)
Kamouraska	A. Berthelot* (R.)	Sherbrooke Town	E. Hale* (G.)
Leinster	J. DeWitt* (R.)	Terrebonne	L. H. Lafontaine (R.)
L'Islet	E. P. Taché* (R.)	Vaudreuil	J. P. Lantier (R.)
Ottawa County	D. B. Papineau* (G.)	Verchères	J. Leslie* (R.)

The contest between the two major political interests is apparent in the following sixteen ridings of Canada East:

Beauharnois	E. Colville (G.), C. DeWitt (R.), Ovide LeBlanc (R.)
Huntingdon	B. H. LeMoine (R.), A. Cuvillier* (G.)
Lotbinière	J. Laurin (R.), J. B. J. Noel* (G.)
Megantic	D. Daly* (G.), Thomas William Lloyd (R.)
Missisquoi	J. Smith (G.), Dr. Leonard Brown (R.)
Montreal County	A. Jobin* (R.), D. B. Viger (G.)
Montreal (2 seats)	G. Moffatt (G.), L. T. Drummond (R.)
	C. C. S. DeBleury (G.), P. Beaubien* (R.)
Quebec County	P. J. O. Chauveau (R.), J. Neilson* (G.)
Richelieu	W. Nelson (R.), D. B. Viger* (G.)
St. Hyacinthe	T. Boutillier* (R.), L. A. Dessaulles (G.)
St. Maurice	F. Desaulniers (R.), J. E. Turcotte* (R.)
Shefford	S. S. Foster* (G.), John E. Mills (R.)
Sherbrooke County	S. Brooks (G.), J. Moore* (R.)
Stanstead	J. McConnell (G.), M. Child* (R.)
Yamaska	L. Rousseau (R.), J. G. Barthe* (G.), M. Fourquin dit Leveille (?G.)

In Champlain: L. Guillet (R.) vs. H. Judah* (R.); in Montmorency: J. Cauchon (R.) vs. F. A. Quesnel* (R.); and in Nicolet: A. P. Methot (R.) vs. Legendre (?) —the contests seemed to lie between men of similar outlook, and probably depended upon personalities and local issues. In the last three ridings of Canada East, lack of information makes interpretation difficult:

Drummond	R. N. Watts* (G.), Christopher Dunkin (Indep.)
Three Rivers	E. Grieve (G?), Moses Hart (?)
Two Mountains	W. H. Scott (G.), Dr. Leonard Dumouchel (?), G. W. Hoyle (?)

In Canada West only five ridings returned members by acclamation: Brockville, G. Sherwood* (G.); Haldimand, D. Thompson* (R.); Huron, W. Dunlop* (G.); Prescott, N. Stewart (G.); Russell, A. Petrie (G.). Thirty-one ridings clearly showed governors partisans aligned against reformers:

Dundas	G. MacDonell (G.), Rose (R.), J. Cook* (R.)
Durham	J. T. Williams* (G.), J. Smith (R.)
Frontenac	H. Smith* (G.), Augustus Thibido (R.), Marks (G.)
Glengarry	J. S. Macdonald* (R.), Dr. Grant (G.)
Grenville	H. D. Jessup (G.), J. Holden (R.), Wells (?)
Halton East	G. Chambers (G.), J. Wetenhall (R.), C. Hopkins* (R.)
Halton West (Waterloo)	J. Webster (G.), J. Durand* (R.)
Hamilton	A. N. MacNab* (G.), Geo. F. Tiffany (R.)
Hastings	E. Murney* (G.), Yager (R.)
Kent	S. B. Harrison (R.), J. Woods* (G.)
Kingston	J. A. Macdonald (G.), A. Manahan (R.)
Lanark	M. Cameron* (R.), Alex. Fraser (G.)
Leeds	O. R. Gowan (G.), William Buell (R.)
Lennox & Addington	B. Seymour (G.), David Roblin (R.)
Lincoln South (Welland)	J. Cummings (G.), G. McMicken (R.)
London	L. Lawrason (G.), John Duggan (R.)
Middlesex	E. Ermatinger (G.), W. Notman (R.), T. Parke* (R.)
Niagara	W. H. Dickson (G.), H. J. Boulton* (R.)
Norfolk	I. W. Powell (R.), Dr. David Dunscombe (G.)
Northumberland North (Peterborough)	A. H. Meyers (G.), Jeffrey (R.)
Northumberland South	G. B. Hall (G.), Col. C. J. Baldwin (R.)
Oxford	R. Riddell (G.), F. Hincks* (R.)
Prince Edward	J. P. Roblin* (R.), D. B. Stevenson (G.)
Stormont	D. A. MacDonell (R.), A. McLean* (G.), Dr. Archibald (?)
Toronto (2 seats)	H. Sherwood (G.), J. H. Dunn* (R.)
	W. H. Boulton (G.)
Wentworth	Hermanus Smith* (R.), Michael Aikman (G.), Williamson (G.)
York 1 (South)	J. H. Price* (R.) W. R. Graham (G.)
York 2 (West)	G. Duggan* (G.), W. H. Blake (R.)
York 3 (East)	J. E. Small* (R.), Geo. Monroe (G.)
York 4 (North)	R. Baldwin (R.), Wm. E. T. Corbett (G.)

In Lincoln North, W. H. Merritt, the sitting member, a reformer, was returned over J. C. Rykert, another reformer. In three further ridings the two opponents were of tory or conservative outlook and might have been expected to support the governor:

Bytown	W. Stewart (G.), G. B. Lyon (indep. moderate)
Carleton	J. Johnston* (G.), Capt. Lyon (G.)
Cornwall	Rolland Macdonald (G.), S. Y. Chesley* (G.)

Finally, the lines drawn in the last two ridings are confused:

Essex	J. Prince* (Indep.), Wingfield (?), Lachlin (?), Elliot (?)
Simcoe	W. B. Robinson (G.), W. Ritchie (?), Armstrong (?), E. Steele* (Indep.)

Although the final alignment of political groups and doubtful members could only be determined by critical divisions in the ensuing session, some trends were immediately visible in the election results. Baldwin and his associates had been decisively defeated in Canada West, while in Canada East Lafontaine's "Liberals" had increased their power. D. B. Viger, who had come out for the governor in late 1843, and his associates Noel, Neilson, Cuvillier, Barthe, Turcotte, and D. B. Papineau had fared very badly, only the last named being returned. There was to be no "French-Canadian" governor's party. Of the Eastern Township and urban seats, where the governor might most expect support, Quebec City was lost, but Montreal, Three Rivers, Sherbrooke Town and County, Megantic, Missisquoi, Shefford, Stanstead, and Drummond were held, or regained from wavering supporters. Beauharnois and Two Mountains were also apparently still under the governor's control. The long-term prognosis for official anti-French parties in Canada East was not good, however, for in the face of officially sponsored opposition the French-Canadian party was making progress. In Canada West the governor had gained some seventeen seats for his support to add to the ten already held at the dissolution of the first parliament. Two of the late executive councillors, J. H. Dunn and F. Hincks, and the veteran reformers H. J. Boulton, J. Cook, J. Durand, and C. Hopkins were defeated.

While the governor's adherents might be jubilant over the victory in Canada West, the result, on balancing the returns from the two sections of the province, was a very closely drawn affair. The matter was not long awaiting exact definition, for the first session of the second parliament met on November 28, 1844, and proceeded to a division in choosing Sir Allan N. MacNab as speaker.[14] Again on December 6 and 9 there were two more major divisions, the first[15] moved by Baldwin and M. Cameron being an amendment to the address in reply to the speech from the throne, and the second,[16] a motion by Baldwin and Price for papers from the members of the late Executive Council concerning the state of the Receiver-General's Department and the Post Office. Taken together, these three divisions serve well as a basis for reconstructing the alignment of the Legislative Assembly early in the second parliament (see Table 6). The governor's Upper Canadian supporters had nearly doubled in number since the last session of the old parliament and now numbered twenty-eight. The French-Canadian group numbered twenty-five. The reformers had shrunk to but a dozen members, while the governor's Lower Canadian supporters had dropped from some seventeen on December 2, 1843, to only thirteen or fourteen.[17] With all members present in the House the governor could expect to have a majority of about three votes (42 to 39) on the basis of these early divisions.[18]

The policies of the governor and his advisers had rewarded him with a new parliament which, barring some major disturbance, might support him in a conservative programme of legislation and administration. A rapid survey of the business of the three sessions of this parliament discloses the transaction of just such a programme. The over-all alignment of members into four groups—Upper Canadian Reformers and Lower Canadian French in opposition, and Tory-Conservatives from Canada West and an almost exclusively Anglo-Saxon group from Canada East in support of the governor—remained recognizable throughout the three sessions of 1844-5, 1846, and 1847. Yet it would be wrong to generalize in terms of strictly disciplined parties at this stage. Almost any division, unless it had the importance of a "confidence" vote, disclosed a varying number of members dividing apart from their usual comrades; but it is not possible either to discover in this tendency the formation of new homogeneous political groups, or to tag these members as independents.

v

It may be stated that responsible government was put plainly into effect in Canada in 1848, and demonstrated beyond dispute in the handling of the Rebellion Losses Bill in 1849. What, then, can be said of the relationship between the executive and the legislative branches of government during the second parliament of the Union that sat before, from 1844 to 1847? Essentially it is evident that the initiative and rallying centre for forming an alternative to the Baldwin-Lafontaine "system" at that time lay in the office of the governor-general. The composition of the new Executive Council in 1844 was hardly the result of an alternative political group, or alliance, thrusting its leaders into power. The arrangements which obtained in 1844-5 were the result of long and patient calculation by Sir Charles Metcalfe and a small number of advisers, identifying individual men who might fulfil the functions of an Executive Council, and bending every effort that lay within the influence of the governor-general's office to secure a favourable outcome in the 1844 general election. While a good measure of public sentiment and a number of capable public men were not in sympathy with the late councillors, the actual initiating of governmental business was organized and directed from the governor's office.

And in the course of governmental activity during the remainder of Metcalfe's term[19] it is not clear that the governor's hand was relaxed from intimate contact with day-to-day problems and their decision. W. H. Draper most nearly fulfilled the role of prime minister and government leader in the Assembly; yet he was more servant and adviser, than authoritative leader of both party and policy. The Executive Council, too, continued to be an assemblage of individuals rather than a coherent expression of major political groups in the House. Two further appointments were made to the Council by Metcalfe: W. B. Robinson, of Compact Tory connections, in late 1844, and William Cayley, a more moderate conservative, in August 1845.

Canadian political life in the years 1841 to 1845, under the Act of Union, had been filled with controversy and muddle. Yet as an experimental period, it had demonstrated some basic tendencies that were to remain valid at least down to Confederation. With his goal in practical measures and in playing down "parochial" political alliances, Sydenham had attempted to canalize the energies of moderate, middle-of-the-road opinion. But his techniques of using official influence and of working against political party traditions proved in need of revision after he had left the scene. And although Sir Charles Bagot's appointment of new executive councillors in 1842 had carefully fallen short of appointing a completely new politically homogeneous "cabinet," the effect of his action was to shape a strong political relationship between the Executive Council and the Legislative Assembly. It is true that his Council was supported by many moderates and at times by men of the "right"; nevertheless, the basis of governmental activity was the group of Lafontaine-Baldwin men in the Council, abetted by their groups of supporters in the Assembly. Then in Metcalfe's régime, the potential strength of party forces controlling the Assembly and influential in the Executive Council began to erode the powers and initiative of the governor-general to an extent that seemed dangerous both to Metcalfe and to the British government. When these tendencies came to a head in late 1843, the Council left from Bagot's day proved to have strong inner unity, and except for Daly, did act together, as their resignation showed.

Up to the end of November 1843, progress in constructing a disciplined political party group in the Assembly had been largely confined to Reformers and French-Canadians. It had seemed necessary to Metcalfe to experiment in redressing the balance by seeking to erect an alternative (party) grouping. The alignment of groups in the first session of the second parliament (1844-5), however slim the ministerial majority, offered proof that some alternative was possible. Sydenham's plan to avoid "parties" had been frustrated, in short; by 1845, public life was essentially conducted in partisan terms. But Metcalfe also had used much of the prestige of his own office to secure the result, and the partisan alternative to the Lafontaine-Baldwin alliance was as yet a very new creation, hardly conscious of the needs of compromise and discipline to make itself effective as a political organization. Still, by 1844, the "right" wing of politics in Canada West was no longer exclusively a continuation of the Compact Tory tradition. It seemed to have gathered to itself some "moderates," new men whose public lives had begun when Compact Toryism was losing its effective meaning. But at this time the source of support from Canada East for a political organization of the "right" so far remained in doubt.

When the strong personality of Metcalfe, the architect of the second parliament's alignment of forces, was withdrawn from Canada in November 1845, the various elements in the political complex were left to find their own equilibrium. Some clue to the course of events might be sought in an analysis of the proceedings of the remaining sessions of the second parliament.

The membership of the House continued to change from time to time, but the effect upon political alignment was not great. Three changes in 1845 constituted gains for the governor's party, while in July 1847 there was a Liberal victory in Dorchester.

January 14, 1845, Saguenay: M. P. S. LaTerrière vice A. N. Morin (double return) (no change)
February 7, 1845, Kent: J. Woods vice S. B. Harrison (Tory gain)
February 13, 1845, London: W. H. Draper vice L. Lawrason (no change)
March 14, 1845, York 3: G. Monroe vice J. E. Small (unseated) (Tory gain)
July 14, 1845, Three Rivers: D. B. Viger vice E. Grieve (no change)
September 15, 1845, Dorchester: J. A. Taschereau vice P. E. Taschereau (Tory gain)
February 28, 1846, Huron: W. Cayley vice W. Dunlop (no change)
June 23, 1846, Carleton: G. Lyon vice J. Johnston (apparently no change)

July 1, 1846, Prince Edward: R. B. Conger vice J. P. Roblin (no change)
August 17, 1846, Cornwall: J. H. Cameron vice R. Macdonald (no change)
May 6, 1847, L'Islet: C. F. Fournier vice E. P. Taché (no change)
June 10, 1847, Missisquoi: W. Badgley vice J. Smith (no change)
July 3, 1847, London: J. Wilson vice W. H. Draper (no change)
July 12, 1847, Dorchester: F. Lemieux vice J. A. Taschereau (Reform gain)

The session of 1846, held under the administration of Lord Cathcart, was not notable for any significant crisis in the Legislative Assembly. However, there were hints, of some slackening in the cohesion of the government ranks, as odd votes were cast now and then with the opposition.[20] By the session of 1847, when Lord Elgin had become governor-general, the tempo of political rivalry had risen, and there were several divisions that seemed clearly to be testing the confidence of the House[21] (see Table 7).

In spite of the hazards of by-elections and other stresses of the era, the government entered the third session with the expectation of a narrow majority of two or three. The most striking changes since 1845 now occurred in the secession of W. H. Scott (Two Mountains) and R. N. Watts (Drummond) to the opposition, although this was partly offset by the ministry gaining the support, at least temporarily, of R. Christie (Gaspé). It is also perhaps a symptom of the weakness in government ranks that three of the executive councillors, J. H. Cameron (Cornwall), W. Cayley (Huron), and W. Badgley (Missisquoi) had been unknown to the House in 1845, and that a fourth, J. A. Macdonald (Kingston), had first entered public life at the 1844 general election. The confidence divisions at the end of the session in July 1847 saw two more government members, Gowan (Leeds) and Monroe (York 3), cross the House, and a third, Ermatinger (Middlesex), divide with the opposition once on the question of the House going into Committee of Supply. These members could have tipped the balance of power against the government had the session continued and a full slate of members attended.

The explanation of this crumbling of the ministerial majority lies in the conflicts and stresses within the groups of members who had been the government's supporters. Sufficient common ground had been found among them in 1844, in opposing the partisans of Lafontaine and Baldwin and in rallying to the support of the governor in his distress; but these links were largely negative. The effort of Draper and his associates to implement any positive policy raised issues of leadership and co-operation that proved to be beyond solution.

The appointments to the Executive Council of Cayley in August 1845 and of J. A. Macdonald and J. H. Cameron in May 1847 might seem to imply attempts to marshal a moderate conservative group in support of the government to leaven the lump of Compact Tories. Yet this generalization must not be pressed, for on Draper's withdrawal from the Executive Council just before the 1847 session, it was Henry Sherwood, of Compact Tory association, who became attorney-general (Canada West) and, presumably, leader of that wing of the Council. The Upper Canadian supporters of the government remained up to and through the elections of 1847 a loose association of moderate independents, small groups of conservative members, and several shades of Tory.

While virtually no progress was made on the government side in inducing representative French Canadians to leave the following of Lafontaine and A. N. Morin,[22] the reshuffling of offices during the years 1845-7 did at least add a few French-Canadian names to the official roster. D. B. Viger resigned in June 1846, and D. B. Papineau in December 1847. F. P. Bruneau, an original member of the Legislative Council of the Union, assumed the duties of receiver-general on December 8, 1847, and served till the resignation of the Executive Council on March 10, 1848. Two other French Canadians in turn filled the post of solicitor-general (Canada East), a non-ministerial appointment in these years. J. A. Taschereau was appointed on August 21, 1845, after the office had been vacant since T. C. Aylwin's resignation in December 1843, and after a second vacancy of over six months, J. E. Turcotte assumed the duties from December 8, 1847, till March 13, 1848. These appointments did constitute definite breaches in the solidarity of French-Canadian ranks.[23]

CHAPTER TWO

OLD RADICALS, NEW ULTRAS

AFTER THE SESSION of 1847 had demonstrated the growing instability of its support in the Legislative Assembly, the government decided upon a dissolution and a new election. A precedent was set when the new governor-general, Lord Elgin, carefully avoided involvement in the contest and refused even by implication to designate the administration's supporters as an official party.

I

In Canada West, the issues involved in the resignation of the Executive Council on November 28, 1843, still remained the principal themes in the contest. Robert Baldwin's supporters opposed "Ministerialists," now often called "Conservatives," in the general alignment of the contest. There is virtually no sign in this election of a "Clear Grit" type of movement, running radical candidates in opposition to Baldwin Reformers. In Canada East, the political climate was of another order. In the predominantly French-Canadian ridings of Lower Canada, there was seldom any question about electing a fellow national. But if the racial issue was tacitly solved and Anglo-Saxon candidates largely eliminated, the basis of contests began to narrow down to the precise viewpoint and persuasion of the French-Canadian candidate. The beginnings of a concerted radical movement are observable in this election, and the newspaper *L'Avenir*, which was to broadcast this new viewpoint and do much to co-ordinate the movement as it grew, began its vivacious and caustic commentary in the summer of 1847. In order to canalize more moderate opinion a movement was launched in Quebec City under the name "l'Association de la Réforme et du Progrès."[1]

It seems clear that, while there was in Canada West a definite threat from the right which imposed a need for solidarity among "Reformers," in Canada East the "British-Official" party threat had virtually disappeared, and tensions between the left and the right of French-Canadian opinion were beginning to be noticeable. It would remain for the sessions of parliament to disclose the extent to which these domestic strains would affect French-Canadian solidarity in the House. In the more predominantly English-speaking ridings of Lower Canada, political rivalry assumed a form very similar to that in Canada West, with "Conservatives" opposed to "Liberals."[2]

In Canada West the general pattern of the contests in the 1847-48 general election was much like that in 1844. In twenty-eight ridings there was a "party battle" between a conservative and a reform candidate. But again it was clear that these generic terms had to be interpreted loosely. In four ridings of the twenty-eight, where more than two candidates offered themselves, the general "two party" alignment did not seem to be altered. (The starred candidates are those who were representing the same riding at the dissolution of the second parliament):

Bytown	J. Scott (R.), John Brown Lewis (C.)
Brockville	G. Sherwood* (C.), W. Buell (R.)
Cornwall	J. H. Cameron* (C.), Dr. R. McDonald (R.)
Dundas	J. P. Crysler (C.), P. Shaver (R.)
Durham	J. Smith (R.), G. Duggan (C.)
Glengarry	J. S. Macdonald* (R.), McMartin (C.)
Grenville	R. Burritt (R.), H. D. Jessup* (C.)
Halton	J. Wetenhall (R.), G. Chambers* (C.)
Hastings	B. Flint (R.), E. Murney* (C.)
Huron	W. Cayley* (C.), John Wellington Gwynne (R.)
Kent	M. Cameron (R.), J. H. Cameron (C.)
Kingston	J. A. Macdonald (C.), K. MacKenzie (R.)
Leeds	W. B. Richards (R.), O. R. Gowan* (C.)
Lennox & Addington	B. Seymour* (C.), Miller (R.)
Lincoln	W. H. Merrit* (R.), J. W. O. Clark (C.)
Middlesex	W. Notman (R.), E. Ermatinger* (C.)
Norfolk	H. J. Boulton (R.), D. Dunscombe (C.)
Northumberland	A. H. Meyers* (C.), W. Weller (R.)
Oxford	F. Hincks (R.), P. Carroll (C.), Campbell (Indep.)
Prince Edward	D. B. Stevenson (C.), R.B. Conger (R.)
Stormont	A. McLean (C.), D. A. Macdonell* (R.)
Waterloo	J. Webster* (C.), A. J. Fergusson (R.)
Welland	D. McFarland (R.), J. Cummings* (C.), Schofield (?)
Wentworth	Hermanus Smith* (R.), M. Aikman (C.), Williamson (C.)
York South	J. H. Price* (R.), J. W. Gamble (C.)
York West	J. C. Morrison (R.), G. Duggan* (C.), Col. E. W. Thompson (?)
York East	W. H. Blake (R.), G. Monroe* (C.)
York North	R. Baldwin* (R.), H. Scobie (C.)

A further six members from Canada West were returned by acclamation:

Essex	J. Prince* (Indep.)		London	J. Wilson* (C.)
Frontenac	Henry Smith* (C.)		Niagara	W. H. Dickson* (C.)
Hamilton	A. N. MacNab* (C.)		Simcoe	W. B. Robinson* (C.)

In the remaining seven ridings of Canada West the alignment of candidates in in terms of "party" was confused. The Toronto *Globe*, for example, on January 12, 1848, referred to T. H. Johnson in the Prescott election as a "loose fish." In the same paper on January 1, there was a letter complaining of Radenhurst's insistence upon running in Lanark, when Bell had been chosen as the reform candidate. G. B. Lyon in Russell, who was later to change his name to Fellows, appeared to pursue an independent conservative course in the subsequent sessions of parliament until his resignation in connection with election corruption in 1860.

Carleton	E. Malloch (C.), J. Robertson (R.), G. Lyon* (C.)
Haldimand	D. Thompson* (R.), Fraser (R.), McKinnon (C.?), Boulton (?)
Lanark	R. Bell (R.), Radenhurst (R.), McMartin (C.)
Peterborough	J. Hall (R.), J. Langton (C.), Birdsell (C.)
Prescott	T. H. Johnson (Indep.), N. Stewart* (C.), D. McDonald (R.)
Russell	G. B. Lyon (later Fellows) (Indep.), A. Petrie* (C.)
Toronto (2 seats)	H. Sherwood* (C.), J. Beaty (C.)
	W. H. Boulton* (C.), D. Bethune (?)

The reformers appeared to gain fifteen seats and lose but two—a victory to rival Metcalfe's in 1844.

In only ten ridings of Canada East was there a "two party" battle between two candidates, and none of these ridings, except Champlain, was a predominantly French-Canadian area:

Beauharnois	J. DeWitt (L.), L. G. Brown (C.)
Champlain	L. Guillet* (L.), J. E. Turcotte (C.)
Megantic	D. Daly* (C.), Robt. Layfield (L.)
Missisquoi	W. Badgley* (C.), Chandler (L.)
Montreal City (2 seats)	L. H. Lafontaine (L.), J. G. MacKenzie (C.)
	B. Holmes (L.), W. Lunn (C.)
Shefford	L. T. Drummond (L.), S. S. Foster* (C.)
Sherbrooke County	S. Brooks* (C.), John Moore (L.)
Stanstead	J. McConnell* (C.), M. Child (L.)
Two Mountains	W. H. Scott* (L.), Wainwright (C.)

In a further six ridings which had unusual contests, either through the presence of independent candidates or the number of contestants, at least five presented a clash between candidates of the political right and the political left:

Bonaventure	W. Cuthbert (C.), J. LeBoutillier* (C.), J. R. Hamilton (C.)
Gaspé	R. Christie* (Indep.), Martel (L.)
Portneuf	A. J. Duchesney (L.), Belleau (L.), Taschereau (C.)
St. Maurice	L. J. Papineau (Indep.), J. E. Turcotte (C.)
Vaudreuil	J. B. Mongenais (L.), J. P. Lantier* (L.), Dr. Valois (L.),
	R. U. Harwood (C.)
Yamaska	M. F. Fourquin dit Leveille (L.), I. Gill (L.), J. W. Wurtelle (C.)

Thus, in only about one-third of the ridings of Canada East was there a "party" contest. A further third of the ridings confirmed their previous choice and returned the sitting member by acclamation. The return of Gugy from Sherbrooke Town alone marked a new member returned by acclamation:

Bellechasse	A. N. Morin* (L.)	Quebec County	P. J. O. Chauveau* (L.)
Dorchester	F. Lemieux* (L.)	Quebec City (2 seats)	T. C. Aylwin* (L.)
Drummond	R. N. Watts* (L.)		J. Chabot* (L.)
Lotbinière	J. Laurin* (L.)	Richelieu	W. Nelson* (L.)
Montmorency	J. Cauchon* (L.)	Sherbrooke Town	B. C. A. Gugy (C.)
Montreal County	A. Jobin* (L.)	Terrebonne	L. H. Lafontaine* (L.)
Ottawa County	J. Egan (C.)	Verchères	J. Leslie* (L.)

And in the remaining twelve ridings, roughly a third of the representation from Canada East, the candidates all represented one shade or another of liberalism and might be expected to support the Baldwin-Lafontaine position in the Legislative Assembly no matter what the outcome of the election. On February 12, 1848, L'Avenir described the five contests in italics below as lying between equally desirable Liberals:

Berthier	D. M. Armstrong* (L.), Von der Velden (L.)
Chambly	P. Beaubien (L.), ...?... (L.)
Huntingdon	T. Sauvageau (L.), J. B. Varin (L.)
Kamouraska	P. C. Marquis (L.), J. C. Chapais (L.), Fraser (?L.)
Leinster	N. Dumas (L.), L. M. Viger (L.)
L'Islet	C. F. Fournier* (L.), Fortier de l'Islet (L.)
Nicolet	T. Fortier (L.), Desilets (L.), Legendre (L.)
Rimouski	J. C. Taché (L.), L. Bertrand* (L.)
Rouville	P. Davignon (L.), R. A. Hubert (L.)
St. Hyacinthe	T. Boutillier* (L.), L. V. Sicotte (L.)
Saguenay	M. P. S. LaTerrière (L.), R. S. M. Bouchette (L.)
Three Rivers (no return)	A. Polette (L.), P. B. Dumoulin (L.)

Unlike the great change in the political complexion of Canada West, the outcome of the voting in Canada East was a "Liberal" gain of perhaps four seats—Beauharnois, Shefford, and the two seats of Montreal City.

The first full confirmation of the new pattern of strength in the House was given on February 25, 1848, when A. N. Morin was elected speaker[3] in preference to MacNab, the government's candidate. On March 3 came two further divisions, one on want of confidence in the administration[4] and the other amending the address in reply to the speech from the throne,[5] that complete the basis for making a sound analysis of the position of members of the Legislative Assembly prior to the resignation of the Daly-Sherwood Council (see Table 8). The Baldwin-Lafontaine coalition then appeared to command fully two-thirds of the seats in the House and a clear majority from both Canada East and Canada West. The government's regular supporters from the lower section now numbered but five, and from Upper Canada had fallen to eighteen. Thus, since the divisions in question were 19 to 54, 54 to 20, and 53 to 22, the existing government could expect to be in a minority of 25 to 56 in a full House.[6] There remained no alternative course but for the Council to resign, which they did on March 10. The governor-general now implemented a complete change in the administration, calling upon Lafontaine to nominate a new slate of executive councillors on the same day.

The session of 1848 lasted only another thirteen days to transact necessary routine business. Since the newly appointed administration was out of the House seeking re-election and had no time to formulate a legislative programme, there were no further incidents in the session having a bearing upon party alignment. The experiment launched by Metcalfe and Draper to construct a Tory-Conservative basis for government had petered out, not only for want of solidarity among Upper Canadian supporters, but also for lack of a Lower Canadian wing. The turn of public opinion in 1847 denied them significant support from Canada West. Not until the fifth parliament, six years later, was a new effort made to form a government from elements on the conservative or "right" wing of politics, and at that time a new solution was found to the problem of securing major support from Canada East.

II

By January 1849, the new reform ministry (see Fig. I) was prepared to meet parliament, and the second session was summoned for the eighteenth of the month. After years of adversity and the repeated collapse of promising hopes through lack of cohesion within the group or the unexpected policies of governors-general, a Liberal-Reform coalition commanding a majority of the representatives of the two sections of the province was entering upon some seventy-eight months in office. Until October 27, 1851, the leadership was to lie with Lafontaine and Baldwin; after that date, with a reorganized council, Hincks and A. N. Morin were to succeed to the direction of policy.

While the 1848 session had seen a pause in which Reform gathered the reins of power, the 1849 session evinced continued unity among the party's rank and file, while there occurred a great burst of new reforming legislation. But by 1850, disunity was already manifest in the straining of a new radical wing of reformers toward fresh and farther goals. In the Hincks-Morin era that followed, the tension between the radical and moderate wings of the reform movement was for a time accommodated; but in 1854 it destroyed the whole Reform system of power.

While the range of business undertaken in the great reforming session of 1849

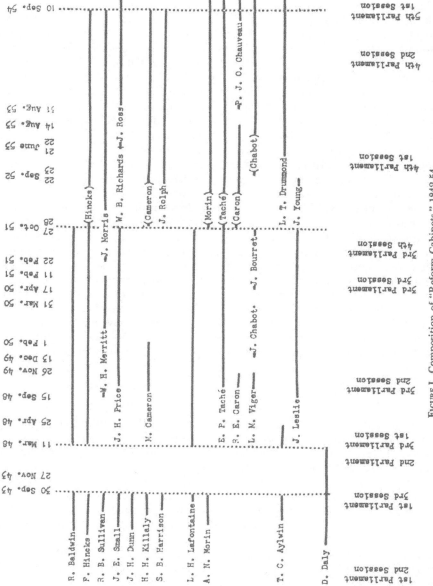

FIGURE I. Composition of "Reform Cabinets," 1842-54.

covered many fields, three subjects proved particularly controversial: the questions remaining from the 1837-8 rebellions in Lower Canada,[7] the provision of new municipal machinery for Canada West,[8] and the arrangement of a new non-sectarian organization for the University of Toronto.[9] They provide a useful insight into the alignment of political groups in this period. In general, the division lists disclose a consistency of view among the members of the Assembly; in fact, a degree of party discipline which had not been approached in any previous period since the Union.

The representation in the Legislative Assembly during the 1849 session (see Table 9) is almost unaltered from that of the previous year, except that by-elections and adjustment in returns had had the effect of increasing the number of the new government's supporters by three. The changes were as follows:

April 7, 1848, Verchères: G. E. Cartier vice J. Leslie (no change)
April 14, 1848, Terrebonne: L. M. Viger vice L. H. Lafontaine (double return) (reform government gain)
April 26, 1848, Three Rivers: A. Polette returned (no return at general election) (government gain)
June 9, 1848, Quebec City: F. X. Méthot vice T. C. Aylwin (no change)
February 8, 1849, Waterloo: A. J. Fergusson vice J. Webster (unseated) (government gain)
April 17, 1849, Sherbrooke County (during second session): A. T. Galt vice S. Brooks (no change—Galt independent)

Since D. Daly had resigned and left the country, Megantic remained vacant until May 1, 1850, when Dunbar Ross was elected. This resulted ultimately in a government gain.

Badgley, and Brooks until his death on March 22, 1849, continued to assert the old Lower Canadian "British Party" viewpoint. Daly had withdrawn from public life, and McConnell wavered in his allegiance, supporting the Reformers' University Bill. L. J. Papineau pursued an individual course, giving only partial support to the Reform administration. Only in the case of the divisions at various stages in the progress of the Rebellion Losses Bill was there a marked deviation from voting on party lines. Two Upper Canadian Reformers, T. H. Johnson (Prescott) and James Smith (Durham), voted against the bill, while four Upper Canadian Reformers, Burritt (Grenville), Lyon (Russell), J. S. Macdonald (Glengarry), and Wetenhall (Halton), absented themselves from the later crucial divisions on this measure. Although J. Wilson (London) was much absent from the division rolls in this session, it seems clear that he crossed the House and aligned himself with the Reformers in late March 1849. Egan, from Ottawa County in Canada East, who was already suspect in his loyalty to the Reform government, was absent from all divisions on the Rebellion Losses Bill.

III

While the Reform government was pursuing its policies with vigour and success in 1849, new radical themes were being advanced in the House which were to have growing importance in the future. L. J. Papineau proposed two amendments during the course of the debate on the speech from the throne. In one, in which he was seconded by La Terrière (Saguenay), he mentioned "the deep and general agitation which has urged the most enlightened nations of Europe to the noblest exertions . . . to alter and reform their vicious governments. . . .[Canadians had] . . . a right to be endowed with political institutions much more free and liberal than the defective constitution imposed on them." His motion concluded with a request for the extension of the elective principle. On division,[10] only the independent members Robert Christie (Gaspé) and John Prince (Essex) joined the mover and seconder in supporting the motion. The second proposition by Papineau was seconded by Robert Christie, and stated that alteration in the scheme of representation was good if carried out on equitable principles, and suggested the principle of representation according to population. On the division which followed,[11] H. J. Boulton (Norfolk) and Joseph Laurin (Lotbinière) joined the movers in support of the motion, though Prince was absent and LaTerrière voted against it. These two propositions, divided upon on January 24, 1849, mark the beginning of a movement in the Legislative Assembly that was eventually to culminate in a Rouge party in Canada East, and in a new more radical reform alliance in the two sections of the province.

Although the Reform government continued to enjoy a strong "working majority" throughout the remaining two sessions of the third parliament on questions that involved the life and continuity of the administration, there was a spate of more and more liberal propositions in 1850 and 1851. At the same time, by-elections in this period returned some new members of a strongly liberal bent and showed a marked tendency to favour the "left." Three government officers secured re-election:

January 11, 1850, Glengarry: J. S. Macdonald re-elected on becoming solicitor-general (U.C.)
January 29, 1850, Quebec City: J. Chabot re-elected on becoming chief commissioner of public works
May 4, 1850, Lincoln: W. H. Merritt re-elected on becoming chief commissioner of public works

But one government appointee failed of re-election: March 18, 1850, Halton: C. Hopkins (advanced reformer) defeated Wetenhall, appointed asst. commissioner of public works.

The other by-elections were:

September 25, 1849, Chambly: L. Lacoste vice P. Beaubien (no change)
December 4, 1849, York East: P. Perry vice W. H. Blake (advanced reformers, but Perry tending to go beyond government policy)
January 21, 1850, London: J. Wilson re-elected (having crossed from conservatives to support of the Reform government, was confirmed in confidence of his constituents)
March 9, 1850, Sherbrooke County: J. S. Sanborn (annexationist) vice A. T. Galt (independent supporter of reform administration)
May 1, 1850, Megantic: D. Ross (liberal, Quebec merchant, etc.) vice D. Daly (symbol of Toryism)
February 1, 1851, Kamouraska: L. Letellier (advanced liberal) vice P. C. Marquis (moderate liberal)
April 21, 1851, Haldimand: W. L. Mackenzie (independent, liberal) vice D. Thompson (administration supporter)

The reappearance of W. L. Mackenzie, Caleb Hopkins, and Peter Perry was to reinforce left-wing reform opinion with something of the spirit of the late 1830's. Luc Letellier was also to follow a distinctly liberal course through the next few decades, while Sanborn, elected on a specifically annexationist platform, was to pursue an erratic course through the next two parliaments, but always on the liberal side of the House.

During the sessions of 1850 and 1851, the agitation of the more advanced wing of reformers might be summarized under four heads: advocacy of independence and annexation to the United States; advocacy of amendment of the Canadian governmental system in accordance with current liberal theories; advocacy of amendment of the legal system in the direction of a "poor man's law"; and criticism of financial policy.

In the opening days of the third session in May 1850, four independent members, L. J. Papineau (St. Maurice), McConnell (Stanstead), Sanborn (Sherbrooke County), and Prince (Essex), were joined by Malcolm Cameron, until a few weeks before a member of the government, and by the two continuing government men, DeWitt (Beauharnois) and Holmes (Montreal City), in supporting the proposition that Canada should become independent.[12] The annexation idea was not, however, a recurring theme for debate and division.

Only a week later H. J. Boulton (Norfolk) and Hopkins (Halton) offered an amendment to the address in reply to the speech from the throne, advocating increase in parliamentary representation based on population, a more extended franchise, and an elected Legislative Council.[13] This resolution had a broader appeal and was supported by W. H. Boulton (Tory, Toronto) and Robert Christie (Independent, Gaspé), as well as by the supporters of the motion on independence. As the sessions of 1850 and 1851 proceeded, these members, joined later by W. L. Mackenzie, continued to advocate various measures for constitutional reform. A motion by H. J. Boulton (Norfolk) and Hopkins (Halton)[14] advocating increased power for county councils in Canada West had as broad a response as any of these propositions, and included in its support (as well as the regular advocates of constitutional reform mentioned above) Bell (Lanark), J. Scott (Bytown), and Johnson (Prescott), who were regular supporters of the Reform administration.

Not all the enthusiasts for constitutional amendment were equally dedicated to reform in the public law and its practice. Typical are four propositions which provide an insight into the views of members, namely, the destruction of the Court of Chancery in Upper Canada,[15] the Goods and Chattels Exemption from Seizure Bill,[16] the Homestead Seizure Prevention Bill,[17] and the Bill to abolish Queen's Council and to let citizens plead.[18] H. J. Boulton (Norfolk), M. Cameron (Kent), Hopkins (Halton), Perry (York East), W. L. Mackenzie (Haldimand), DeWitt (Beauharnois), Holmes (Montreal City), Letellier (Kamouraska), McConnell (Stanstead), and Sanborn (Sherbrooke County) were consistent advocates of these innovations in the law. W. H. Boulton (Toronto), Prince (Essex), and R. Christie (Gaspé), enthusiastic constitutional reformers, did not support this legal reform. But, as in the case of constitutional reform, there was a group of members who cast one or more odd votes on behalf of these measures.[19] It was the attack on the Court of Chancery on June 26, 1851, led by W. L. Mackenzie and Hopkins, with the support of most of these reformers intent upon legal reform—and on this occasion joined by the rank and file of the Upper Canadian Tory-Conservative opposition—that placed Baldwin in a minority in Canada West and led him to give up his leadership of the Reformers.

The attacks on the Reform government's financial policy were led by the same few who led in advocating constitutional amendment and legal reform; but financial criticism is a common device of any opposition at any time, and it followed naturally that nearly all opposition members joined in the battle for economy and stricter control of appropriation. The outstanding critics of government financing were Burritt (Grenville), McFarland (Welland), J. Smith (Durham), D. Thompson (Haldimand), Letellier (Kamouraska), and W. H. Scott (Two Mountains).

It is well known that the Baldwin-Lafontaine administration was progressively subject to internal strains as left-wing supporters pressed insistently for more progressive policies. Ultimately, some twenty-eight government members were involved to a greater or less extent in this advocacy (see Table 10). When the government, for example, sponsored a bill to abolish primogeniture in Upper Canada, there was no dissenting voice from Reform ranks,[20] while the principle of sponsoring the Grand Trunk Railway's construction called forth heated opposition among Reform members.[21] Yet in 1850 the government was sustained handsomely in the official version of the address in reply to the speech from the throne, and in 1851 there was no division on the question. Legislation concerning Clergy Reserves,[22] amending the University Act,[23] salaries of civil servants,[24] amendment of customs duties,[25] representation in the Legislative Assembly,[26] and so on, confirmed the continuing strength of the administration's support. But the small group of H. J. Boulton, M. Cameron, C. Hopkins, P. Perry, and W. L. Mackenzie had emerged in these sessions as a group of Ultra-Reformers, clearly in opposition to the Lafontaine-Baldwin government, and their views attracted the sympathy of a significant number of rank-and-file Reformers.

The fourth session of the third parliament was prorogued at the end of August 1851, and by late October Hincks had succeeded in reconstructing the Executive Council and looked forward to a new general election.

IV

While the Hincks-Morin government, which enjoyed power from late 1851 till September 1854, was in many ways an extension of the Lafontaine-Baldwin régime, the Liberal-Reform alliance in both sections of the province was subject to considerable tension which challenged the ability of the new leaders. As a more detailed discussion of party cohesion follows at a later stage, it is perhaps sufficient here to note the composition of the new ministry. F. Hincks, A. N. Morin, E. P. Taché, and James Morris continued to hold office. Dr. John Rolph and Malcolm Cameron were brought into office as representatives of advanced reform opinion in Canada West, while John Young and L. T. Drummond were sufficiently strong liberals to appeal to advanced opinion in the lower section of the province. W. B. Richards represented the strongly liberal strain of Leeds and Grenville reformers, while R. E. Caron, from the Legislative Council, enjoyed the confidence of moderate French Canadians and had previous experience in office. The new Executive Council (see Fig. I) went far to fulfil the expectation that it would bridge the major dissensions in the reform ranks.

The general election of 1851 made it quite obvious that old political affinities and associations were giving place to a new groping for alignment. Perhaps the most striking feature of the election is the fact that the contests in at least fifteen ridings of Canada East saw a Rouge candidate (R.) or a strong Liberal (SL.) offering himself:

Beauharnois:	O. LeBlanc (L.), Parsons (?), J. DeWitt* (SL.)
Berthier	J. H. Jobin (R.), P. E. Dostaler (SL.)
Champlain	T. Marchildon (SL.), L. Guillet* (L.), J. B. E. Dorion (R.)
Huntingdon	J. B. Varin (L.), Lanctot (R.)
Kamouraska	J. C. Chapais (L.), L. Letellier* (SL.)
Montreal County	M. F. Valois (SL.), A. Jobin* (L.)
Montreal City (2 seats)	J. Young (SL.), L. J. Papineau (R.), Devins (?)
	W. Badgley (C.), LaRocque (?), Gedeon Durocher (?)
Richelieu	A. N. Gouin (L.), Dufresne (R.), Durocher (L.)
Rouville	J. N. Poulin (L.), E. R. DeMorse (?), Seurette (S.L.?)
St. Hyacinthe	L. V. Sicotte (SL.), Chas. Tetû (SL.)

Saguenay	M. P. S. LaTerrière* (SL.), Dr. Harvey (of Malbaie)(?)
Shefford	L. T. Drummond* (L.), J. O'Halloran (SL.)
Sherbrooke County	J. S. Sanborn* (SL.), J. H. Pope (L.)
Vaudreuil	J. B. Mongenais* (L.), Sauvé (R.), R. U. Harwood (C.), DeLesderniers (?)

The same sort of phenomenon appeared in at least fourteen ridings of Canada West, where Ultra-Reformers (U.) of one sort or another stood for election:

Cornwall	R. McDonald (U.), Dr. James Dickson (?C.)
Haldimand	W. L. Mackenzie* (U.), McKinnon (C.)
Halton	J. White (U.), Dr. Hamilton (C.)
Huron	M. Cameron (U.), W. Cayley* (C.)
Kent	G. Brown (U.), A. Rankin (R.), E. Larwill (C.)
Lincoln	W. H. Merritt* (R.), Morse (U.), J. C. Rykert (R.)
Middlesex	C. Willson (C.), W. Notman* (R.), Grover (?U.)
Norfolk	J. Rolph (U.), Hunt (C.)
Waterloo	A. J. Fergusson* (U.), Wright (C.)
Welland	T. C. Street (C.), D. McFarland* (R.), Duncan (U.)
Wentworth	D. Christie (U.), M. Aikman (C.)
York South	J. W. Gamble (C.), J. H. Price* (R.), Gibson (?U.)
York West	G. Wright (C.), J. C. Morrison* (R.), Graham (?U.)
York North	J. Hartman (U.), R. Baldwin* (R.), H. Scobie (C.)

In affixing these names of strong Liberal, Ultra-Reformer and so forth, to various candidates, it must be noted that there is no simple test by which these men could be categorized, nor must it be supposed that all "ultras" or all "strong Liberals" divided together on any or all issues. On the other hand, it is quite clear that the more left-wing elements in both sections of the province, who had first become noticeably active in the Legislative Assembly in 1850, were now clearly active at the polls.

In the case of Canada West, in spite of the rise of Ultra-Reformers, that is, the "Clear Grit" movement, it is still possible to trace the lines of a political duel between a candidate of the left and one of the right in the great majority of ridings. In the fourteen ridings cited above, seven of the contests were complicated by the presence of a "Ministerial Reformer" as well as an Ultra. In a further eighteen ridings, there were contests between "Ministerial Reformers" and Conservatives:

Bytown	D. McLachlin (R.), W. Stewart (C.)
Durham	J. Smith* (R.), Francis Burton (C.)
Frontenac	Henry Smith* (C.), Kenneth McKenzie (R.)
Hamilton	A. N. MacNab* (C.), S. B. Freeman (R.)
Hastings	E. Murney (C.), B. Flint* (R.)
Kingston	J. A. Macdonald* (C.), Counter (R.)
Lanark	J. Shaw (C.), Radenhurst (R.)
Leeds	W. B. Richards* (R.), O. R. Gowan (C.)
Lennox & Addington	B. Seymour* (C.), D. Roblin (R.)
London	T. C. Dixon (C.), J. Wilson* (R.)
Northumberland	A. A. Burnham (C.), John R. Clark (R.)
Oxford	F. Hincks* (R.), Vansittart (C.)
Peterborough	J. Langton (C.), J. Hall* (R.)
Prescott	T. H. Johnson* (R.), Neil Stewart (C.)
Prince Edward	D. B. Stevenson* (C.), R. B. Conger (R.)
Simcoe	W. B. Robinson* (C.), Alfred Wilson (R.)
Stormont	W. Mattice (R.), French (C.)
York East	Amos Wright (R.), Thomson (C.)

Six members were returned by acclamation:

Carleton	E. Malloch* (C.)	Grenville	W. Patrick (R.)
Dundas	J. W. Rose (R.)	Niagara	F. Hincks (R.)
Glengarry	J. S. Macdonald* (R.)	Russell	G. B. Lyon (Fellows) (Indep.)

In the Essex election the Independent, Colonel John Prince, the sitting member, was unsuccessfully opposed by Francis Caron, presumably a reformer or liberal, while in Brockville and Toronto the two Sherwoods were defeated by more moderate conservatives, marking the defeat of old Toryism:

Brockville	G. Crawford (C.), G. Sherwood* (Tory-C.)
Toronto (2 seats)	G. P. Ridout (C.), H. Sherwood* (Tory-C.)
	W. H. Boulton* (C.), O'Neill (R.), Capreol (?)

In Canada East, the general election did not reflect very much of the spirit of division between right and left; only in Megantic and Missisquoi, together with Montreal City which was cited above, did Conservative oppose Liberal:

Megantic	J. G. Clapham (C.), D. Ross* (L.)
Missisquoi	S. Paige (L.), W. Badgley* (C.), Abel L. Taylor (?)

In a further ten ridings, the contests lay between men of moderate position who might have supported the ministry, whether marked as Liberal (L.), Moderate (M.) or, in the case of Hamilton in Bonaventure, Conservative (C.):

Bellechasse	J. Chabot (L.), M. B. Pouliot (?), Fortier (?), Faucher (?)
Bonaventure	D. LeBoutillier (M.), J. R. Hamilton (C.)
Drummond	J. McDougall (M.), Marler (C.)
Leinster	L. M. Viger (L.), Poirrier (L.)
Lotbinière	L. Laurin* (L.), H. G. Joly (L.), Poudrier (?)
Nicolet	T. Fortier* (L.), J. E. Pacaud (?)
Quebec County	P. J. O. Chauveau* (L.), Chas. Panet (L.)
St. Maurice	J. E. Turcotte (L.), Desaulniers (L.), Clouthier (?)
Stanstead	H. B. Terrill (L.), M. Child (L.)
Yamaska	P. B. Dumoulin (L.), Fourquin dit Leveillé (L.), J. G. Barthe (L.)

Seven members were returned by acclamation:

Dorchester	F. Lemieux* (L.)	Three Rivers	A. Polette* (L.)
L'Islet	C. F. Fournier* (L.)	Two Mountains	W. H. Scott* (L.)
Ottawa County	J. Egan* (M.)	Verchères	G. E. Cartier* (L.)
Rimouski	J. C. Taché* (L.)		

In the remaining eight ridings not dealt with above, information is not complete, but the contests do not appear to alter the general scheme of the election:

Chambly	L. Lacoste* (L.), Willett (?)
Gaspé	R. Christie* (Indep.), Kavinagh (?)
Montmorency	J. Cauchon* (L.), Guay (?)
Portneuf	U. J. Tessier (L.), Fiset (?), Angers (?)
Quebec City (2 seats)	G. O. Stuart (Indep. C.), F. X. Methot* (L.)
	H. Dubord (Indep. L.), Maguire (?)
Sherbrooke Town	E. Short (L.), Griffith (?)
Terrebonne	A. N. Morin (L.), A. B. Papineau (?)

An approximate statement of the trend of the election in Canada West would show twenty-seven seats unchanged, and eight Conservative, four Ministerial, and three Ultra-Reform gains; there was virtually no change in the general alignment, only a small erosion of dependable ministerial strength. Previously, the ministerial group in Canada East had been stronger than that in the West, and while it did suffer a set back, the general effect of the election was to leave the relative strength of parties unchanged.

The results of the 1851 general election were eventually tested when the new Legislative Assembly divided upon the choice of J. Sandfield Macdonald as speaker.[27] The division, showing fifty-five in favour of the government's candidate and only twenty-three opposed, seemed to augur well for the success of the reconstructed ministry. But the fact that this parliament did not drag on through three or four sessions may help to account for such unity as does appear upon the surface of its proceedings in the 1852-3 session. As in the late sessions of the previous parliament, there was in the 1852-3 session no doubt of the government's retaining a solid majority for transacting the major items of its programme; but at the same time a little knot of Ultra-Reformers and Independents continued to snipe at various phases of government activity and to advance propositions for constitutional, legal, and financial reform.

On the question of settling Clergy Reserves, for instance, all reformers and most French-Canadian members supported the administration, the Conservatives presenting a nearly solid opposition.[28] The whole idea of railway building called forth quite a different response from the House. It was evident that the question of railway promotion cut across the usual lines of division, and that for many it was not a clear case of being either for or against railways in general terms. Each railway bill called forth its own supporters and its own opponents. The implementing of the plans for the Grand Trunk Railway was a principal policy of the Hincks-Morin ministry, yet the division on the final passing of the bill[29] showed many absences and abstentions. Only six Ministerial Reformers divided in its favour[30] and four of them were ministers, while W. L. Mackenzie and George Brown opposed it. Conservative opinion was also divided, seven favouring the bill, while Gamble (York South), J. A. Macdonald (Kingston), and Malloch (Carleton) opposed it. The bill passed by virtue of support from Canada East, where fourteen members divided in its favour, and only Dubord (Quebec City), Marchildon (Champlain), and J. Young (Montreal) opposed it. A motion some time later by D. Christie (Went-worth) and Amos Wright (York East), both advanced reformers, respecting the Brantford and Malden Railway[31] provided an interesting contrast. Almost all reformers supported the motion, most conservatives opposed it, and the French-Canadian group was split, nine of them voting "nay."

It is when we examine the divisions that followed motions by the Independent Reformers, George Brown and W. L. Mackenzie, that the continuing stresses among the administration's supporters become apparent. On September 7, 1852, Hincks and Chauveau proposed a six months "hoist" for a Bill to Restrict the Acceptance of office, sponsored by W. L. Mackenzie and Hartman (York North). Thirteen members supported Mackenzie and Hartman in the face of Hincks' known view and represent a fair sample of the eager spirits of the House who frequently demonstrated enthusiasm for radical innovation. George Brown (Kent), an Independent, D. Christie (Wentworth), Hartman (York North), White (Halton), and Amos Wright (York East), Ministerial Reformers, and the three Conservatives W. H. Boulton (Toronto), Gamble (York South), and Malloch (Carleton), formed the group from Canada West. From Canada East, Dubord (Quebec City), Jobin (Berthier), L. J. Papineau (Two Mountains), and Valois (Montreal County), all Radicals, and Clapham (Megantic), a Ministerialist, supported the bill and opposed its being shelved. (In Table 11, there is a representation of the alignment of members at this time.)

The degeneration of the ministry's position toward the end of the 1852-3 session is perhaps best illustrated by the reaction on April 6, 1853, to a bill sponsored by Brown and Fergusson (Waterloo) to abolish rectories. From Canada East, Jobin

(Berthier), Marchildon (Champlain), and J. Young (Montreal City) supported the bill; all other Lower Canadians and the Upper Candian Conservatives opposed it. But the ranks of the Reform group, with the exception of Patrick (Grenville) and the ministers Cameron and Richards, voted in its favour.[32]

The short session of this parliament that followed in June of 1854 was to witness such violent reaction to the Hincks government that one would suspect that the radical element in the House had meanwhile been reinforced by new success in by-elections. But, in fact, any changes in membership during the course of the fourth parliament had little effect upon the alignment of groups. The changes were as follows:

July 9, 1852, Two Mountains: L. J. Papineau (Rouge) vice W. H. Scott ("English" Liberal) (gain for Rouge group)
November 23, 1852, Stanstead: T. L. Terrill vice H. B. Terrill (both "English" Liberals) (no change)
March 8, 1853, Sherbrooke Town: A. T. Galt vice E. Short (both "English" Liberals) (no change)
April 28, 1853, Toronto: H. Sherwood vice W. H. Boulton (both "Tories") (no change)
July 13, 1853, Leeds: J. DeLong vice W. B. Richards (both Moderate Reformers) (no change)
September 25, 1853, Niagara: J. C. Morrison vice F. Hincks (both Moderate Reformers) (no change)

A full year intervened between the close of the 1852-3 session and the calling of a new one on June 18, 1854. The activities of the government in the interim had not prevented the growing schisms in the ranks of its suporters, and on the opening of parliament it was met on all sides by excited opposition. The strong current of dissatisfaction in Reform ranks was communicated to the Lower Canadian members and the Conservatives. Only three divisions occurred in the short five-day session, and they pose a problem in logic if they are to be analysed to show the viewpoints of all the participating members. On June 19, 1854, H. Sherwood (Conservative, Toronto), seconded by J. A. Macdonald (Conservative, Kingston), moved an amendment to a resolution in the address in reply to the speech from the throne expressing the "regret we feel that Parliament had not been convened at an earlier date."[33] The motion was lost 29 to 40; but it iden-tified, as being in want of confidence in the ministry, George Brown (Kent), an Independent Reformer, eighteen western conservatives, and from Canada East, Badgley (Montreal), Cauchon (Montmorency), Clapham (Megantic), Jobin (Berthier), LaTerrière (Saguenay), Marchildon (Champlain), Polette (Three Rivers), Sanborn (Sherbrooke County), Stuart (Quebec), and Valois (Montreal County).

On the following day, Hartman (York North), seconded by Sicotte (St. Hya-cinthe), proposed a similar motion[34] indicating that the House "regrets that His Excellency has not been advised to recommend, during the present session, a measure for the secularization of the Clergy Reserves, and also a measure for the abolition of Seigniorial Tenure." This motion was also lost, but those voting "yea" included many Reformers (but few Conservatives), and the Lower Canadian group identified did not correspond exactly to the previous division. This second division disclosed that Brown (Kent), Fergusson (Waterloo), Hartman (York North), R. McDonald (Cornwall), W. L. Mackenzie (Haldimand), Mattice (Stormont), J. W. Rose (Dundas), White (Halton), and Amos Wright (York East) were now of the anti-ministerialist Reform group. Langton (Peterborough) and Lyon (Russell) of the Conservative group also voted for the motion. And in Canada East, Jobin (Berthier), Marchildon (Champlain), Sanborn (Sherbrooke County), Sicotte (St.

Hyacinthe), and J. Young (Montreal City) could be identified as strong Liberals or Rouges.

The third division[35] occurred on the same day (June 20), on a motion, somewhat similar to the preceding one in wording, by Sicotte seconded by Cauchon. It was regarded by all as a final vote of non-confidence in the Hincks-Morin government. The motion was passed by a vote of 42 to 29. It had succeeded in including all the members who had voted against the ministry in the two previous divisions, with the exception of Sanborn (Sherbrooke County) and A. Wright (York East), and in addition had secured for the opposition Dubord (Quebec City), Gouin (Richelieu), Lacoste (Chambly), LeBlanc (Beauharnois), J. McDougall (Drummond), and Tessier (Portneuf). Ten members did not divide at the session so that it is not possible to indicate all their probable views at this time (see Table 12). However, ignoring six of the absent members,[36] the House seemed to be aligned with twenty Lower Canadian, eight Upper Canadian, and two independent members in support of the Hincks-Morin government. Twenty conservatives and about eleven Eastern Canadian members seemed to oppose the government from the right. On the left, and newly urgent in their opposition, lay nine Reformers of Canada West and seven Rouges and advanced Liberals from Canada East. In the end, the opposition from the right outnumbered the Ministerialists; yet it was the breaking away of the seceding group of reformers that had been the significant move that demolished the government's position. While the government was in a distinct minority in Canada West, it was within a vote of two of a majority in the East.

As the Executive Council was already experiencing strains between Rolph and M. Cameron, the two advanced Liberals, and between these two and the remainder of the Council, it did not seem feasible to hope for an appeasement of urgent reforming currents by a new reconstruction of the administration. The parliament was precipitously prorogued on June 22 and dissolved the following day, it having been determined to hazard the ministry's life in a new general election.

CHAPTER THREE

THE WATERSHED

THE COLLAPSE of the Reform administration in June 1854, its continued distress in the first session of the fifth parliament, and its supersession by a new government dependent upon an altered basis of support in the Legislative Assembly together constitute a well-recognized watershed in the alignment of political groups in this era. While an interpretation of these events follows at a later stage of this narrative, it is necessary to present here a fairly detailed analysis of the crisis of 1854.

I

An act had been passed in 1853 that enlarged the Legislative Assembly from 84 to 130 seats, and laid down the details of the consequent redistribution of ridings. In attempting to discuss the general election of 1854 against the background of previous contests, there is the difficulty of dealing with 46 additional ridings.[1]

A first casual view of the elections in 1854 shows a large proportion of contests between two candidates, but when an effort is made to identify the men, it becomes clear that the traditional rivalry of Reformers and Conservatives in Canada West is again complicated, as it was in 1851, by a differentiation between Ministerial Reformers (MR.) and Ultra-Reformers (UR.) who opposed the ministry. At least eighteen candidates in Canada West seem to be Ultra-Reformers and some thirty-three were Ministerialists, while the Conservatives entered at least thirty-six. In Canada East there was a larger effort than in 1851 by Rouges (R.) and Independent Liberals (Lib.) opposing the government, not less than twenty-two being identified. In nearly every contested riding there was a candidate, either a Ministerialist (Min.) or a Moderate, who might be expected to support the ministry. The continuation of a Tory-Conservative cause (C.) in Canada East was confined to the "urban" and "English" ridings.

In nine ridings of Canada West members were returned by acclamation, and in a number of cases these were the sitting members at the dissolution of the fourth parliament. The redistribution of the seats and the enlargement of the representation in the Legislative Assembly make it difficult to mark "sitting members" with an asterisk as in the previous similar lists. In the analysis of the 1854 general election the asterisk is used to designate a candidate who sat for any riding at the close of the previous parliament.

Glengarry	J. S. Macdonald* (UR.)	Peterborough	J. Langton* (C.)
Kingston	J. A. Macdonald* (C.)	Prescott	H. W. McCann (C.)
Lincoln	W. H. Merritt* (MR.)	Simcoe South	W. B. Robinson* (C.)
Niagara	J. C. Morrison* (MR.)	Welltington South	A. J. Fergusson* (UR.)
Oxford North	D. Matheson (C.)		

Twenty-four ridings seemed to witness contests between Conservatives and a Reform candidate of some shade of opinion:

Cornwall	Roderick McDonald* (UR.), Dr. Jas.Dickson (C.)
Dundas	J. P. Crysler (C.), J. W. Rose* (UR.)
Durham East	F. H. Burton (C.), Jas. Smith* (MR.)
Elgin East	G. Southwick (MR.), E. Ermatinger (C.)
Grenville South	W. Patrick* (MR.), McMillan (C.)
Grey	G. Jackson (C.), A. Rankin (MR.), Carney (?), Blyth (?)
Halton	G. K. Chisholm (C.), J. White* (UR.)
Hamilton	A. N. MacNab* (C.), I. Buchanan (MR.)
Huron & Bruce	W. Cayley (C.), McQueen (MR.)
Kent	E. Larwill (C.),A. McKellar (UR.), Waddell (?), J. Woods (C.)
Lanark North	R. Bell (MR.), A. W. Playfair (C.), Buell (UR?)
Leeds & Grenville North	B. R. Church (MR.), F. Jones (C.), Whitmarsh (C.), Kelly (?)
Leeds South	J. DeLong* (MR.), B. Tett (C.)
Lennox & Addington	D. Roblin (MR.), B. Seymour* (C.)
London	J. Wilson (MR.), T. C. Dixon* (C.)
Ontario North	J. Gould (MR.), O. R. Gowan (C.), T. N. Gibbs (C.), McDonell (?), Thompson (?C.)
Ottawa (Bytown)	A. Yielding (C.), Friel (?MR.)
Peel	J. C. Aikins (UR.), G. Wright* (C.)
Prince Edward	D. B. Stevenson*(C.), McCuaig (MR.)
Stormont	W. Mattice* (UR.), Grant (?C.)
Waterloo South	R. Ferrie (UR.), Tiffany (?C.)
Welland	J. Frazer (MR.), T. C. Street* (C.)
Wellington North	W. Clarke (C.), Barron (R?)
York West	J. W. Gamble* (C.), Tyrrell (MR.)

In another thirteen ridings there were contests between two candidates from the same general political movement. These demonstrate the internal stresses within both the Conservative and the Reform camps at this period. The contest for the two Toronto seats saw five Conservatives offering:

Brant East	D. McKerlie (MR.), D. Christie* (UR.)
Brockville	G. Crawford* (Moderate C.), G. Sherwood (Tory-C.)
Carleton	W. F. Powell (C.), E. Malloch* (C.)
Haldimand	W. L. Mackenzie* (UR.), McKinnon (MR?)
Hastings North	E. Murney* (C.), G. Benjamin (C-Orangeman)
Hastings South	B. Flint (UR.), L. Wallbridge (MR.)
Lambton	G. Brown* (UR.), M. Cameron* (MR.)
Norfolk	J. Rolph* (MR.), Ritchie (UR.)
Waterloo North	M. H. Foley (MR.), W. McDougall (UR.)
York North	J. Hartman* (UR.), J. H. Price (MR.), Brothers, Hunter (Latter two: no votes)
York East	Amos Wright* (UR.), J. S. Hogan (MR.)
Toronto (2 seats)	J. H. Cameron (C.), H. Sherwood* (C.)
	J. G. Bowes (C.), G. P. Ridout* (C.), W. H. Boulton (C.)

Finally, the remaining nineteen ridings of Canada West present problems of interpretation, because of unidentified candidates or unusual political conditions within the area:

Brant West	H. Biggar (MR.), O'Reilly, Griffin
Durham West	H. Munro (MR.), Lowe
Elgin West	G. MacBeth (C.), McIntyre
Essex	A. Rankin (MR.), J. Prince* (Indep.), Peel
Frontenac	Henry Smith* (C.), Strange
Lanark South	J. Shaw* (C.), Cameron
Middlesex East	W. Niles (MR.), Norton
Middlesex West	J. Scatcherd (UR.), Ferguson, Keefer, Wilson (?)
Northumberland East	J. Ross (MR.), Boucher
Northumberland West	S. Smith (MR.), Boulton
Ontario South	J. M. Lumsden (UR.), Farwell
Oxford South	F. Hincks* (MR.), Miller (?UR.), P. Carroll (C.)

Perth	T. M. Daly (C.), Mitchell
Renfrew	F. Hincks (MR.), McKea, McKennon
Russell	G. B. Lyon* (Fellows) (?C.), R. Bell (C.), Stewart
Simcoe North	A. Morrison (MR.), Sanson
Victoria	Jas. Smith (MR.), Boyd
Wentworth North	R. Spence (MR.), Miller
Wentworth South	S. B. Freeman (UR.), Wetenhall, Williamson (C.)

In Canada East, fifteen members were returned without contests:

Bagot	T. Brodeur (Min.)	Pontiac	J. Egan* (Min.)
Bellechasse	J. Chabot* (Min.)	Quebec County	P. J. O. Chauveau* (Min.)
Chicoutimi & Tadoussac	A. N. Morin* (Min.)	St. Hyacinthe	L. V. Sicotte* (Lib.)
Dorchester	B. Pouliot (Min.)	Shefford	L. T. Drummond* (Min.)
Iberville	C. J. Laberge (R.)	Sherbrooke	A. T. Galt* (Mod. Indep.)
Jacques Cartier	M. F. Valois* (R.)	Two Mountains	J. B. Daoust (Min.)
Joliette	J. H. Jobin* (R.)	Yamaska	I. Gill (Min.)
Levis	F. Lemieux* (Min.)		

The dynamic element in the general election was the continuing emergence of a political left made up of Rouges, who were the organized group in association with the Dorions, and other liberals who opposed the policies of the Hincks-Morin ministry. A Rouge or Liberal appeared in each of the following twenty-two contests:

Beauharnois	C. Daoust (R.), O. LeBlanc* (Min.)
Berthier	P. E. Dostaler (Min.), E. U. Piché (R.), Bondy
Chambly	N. Darche (R.), J. B. Jodoin (Min.)
Champlain	T. Marchildon* (R.), Pacaud, Dr. Rousseau
Châteauguay	J. DeWitt (Lib.), Primeau
Compton	J. S. Sanborn* (Lib.), J. H. Pope (Min.)
Hochelaga	J. Laporté (Min.), Valois (R.)
Huntingdon	R. B. Somerville (Lib.), Davidson
Kamouraska	J. C. Chapais* (Min.), Luc Letellier (Lib.)
L'Assomption	J. Papin (R.), Simeon Morin (Min.)
Laval	P. Labelle (Min.) Belanger (R.)
Lotbinière	J. O'Farrell (Lib. Indep.), Joseph Laurin* (Min.)
Montreal (3 seats)	A. A. Dorion (R.), Baudry
	L. H. Holton (Lib.), W. Badgley* (C.)
	J. Young (Lib.), Bristow
Napierville	J. O. Bureau (R.), Laviolette
Ottawa County	A. Cooke (R.), T. McGoey (Min.)
St. John's	F. Bourassa (R.), Jobson
Saguenay	P. G. Huot (Indep. Lib.), Jean Langlois
Temiscouata	B. Dionne (Min.), J. B. Pouliot (Lib.)
Terrebonne	G. M. Prévost (R.), A. N. Morin (Min.)
Three Rivers	A. Polette* (Lib.), P. B. Dumoulin (Min.)

By contrast, only nine ridings of Canada East seemed to present any "rightist" opposition to the ministry, either in the form of old Tories and Conservatives in "English" ridings, or in several cases by the temporary estrangement of French Canadians like Cauchon, Dufresne, and Casault:

Argenteuil	S. Bellingham (Min.), Robt. Simpson (C.)
Gaspé	J. LeBoutillier (C.), Peter Winter (Min.), R. Christie* (Indep.)
Megantic	W. Rhodes (Min.), J. G. Clapham* (C.), J. O'Farrell (Lib. Indep.-2 votes)
Missisquoi East (Brome)	J. M. Ferris (C.), B. C. A. Gugy (C.)
Montcalm	J. Dufresne (Mod. Indep.), Aime Dugas, Marcel Poirier (Min.), Alex. Daly
Montmagny	N. Casault (Mod. Indep.), Telephore Fournier (?Lib.)
Montmorency	J. Cauchon* (Mod. Indep.), Glackemeyer (?Lib.)
Stanstead	T. L. Terrill* (Min.), J. McConnell (C.)
Vaudreuil	J. B. Mongenais* (Min.), R. U. Harwood (C.)

Of the remaining nineteen ridings of Canada East, thirteen saw a contest between
a supporter of the ministry and one other candidate who has not been identified
politically; the remaining contests were either multilateral, or disclosed unusual
situations:

Beauce	D. Ross (Min.), Belanger
Bonaventure	J. Meagher (Min.), Macdonald
Laprairie	T. J. J. Loranger (Min.), Beaudouin
L'Islet	C. F. Fournier* (Min.), Pelletier
Maskinongé	J. E. Turcotte* (Min.), Gauvreau
Missisquoi West	H. H. Whitney (Min.), Seymour, Smith (?C.), Badgley (C.)
Nicolet	T. Fortier* (Min.), Rousseau, Chailly
Portneuf	J. E. Thibaudeau (Min.), Dery
Quebec City (3 seats)	C. Alleyn (Min.), G. O. Stuart* (Mod. Indep.)
	J. Blanchet (Min.), G. H. Simard (Mod. Indep.)
	J. Chabot (Min.), H. Dubord* (Lib.)
Richelieu J. B. Guévremont (Mod. Indep.), Dorion (R.), A. N. Gouin* (Min.), Dufresne (R.)	
Rimouski	J. C. Taché* (Min.), Joseph Garon
Rouville	J. N. Poulin* (Min.), Blanchet
St. Maurice	L. L. L. Desaulniers (Min.), Richer
Sherbrooke & Wolfe	W. L. Felton (Min.), Aylmer
Soulanges	L. H. Masson (Min.), Bastien
Verchères	G. E. Cartier* (Min.), Massue

Although the results of the elections seemed to indicate the return of over a dozen
Ultra-Reformers and some eighteen Rouges and Lower Canadian opposition
liberals, and although the Conservatives had won about two dozen seats, it was not
at all clear that the ministry had failed to find a new majority. And if the opening
divisions in the new parliament had disclosed a minsterial majority, some doubtful
members would most probably have rallied to its support.

But on September 5, 1854, G. E. Cartier, the government's candidate for the
speakership, was defeated by 62 votes to 59, and L. V. Sicotte, an Independent
Liberal from Canada East, was chosen in his stead.[2] When the House approached
the regular business of the session on September 7,[3] the Hincks-Morin government
lost to the opposition its initiative in ordering the course of debate. By September
10, F. Hincks (Oxford South), J. Morris (legislative councillor), M. Cameron (defeated in Lambton by G. Brown), and J. Rolph (Norfolk), Upper Canadian members of the Executive Council, resigned and were succeeded on September 11 by Sir
A. N. MacNab (Hamilton), W. Cayley (Huron & Bruce), and J. A. Macdonald
(Kingston), three Conservatives, and R. Spence (Wentworth North), a Moderate
Reformer. J. Ross (a legislative councillor from Canada West) and the Canada
East members of the Executive Council retained their portfolios. By September
20, the reconstructed ministry was being supported by handsome majorities of
70-33 and 62-29 in the debate on the speech from the throne.[4]

An analysis of the divisions on September 5, 7, and 20, discloses a fundamental
rearrangement of political groups in the House to support the new Morin-MacNab
ministry, and also provides evidence for reconstructing the results of the general
election.

At the close of the June session, the Lower Canadian supporters of the ministry
had just barely constituted a majority of the members present from their section
(nineteen). The Conservatives from Canada West just equalled them, with nineteen votes. The Upper Canadian Reformers were divided evenly, eight votes being
cast for and eight against the ministry, while the Liberal and Rouge opposition

from Lower Canada consisted of only six members. A number of independent votes, including the perennial Independents, some Lower Canadian Tories and several French-Canadian members (for example), Cauchon, Dubord, Gouin, and LeBlanc), completed the opposition to the government (see Table 12). The picture following the 1854 general election was not changed in its essentials. Hincksite Reformers and Ministerialists from Canada East had gained slightly at the expense of Conservatives and opposition Reformers. The Rouge and Liberal group from Canada East had gained ground. Cauchon and a group of moderates, and a few Lower Canadian Tories, remained in opposition. While the gains of the Lower Canadian Ministerialists had placed them in an undisputed majority in Canada East, the confusion in Upper Canadian reform ranks remained, and Hincks' own following, though equal in numbers to the Conservatives, did not command a majority of western Canadian members. The supporters of the ministry in early September 1854 constituted a moderate centre which was opposed by significant forces both on its left and on its right; yet Hincks' government was only a member or two short (in a House with full attendance) of commanding an absolute majority of the Assembly (see Table 13).

The reconstruction of the Upper Canadian portion of the Executive Council succeeded in enlisting the support of the Conservatives and other former opponents from the right, but at the same time so strained the adhesion of the Upper Canadian Reformers that six members immediately crossed into opposition. The new Morin-MacNab Council had adopted the late ministry's principal items of legislation concerning Clergy Reserves, the abolition of Seignorial Tenure, and an elective Legislative Council, and this served to hold the confidence of many Reformers for a time. The large moderate group of Lower Canadian members seemed to pass through the adjustments of September 1854 with little disturbance to their solidarity in the House and, apparently, no change in relationship to the Executive Council. Yet, in September 1854, they had absorbed all moderate and rightist opponents and had, in fact, ceased to be a centre party. Not until a later era, after Confederation, were they to be challenged again by a significant group to their right (see Table 14).

The composition of the Executive Council changed several times between September 1854 and July 1858, when the Liberal-Conservative government gave place momentarily to the Brown-Dorion administration. At all times in this period it did preserve the form of a coalition by continuing to have two Reformers from Canada West to act with three Conservatives (see Fig. II). Immediately following September 1854, R. Spence (Wentworth North) and J. Ross (legislative councillor) represented the Reform viewpoint in the cabinet. In early 1856, Ross was replaced by J. C. Morrison (Niagara), and finally, from February 2, 1858, till the resignation of the ministry, J. Ross and Sydney Smith (Northumberland West) were the Reform cabinet ministers. There were two major occasions on which French-Canadian cabinet ministers were changed. A. N. Morin, J. Chabot (Quebec City), and P. J. O. Chauveau (Quebec County), all old-guard followers of Lafontaine, gave place on January 27, 1855, to J. Couchon (Montmorency),[5] Francois Lemieux (Levis), a follower of Lafontaine in the House from 1847, but presently destined to consort with Brown and Dorion in their "short administration," and G. E. Cartier (Verchères), just commencing his remarkable career in office. The second occasion for major cabinet reconstruction was in 1857. In this year Cauchon withdrew from

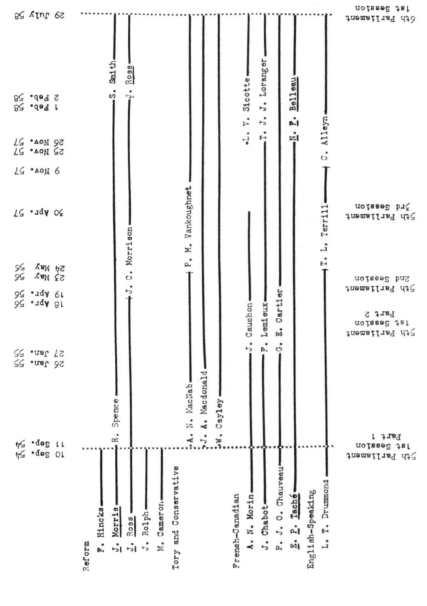

FIGURE II. Composition of Liberal-Conservative Cabinets, 1854-58. NOTE: names of members of Legislative Council underlined.

[41]

office in April, followed by Lemieux, and E. P. Taché in November. By late 1857 Cartier found himself senior surviving executive councillor from Canada East and was securing as his running mates L. V. Sicotte (St. Hyacinthe), essentially a Moderate Liberal, T. J. J. Loranger (Laprairie), a staunch Conservative and a most able lawyer, and N. F. Belleau (legislative councillor), a Moderate. These changes seem to illustrate both a need for men who would hold the confidence of diverse groups of members of the centre and right, and the identification of a new generation who represented a newer tradition not known to Lafontaine. The "Cartier era" in Lower Canada may be dated from November 26, 1857.

The episode in May 1856, when MacNab was dropped from the Council, gives a most revealing insight into the affairs of the coalition in Canada West. Two sets of forces were at work: a reaction of moderate coalition Reformers against the continued leadership in the ministry of a Compact Tory, and the reassertion of a right-wing conservative distrust of J. A. Macdonald and like-thinking moderate Conservatives because of their continued involvement with Reformers of any hue. While enlarged hopes were held out for new confidence on all sides among supporters of the coalition when MacNab was dropped, the actual outcome of the elimination of MacNab was a large demonstration against the continuing ministers and the loss of both Reform and high-Conservative votes for the remainder of the sessions of the fifth parliament.

The most meaningful division at the time of this MacNab crisis occurred on May 30, 1856, when A. A. Dorion (Montreal), seconded by G. Brown (Lambton), moved a formal motion of want of confidence in the reconstructed Taché-Macdonald administration.[6] The fragmentation of political groups at this point is evident. While eighteen Conservatives supported the administration, two (J. H. Cameron and Murney) went into continuing opposition, while three more (Mac-Nab, Matheson, and Powell) were in temporary opposition. Gamble (York West) crossed the House from Conservative ranks to join the Ultra-Reformers in opposition. While the Bleus under Cartier remained in support of the government, two Lower Canadian Conservatives (Felton and Rhodes) and Loranger, who had given only independent support to Cartier since "falling out" with him, voted with the opposition.

The disaffection of Upper Canadian Reformers came close to eliminating the last semblance of a coalition between Reformers and Conservatives. Between early September 1854 and May 30, 1856, eleven Reformers who had initially supported Hincks crossed to join the opposition reformers. On May 30, of fourteen Hincksite Reform members, eight voted against the ministry, two supported it, and four were absent.[7] Subsequently, all but two (H. Biggar and J. Delong) of these Hincksite Reformers continued to give support to the reconstructed Council. It was apparent, however, that the crisis had shaken the coalition severely. Although the reconstructed Taché-Macdonald government did survive until July 1858, managing to weather the elections of 1857, the impression is gained that dynamic politics were being repressed in order to avoid unnecessary strains upon the existing system of power in the House.

The realignment of political forces which was being worked out during the fifth parliament was not decisively reflected in the course of by-elections and changes of membership of the Legislative Assembly during that parliament. The following list of occasions when the membership of the House changed is quite

undramatic. (Hincksite Reformers and Liberal-Conservatives are shown respectively as HR. and LC.)

October 9, 1854, Oxford South: E. Cook (HR.) vice F. Hincks (HR.) (no change)
October 17, 1854, Bellechasse: O. C. Fortier (LC.) vice J. Chabot (LC.) (no change)
March 12, 1855, Brant East: D. Christie (UR.) declared elected in place of D. McKerlie (HR.)
   (Liberal gain)
April 26, 1855, Chicoutimi & Tadoussac: D. E. Price (LC.) vice A. N. Morin (LC.) (no change)
August 7, 1855, Quebec County: F. Evanturel (LC.) vice P. J. O. Chauveau (LC.) (no change)
January 26, 1856, Peterborough: W. S. Conger (LC.) vice J. Langton (LC.) (no change)
March 21, 1856, Renfrew: J. Supple (LC.) vice Hincks (HR.) (little change)
October 4, 1856, Rouville: W. H. Chaffers (Liberal) vice J. N. Poulin (LC.) (Liberal gain)
October 23, 1856, Hastings North: G. Benjamin (LC.) vice E. Murney (Cons.) (LC. gain)
October 27, 1856, Quebec City: G. H. Simard (LC.) vice J. Chabot (LC.) (no change)
February 17, 1857, Rimouski: M. G. Baby (LC.) vice J. C. Taché (LC.) (no change)
April 14, 1857, Quebec City: G. O. Stuart (LC.) vice J. Blanchet (LC.) (no change)
June 23, 1857, Terrebonne: L. S. Morin (LC.) vice G. M. Prévost (Rouge) (Lib-Cons. gain)

All the members appointed to office were consistently re-elected during this
period. In March 1855, however, the Hincksite Reformer McKerlie was unseated
and D. Christie declared the sitting member for Brant East. In October 1856, after
the crisis of the spring of that year, there was a Liberal victory in Rouville, returning W. H. Chaffers in place of J. N. Poulin, while at the same time E. Murney,
a right-wing Conservative who had opposed the moderate policies of J. A. Macdonald and his associates, resigned and was replaced in Hastings North by G.
Benjamin, a ministerial supporter. Toward the end of the parliament's life, the
government gained another seat in Terrebonne, where L. S. Morin replaced G. M.
Prévost, a Rouge, on June 23, 1857.

CHAPTER FOUR

THE MACDONALD-CARTIER SYSTEM

THE GENERAL ELECTION in late 1857 was a first broad testing of public opinion concerning the Liberal-Conservative coalition erected in September 1854.[1]

I

The contests in both sections of the province were for the most part two-sided fights between a candidate who had supported or would support the ministry and a partisan of the left. But there remained traces of some of the older affiliations. Generally the Conservatives and Coalition Reformers of Canada West agreed on a single candidate and avoided dividing the ministerial vote. In five ridings the contest lay between Coalition Reformers and Liberals (opposition reformers).[2] In Canada East the opposition candidates included both out-and-out Rouges of Dorion's association and other Liberals. The contest in some "English" ridings of Canada East had local terminology, but the elected members took sides with the Liberal-Conservatives or the opposition and seemed to adjust themselves, in the House, to the general pattern of left opposing right.

The issues debated at the election centred around the record of the Liberal-Conservative government and the new stirring challenge of "representation by population" from the Liberals of Canada West. In Lower Canada the appeal to the electorate by the opponents of the government rehearsed the programme of the Rouge group, or dealt in personalities and government failings. The returns from the general election in both sections of the province forecast the political trend that was to end in deadlock. The Liberals (Reform movement) in Canada West considerably strengthened their position at the expense of Conservatives and Coalition Reformers, while in Canada East the Rouges and opposition Liberals returned but a handful in face of the augmented ranks of the Bleus (ministerial supporters).

In early July 1858, an experiment was made in forming a Liberal cabinet based upon the expected support of Liberals and Rouges from both parts of the province (see note, Fig. IV). Although the experiment ended in a fiasco, the divisions in the House during the testing of the strength of the short Brown-Dorion administration represent very clearly the political composition of the sixth parliament. After the crisis in July-August 1858, the Liberals continued to mature the full range of their opinion and did win some successes at by-elections, but the alignment of the House underwent no large change.

The crisis of July 1858 was brought on by a division, which cut across normal party lines, concerning the suitability of Ottawa as the capital. Although the J. A. Macdonald-Cartier ministry resigned when its policy favouring Ottawa as the new capital was rejected on division, the subsequent feeling of the House showed quite clearly that it was not ready to support the Brown-Dorion ministry formed on August 2 from Liberal and Rouge elements. While the question of designating a permanent capital city for the province had been a controversy for years, the alignment of members on this issue did not coincide with their normal alignment in dealing with general political issues. The division on August 2 on a motion of want of confidence in the Liberal administration provides an accurate insight into the political affiliation of members (see Table 16).

On August 2, 1858, the members supporting the Liberal-Conservative course consisted of twenty-three Conservatives and five Coalition Reformers from Canada West, and forty-eight members from Canada East, of whom fifteen appear to have been "English." The liberal forces were composed of thirty-three Liberals (and Ultra-Reformers) from Canada West and ten Liberals and Rouges from Canada East. Five Lower Canadian members, three of whom received offices in the Brown-Dorion Council, appear to have crossed the floor of the House during this episode.[3] A. T. Galt (Sherbrooke) had tended, down to July 1858, to vote with the Liberals. On August 2, he voted with the Liberal-Conservatives and was taken into the Council formed by the latter after the crisis. J. S. Hogan, an Independent Liberal from Canada West had voted against the Liberal government on August 2, though thereafter he continued to favour the Liberal side of questions.

The indignation of Liberals and Reformers at the sudden collapse of their hopes and the "double shuffle," in early August 1858, has given rise to some misunderstanding of the exact strength of political groups in the House at this time. The division on August 2 recorded seventy-one rightists and thirty-one leftists who were present at the division. Had all members been present, the division would probably have witnessed seventy-eight opponents and forty-eight supporters of the Brown-Dorion government in the aisles. The actual division in members from Canada West showed the same want of confidence by a majority of two members (27-25), and in projecting the probable division with all members present, the figures become twenty-nine Liberal-Conservatives opposing thirty-three Liberals, a majority of four.[4] The margin in favour of the Liberal-Conservatives was wide enough to maintain their majority in the House, even if C. Alleyn, G. E. Cartier, J. A. Macdonald, and S. Smith had returned to their contituencies on August 6 and not resorted to the "double shuffle."

The Executive Council assembled by George Brown and A. A. Dorion on August 2, 1858, was composed of five members from Canada East and five from Canada West. Of the Lower Canadians, Drummond, Lemieux, and J. E. Thibaudeau had been moderates, voting with the majority of Lower Canadians until shortly before the change of government; the English-speaking community was represented by two ministers, Drummond and Holton. The Upper Canadians were apparently chosen with a view to attracting various wings of the reform movement, for though Mowat was an intimate associate of Brown, the other three represented a different reform tradition. J. Morris gave continuity with the old Baldwin-Lafontaine ministry of 1851 and the Hincks-Morin government that succeeded it. J. S. Macdonald, from the eastern extreme of Upper Canada, represented a more moderate tradition than Brown's, while Foley, though from the western peninsula, was regarded at this time as belonging to J. S. Macdonald's "tail."

II

The Liberal-Conservative ministry which returned to forty-six months of power on August 6 and 7 was largely a continuation of the Council that had resigned on July 29. It continued to comprise representatives of the Conservative and Coalition Reform groups in Canada West, and of French-Canadian Bleus and English-speaking Conservatives in Canada East. The principal leaders, G. E. Cartier and J. A. Macdonald, held office continuously through this period, as did P. M. Van Koughnet (legislative councillor), Sydney Smith and J. Ross (Coalition Reformers), N. Belleau (legislative councillor), L. V. Sicotte, and Charles Alleyn (English-speaking Quebec City lawyer). A. T. Galt (Sherbrooke) who had recently crossed the House from opposition, was taken into the Council at this time. He not only represented the viewpoint of the Eastern Townships and commercial interests in Montreal, but also lent some further support to the idea that the ministry was a coalition of moderates. George Sherwood succeeded W. Cayley, both firm Conservatives. Finally John Rose, who held office from August 7, 1858 till June 12, 1861, though a third Anglo-Saxon from Canada East, through friendship with Macdonald and Montreal business association may have served as a member at large equally acceptable to the Liberal-Conservatives of both sections of the province. There was an evolution in the period (see Fig. III) culminating in the spring of 1862, toward a Council of twelve members rather than the previous ten, in the proportion of four Conservatives, four French-speaking Bleus, and two each of Coalition Reformers and English members from Canada East.

When L. V. Sicotte withdrew late in 1858 to begin a course ending in support of the opposition groups, he was not replaced for over a year, until January 1860, when L. S. Morin became the third French-Canadian cabinet member. For about two years after February of 1860, J. C. Morrison returned to the Council as a third Coalition Reformer. In June 1861, Joseph Cauchon again entered the ministry as a fourth French Canadian. Finally, in 1862, when the ministry was facing the first session of the seventh parliament, several adjustments were made in the Upper Canadian section. Vankoughnet (Conservative) withdrew at the same time as J. C. Morrison, while J. B. Robinson (Toronto, Conservative) and J. Carling (London, Conservative) were appointed. On March 26, J. Ross, who had held office fairly consistently since the Hincks-Morin ministry, was replaced by J. Patton (legislative councillor, probably a Moderate Reformer). With the elimination of Loranger in August and L. V. Sicotte in December 1858, the Lower Canadian group which had followed Lafontaine and Morin was transformed into the Parti Bleu, under the undisputed leadership of G. E. Cartier. The admitting of three new Upper Canadians to the Executive Council in early 1862 marked the occasion when J. A. Macdonald tried to broaden the basis of his support in Canada West by including new blood, though this measure involved the admission of moderate men who did support the principle of "representation by population."

III

There were some twenty changes in the membership of the Legislative Assembly between 1858 and 1861:

March 3, 1958, Renfrew: W. Cayley (C.) vice J. L. McDougald (C.) (no change)
May 14, 1858, Oxford North: W. McDougall (L.) vice G. Brown (L.) (no change)
May 21, 1858, Leeds & Grenville North: O. R. Gowan (C.) vice B. R. Church (R.) (no change)
June 7, 1858, L'Islet: C. F. Fournier (LC.) vice L. B. Caron (L.) unseated (Lib.-Cons. gain)

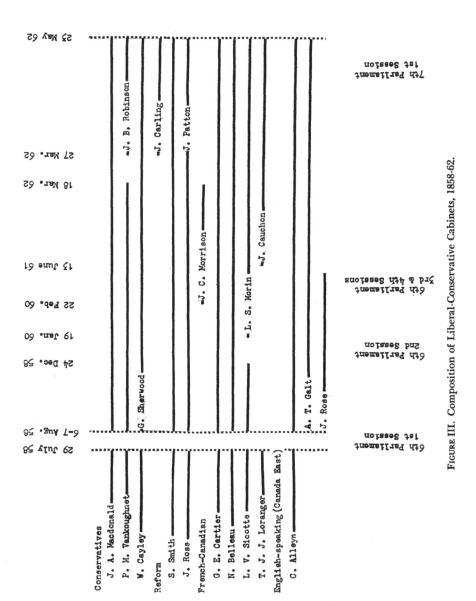

FIGURE III. Composition of Liberal-Conservative Cabinets, 1858-62.

August 5, 1858, Middlesex West: A. P. Macdonald (L.) vice J. Scatcherd (L.) (no change)
September 14, 1858, Shefford: A. B. Foster (LC.) vice L. T. Drummond (L.) (LC. gain)
October 2, 1858, Lotbinière: L. T. Drummond (L.) vice J. O'Farrell (Moderate?) (L. gain)
October 7, 1858, Haldimand: M. Harcourt (L.) vice W. L. Mackenzie (L.) (no change)
December 1, 1858, Brant East: H. Finlayson (L.) vice D. Christie (L.) (no change)
December 14, 1858, Maskinongé: G. Caron (LC.) vice L. H. Gauvreau (LC.) (no change)
February 23, 1859, Wellington North: Jas. Ross (L.) vice C. Allan (L.) (no change)
December 21, 1859, Russell: J. W. Loux (LC.) vice G. B. L. Fellows (LC.) (no change)
January 14, 1860, York North: A. Wilson (L.) vice J. Hartman (L.) (no change)
March 12, 1860, Argenteuil: J. J. C. Abbott (L.) declared elected vice S. Bellingham (LC.) (Liberal gain)
April 16, 1860, Quebec City: P. G. Huot (L.) vice H. Dubord (LC.) (Liberal gain)
May 31, 1860, Middlesex East: R. Craik (L.) vice M. Talbot (C.) (Liberal gain)
November 7, 1860, Lincoln: J. C. Rykert (L.) vice W. H. Merritt (L.) (no change)
November 19, 1860, Lambton: H. F. MacKenzie (L.) vice M. Cameron (R.) (Liberal gain)
November 26, 1860, Vaudreuil: J. B. Mongenais (LC.) vice R. U. Harwood (LC.) (no change)
March 4, 1861, Grey: J. T. Purdy (L.) vice J. S. Hogan (Indep. L.) (no change)

The following members who resigned from the Legislative Assembly were elected to the Legislative Council: D. Christie, Erie, 1858; M. Cameron, St. Clair, 1860; W. H. Merritt, Niagara Division, 1860; R. U. Harwood, Rigaud, 1860.

Thirteen of these changes did not affect the standing of parties, though O. R. Gowan's return in Leeds & Grenville North in succession to B. R. Church saw a Conservative succeed a Coalition Reformer. Two changes, in L'Islet and Shefford in 1858, were ministerial gains, while the Liberal opposition gained five seats, four of them being in Quebec City, Argenteuil, Middlesex East, and Lambton in 1860. There was thus an over-all gain of three seats by the Liberals in this period, with a wave of successes in the year 1860. None of these changes altered, markedly, the standing of parties as they had stood at the beginning of August 1858.

IV

The dissolution of the sixth parliament in June 1861 was not occasioned by a political crisis, but there were growing signs of restlessness within the ranks of the government's supporters. The persistent onslaught by the Liberal opposition from Canada West, particularly in its case for "representation by population," was beginning to erode ministerial support. The recriminations between various groups, both within the Conservative party and without, following upon the visit of the Prince of Wales, also helped to throw political alignments into confusion.

The election campaign in the early summer of 1861 was largely conducted in terms of the record of the Cartier-J. A. Macdonald ministry, with the added agitation in Canada West for some alteration in the system of representation. The contests in most ridings of both sections of the province followed the simple pattern of a government supporter opposed by a Liberal. Although some candidates still presented themselves in Canada West as Coalition (Hincksite) Reformers, this formula was by now nearly meaningless in the broad clash of two generally inclusive political groupings. Yet it does explain the opposition of J. Cockburn (a Conservative) and Sydney Smith (a Coalition Reformer and cabinet minister) in Northumberland West, and A. Hooper (Conservative) and D. Roblin (Coalition Reformer) in Lennox & Addington. It also may explain the apparent aberration in the voting of I. Buchanan (Hamilton), J. W. Dunsford (Victoria), D. McLachlin (Renfrew), and J. C. Rykert (Lincoln), who supported the Liberal-Conservative ministry in the early stages of the seventh parliament, but passed into opposition and gave support to the J. S. Macdonald government in the earlier stages of its life. There was a fairly large number of members returned by acclamation in 1861, especially in Canada East.

In eighty-seven ridings there was little or no change from the previous parliament in the political outlook of the representatives elected. Some sixty-one members retained their seats. The trend of the contests in the remaining ridings saw the Conservatives gain some eight seats in Canada West, while the Bleus in Canada East lost a net total of twelve. As in previous general elections, there was a sufficient number of doubtful members and disputed elections to leave the results indecisive until demonstrated by divisions in the House. It was clear, however, that the Conservative gains in Canada West should at least bring the strength of major groups in that section into balance, while the Ministerial losses in Canada East, though serious, should not leave the opposition in a majority.

The opening division in the seventh parliament on March 20, 1862, concerned the election of J. E. Turcotte (Three Rivers) as speaker and, as usual, was regarded as a guide to the alignment of political groups. The Liberal-Conservatives' candidate was elected speaker by a majority of 66-53. The eleven votes not recorded in this division[5] would have brought the totals to seventy-four government members, fifty-five opposition, and one riding vacant (see Table 17). The Conservatives and Liberals of Canada West had each returned twenty-nine members while a little group of Coalition Reformers gave a margin of six votes to the government. The Lower Canadian Liberal successes at the polls had increased their numbers significantly to twenty-three, but the Bleu group with twenty-seven and the Lower Canadian Conservatives with six firm supporters held a majority in the section. Two further English-speaking members, Dawson and Price, and three French Canadians, Gagnon, Prevost, and Sylvain, added weight to the majority in the early stages of the parliament. Independents, the speaker, and a vacant riding accounted for five seats. The Liberal-Conservative administration had secured a majority from both sections of the province in the 1861 general election, but the margin of safety was not large in Canada West and, accompanied by the upsurge of liberalism in Canada East, the trends were not unlike those in 1854, favouring the right in Upper Canada and the left in Lower Canada.

The very urgent question of altering the representation in the Assembly had received a serious check; yet the exponents of representation by population and of the principle of the double majority initiated long and full debates on these subjects, and seriously strained the more basic alignment of members when thirteen Conservatives, three Coalition Reformers, and one Lower Canadian[6] voted for representation by population. It was on the understanding that the possibility of changes in the distribution of seats would thereafter be an "open question" in the cabinet, that Carling, Patton (legislative councillor), and Robinson were brought into the administration on March 27, 1862. It was hoped, indeed, that the "open question" formula would stave off a ministerial crisis indefinitely.

Although the Liberal-Conservative government did enjoy quite safe majorities on most major items of legislation and seemed to view the Liberals of Canada West, armed with their constitutional platforms, as the principal threat to their existence, it was an almost unprecedented breakdown of Bleu solidarity on the principal item of government legislation that brought on the crisis of May 1862.

It was the defection of fourteen Bleu members on May 20, 1862, in opposing the comprehensive and costly reorganization of the militia that put the Cartier-Macdonald government in a minority (see Table 17).

v

Sandfield Macdonald formed a Liberal administration which took office on May 24, 1862 (see Fig. IV). The Upper Canadian section, in addition to Sandfield Macdonald himself, included J. Morris (Legislative Council) and M. H. Foley (Waterloo North) who had been in Brown's cabinet in 1858. Then there was William McDougall (Oxford North) who was by this time a less intimate lieutenant of George Brown and moving from his outlook, while W. P. Howland (York West) and Adam Wilson (York North) were from Toronto's Liberal commercial group. The ministers from Canada East, with the exception of A. A. Dorion, who alone had been in the 1858 Liberal government, were moderate Liberals who had of late opposed the Bleus, but were not of the true Rouge tradition. L. V. Sicotte (St. Hyacinthe) led this wing of the administration as attorney-general (Lower Canada) and associated himself with Evanturel (Quebec County), McGee (Montreal West), J. J. C. Abbott (Argenteuil), and U. J. Tessier.[7] Some seven months later, A. A. Dorion withdrew from the Council and was succeeded by J. O. Bureau of Napierville who had represented this riding as a Rouge since September 1854.

The cabinet seemed designed to appeal to all shades of Liberals in Canada West, but in Lower Canada it sought to avoid the stamp of a Rouge machine in the hope of attracting moderate supporters away from the Bleu camp. There was no immediate testing of the House's confidence in the new régime and, in fact, there seemed to be a tendency to avoid any issues that might have the weight of votes of confidence. It was not till the close of the second session on May 6, 1863, that there was a full-dress debate on a motion by G. E. Cartier and J. A. Macdonald expressing lack of confidence in the administration. It carried on division by sixty-four to fifty-nine.

As an aftermath to the vote on the Militia Bill and the change of government in May 1862, there had been some readjustments in the allegiance of members. Four Upper Canadian Coalition Reformers and Moderates (I. Buchanan, J. W. Dunsford, D. McLachlin, and J. C. Rykert) had crossed into support of the Liberal régime. From the Bleu group, three members (Gagnon, Prévost, and Sylvain) who had opposed the Militia Bill continued on in the Liberal ranks, and were joined by W. McD. Dawson (Ottawa County) and D. E. Price (Chicoutimi & Saguenay). To counter-balance these nine accessions, only C. Boucher de Boucherville (Chambly) went into opposition to the Liberals. In the eight changes in membership of the House between May 24, 1862, and the close of the seventh parliament, the opposition appeared to win a net gain of three seats.

September 27, 1861, Laval: L. S. Morin (LC.) vice P. Labelle (LC.) (no change)
February 20, 1862, Montcalm: J. Dufresne (LC.) vice J. L. Martin (L.) (LC. gain)
March 17, 1862, Brome: C. Dunkin (LC.) vice M. Sweet (LC.) (no change)
June 20, 1862, Hochelaga: A. A. Dorion (L.) vice J. P. Falkner (L.) (no change)
July 3, 1862, Perth: T. M. Daly (LC.) vice M. H. Foley (L.) (LC. gain)
November 17, 1862, Napierville: P. Benoit (L.) vice J. O. Bureau (L.) (no change)
February 23, 1863, Elgin West: J. Scoble (L.) vice G. MacBeth (LC.) (Liberal gain)
March 9, 1863, Oxford South: G. Brown (L.) vice S. Connor (L.) (no change)

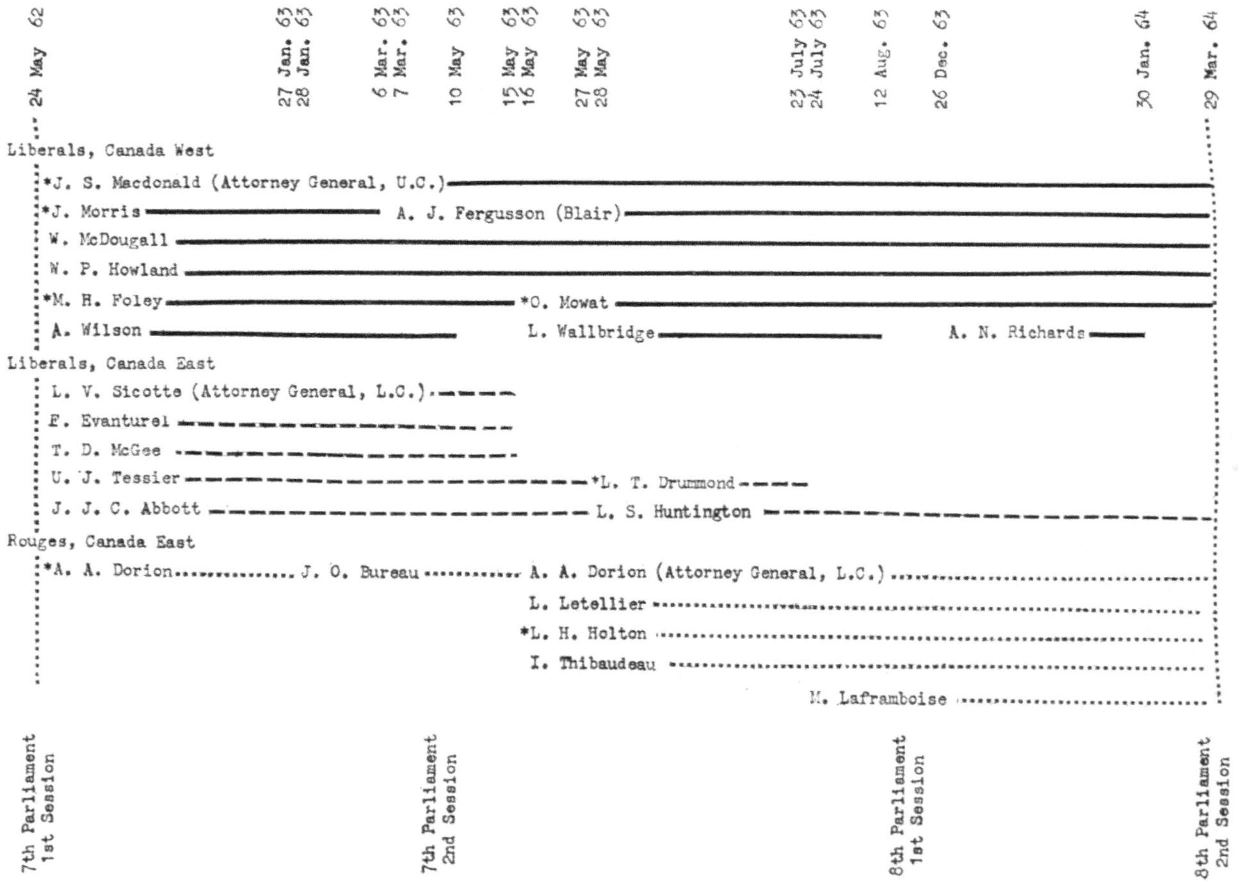

FIGURE IV. Composition of Liberal Cabinets, 1862-64.

NOTE: * indicates members of Brown-Dorion administration Aug. 2-4, 1858. (Brown, Lemieux, and J. E. Thibaudeau of the 1858 Liberal ministry do not appear in this figure.)

April 1, 1863, Laprairie: A. Pinsonneault (LC.) vice T. J. J. Loranger (Indep.) (LC. gain)
April 7, 1863, Essex: J. O'Connor (LC.) vice A. Rankin (L.) (LC. gain)
May 4, 1863, Verchères: C. F. Painchaud (LC.) vice A. E. Kierskowski (L.) (LC. gain)
(The changes in Elgin West, Essex, and Verchères were the result of voiding the original election returns; there were no new elections involved.)

In reconstructing the alignment of groups in 1862 and 1863, it is hard to avoid the conclusion that the J. S. Macdonald-Sicotte government would have been in a minority if a simple vote of confidence had been taken at any stage in its first year in office. Yet the government had survived nearly twelve months before this probability was tested succesfully.

Within ten days of the vote in want of confidence in the Liberal government, on May 6, 1863, the House was prorogued, the government reconstructed, and a new general election called.

CHAPTER FIVE

DEADLOCK

THE LAST STAGES of the party battles of the United Province of Canada in the eighth parliament began when an absolute deadlock in the relative strength and alignment of political groups was demonstrated by the inability of either the Liberals under J. Sandfield Macdonald and A. A. Dorion, or, after March 30, 1864, the Liberal-Conservatives under G. E. Cartier[1] and J. A. Macdonald to form a lasting basis of power in the Legislative Assembly. On the fall of the latters' ministry the normal alignment of groups in the Legislative Assembly was revolutionized when, on June 30, 1864, the great majority of Upper Canadian Liberals joined the Liberal-Conservatives in a temporary coalition in order to change the constitutional framework of the Province of Canada by replacing the existing legislative union with some form of federal union. This coalition retained its resiliency and sense of purpose throughout the third and fourth sessions of the eighth parliament, in the spring and autumn of 1865.

A final stage of evolution, more difficult to analyse, was reached in 1866 in the fifth session. By then the organization of the new Confederation of the British North American provinces was at the stage of detailed legislation of the constitution of the new provinces of Upper Canada and Lower Canada, and so far as the Province of Canada was concerned, Confederation had been accomplished. The original purpose of the coalition of 1864 had been achieved. Thus, in this last session of the Canadian parliament before Confederation, there were definite indications that the coalition was breaking up. The division lists at this time have something of the flavour of the period after the coalition of 1854, in the late fifties, when the groups on the left of the House, from both sections of the province, groped in some disunity for new liberal reforming policies which quite often stemmed from sectional aspirations. To some extent, all parties by 1866 were subject to this new turmoil, as men tried to come to grips with the new political situation which would be presented by a federal constitution.

I

The prospects for the Liberal government in the late spring of 1863 must have appeared fairly promising, for they had succeeded in maintaining an administration for nearly twelve months in a parliament elected under Liberal-Conservative auspices. The hopes for improving their strength in Canada West were bright, and with good management the strength of Lower Canadian support might be improved. It was with the forthcoming election in mind that J. Sandfield Macdonald reconstructed his cabinet in May 1863 (see Fig. IV).

The substitution of Mowat for Foley was a bid to attract the support of those Upper Canadian Liberals (Reformers) who contended that the government's policies had been lukewarm. Mowat was a close associate of Brown and a Toronto "representation by population" man. The admission of Lewis Wallbridge might be expected to attract votes in the same way, for he was quite orthodox in his liberalism and represented a section of eastern Upper Canada which had previously been unrepresented in the cabinet. More striking than these changes in the Upper Canadian section was the total reconstruction of the Lower Canadian section of the cabinet. A. A. Dorion, Letellier (legislative councillor who had previously represented Kamouraska), and Isadore Thibaudeau, all well-recognized staunch Liberals and Rouges, were brought into the government in place of L. V. Sicotte, F. Evanturel, and J. O. Bureau. L. H. Holton, a Liberal of long standing and a leader in Montreal's commercial community, succeeded T. D. McGee. The substitution of L. T. Drummond and L. S. Huntington for U. J. Tessier and J. J. C. Abbott was accomplished a dozen days later. All the displaced ministers were unhappy about their removal from office, and M. H. Foley, L. V. Sicotte, F. Evanturel, T. D. McGee, and J. J. C. Abbott, who were returned to the Legislative Assembly of the eighth parliament, registered strong protests in the early stages of the first session of the eighth parliament.[2]

The general election of 1863 had been largely a two-party battle between Liberals and Liberal-Conservatives in both parts of the province. The only candidates to diverge from strict allegiance to the two major parties were the group of ex-ministers together with Buchanan (Hamilton). J. Y. Bown (Brant East), G. Jackson (Grey), A. Morrison (defeated in Simcoe North), Sydney Smith (defeated in Victoria), and J. C. Rykert (defeated in Lincoln) who were all "latter day" Reformers.[3] In ninety-eight ridings (fifty-one Canada West and forty-seven Canada East) there was no significant change in the viewpoint of the candidate elected in 1863; eighty-five members of the seventh parliament were returned again, twenty-six without opposition. This very large measure of continuity between the seventh and eighth parliaments was unprecedented, and is clear evidence of the firmness of party organization achieved by this time. Although there was a change in the political complexion of the new members elected in thirty-one ridings in 1863, the balancing out of gains and losses resulted in a net increase of nine Liberals in Canada West, as opposed to four Liberal-Conservatives in Canada East. This gain constituted a significant victory for the Liberals in Canada West. The over-all gain of five Liberal seats in the Assembly, however, did nothing to resolve the state of deadlock existing at this period. Whereas the Liberal government in early 1863 was in a minority of two or three, it now found itself expecting a majority of two or three. But so great was the importance of every single vote that a handful of disgruntled ex-ministers or independent-spirited reformers could, and did, shift the balance sufficiently to unseat a government formed by either the right or the left.

II

The division[4] concerning the election of Lewis Wallbridge (Liberal, Hastings South) as speaker seemed to demonstrate a Liberal majority of eight (division 66 to 58); but even this apparent working majority was illusory, for R. J. Cartwright (Lennox & Addington), W. S. Conger (Peterborough), and J. Y. Bown (Brant East), who supported Wallbridge's candidature, were soon to disclose their opposition to the Liberal government.

Three divisions—one on August 29[5] on a motion by Sicotte and Foley condemning the reconstruction of the Liberal government in May of that year, one on September 18[6] regretting the appointment of Sicotte to the judiciary and a third on October 8[7] complaining of the lack of economy in government expenditure mentioned in the speech from the throne—provide a good insight into the party affiliation of members during J. Sandfield Macdonald's tenure of power. The speaker and 123 members (38 Liberals, 20 Conservatives, and 2 Reformers from Canada West; and 25 Liberals and Rouges, 24 Bleus, and 14 English-speaking Conservatives from Canada East) seemed to remain firm in their alignment at this time. The riding of Essex was disputed and unrepresented in the House. In St. Hyacinthe, Sicotte, who opposed the Liberal ministry as reconstructed in 1863, had been replaced by R. Raymond, a Bleu. In terms of government supporters and opposition, the government had the continuing confidence of 38 Liberals from Canada West and 25 Liberals and Rouges from Canada East, a total of 63 votes, while the opposition numbered 61 members (20 Conservatives and 2 Reformers from Canada West, 24 Bleus and 14 English-speaking Conservatives and the member from St. Hyacinthe in Canada East). Four additional members—Poulin (Rouville) and Bown (Brant East), who were more usually in the opposition but voted once in support of the Liberal government, Foley (Waterloo North), a long-term Liberal who joined the opposition temporarily when dismissed from office, and the member for Leeds (South), where in January 1864 D. F. Jones a Conservative defeated A. N. Richards a Liberal—completed the roll of the House, and supplied the final ingredients in producing complete deadlock.

As nearly as may be calculated, of the 128 members to divide, the government might hope after January 1864 to claim 64 votes and the opposition 64. In late March 1864, the Liberal government of J. S. Macdonald and A. A. Dorion resigned, and from March 31 until May 3 the House was adjourned to allow the members of the newly formed Taché-J. A. Macdonald government to seek re-election in their ridings. At this period there were two changes in the membership of the House. M. H. Foley, the new postmaster-general, was not re-elected in Waterloo North but was defeated by I. E. Bowman, a staunch Liberal; and the select committee on the disputed Essex election declared A, Rankin, a Liberal, the sitting member. While Foley's defeat replaced a wavering Reformer with a decided Liberal, this did not upset the deadlock; for in the original analysis above, Foley was credited as usually voting with the Liberal government supporters in the early months of 1864. It was the return of Rankin for Essex which resolved the deadlock in favour of the Liberals just as the Liberal-Conservative government assumed power.

During the approximately six weeks of meetings between May 3 and June 14, 1864, two divisions confirmed the difficulties of carrying on government and give clear proof of the alignment of members. On May 17[8] A. A. Dorion (Hochelaga) and McGiverin (Lincoln) moved an amendment to the motion that the House go into Committee of Supply, and on June 14[9] Dorion and McDougall (Ontario South) moved a critical amendment in the same circumstances. Both divisions were clearly on the question of confidence in the Taché-Macdonald government. On the first occasion, the government was sustained by two votes (62-64); on the latter it was defeated by the same margin (60-58). The solidarity of political grouping remained, and the shift in the balance of power depended upon just two or three members. In the first of the two divisions (May 17, 1864), Rankin (Essex) supported the Taché-Macdonald government, though he subsequently voted consistently as a Liberal. At this time, too, Sylvain (Rimouski) crossed the House to join the

Liberal-Conservatives permanently. Poupore (Bleu, Pontiac), Dunkin (Conservative, Brome), and Wood (Liberal, Brant West) were absent. Had the absent members been present, the House would probably have divided with 66 government members confronting 63 opposition. On the second of the two divisions, Rankin (Essex), who had on the previous division supported the government, was now in the opposition, while Dunkin (Brome), who had been absent on May 17 and had been a consistent Conservative, now voted with the Liberals. Thus, in effect, the change in view of Dunkin and Rankin upset the government. Also contributing to the government's minority in the division of June 14 was the absence of six government members, only five of whom could have been paired with opposition absentees. Abbott was among the six government members not present. As an ex-Liberal minister, and one who was much away and rather independent in his support of the Confederation coalition in the later stages of the eighth parliament, it might be conjectured that he was the unpaired absentee.

III

When J. S. Macdonald's cabinet resigned on March 29, 1864, the new Executive Council constructed by the Liberal-Conservatives contained only three members of the Cartier-Macdonald government that had resigned on May 23, 1862. Yet the composition of the new ministry was on the same lines as its predecessor. It had four Conservatives: J. A. Macdonald, A. Campbell (Cataraqui Division, Legislative Council), J. Simpson (Niagara), and J. Cockburn (Northumberland West); two Reformers: I. Buchanan (Hamilton) and M. H. Foley (Waterloo North); four French Canadians: Sir E. P. Taché (Legislative Council), G. E. Cartier, H. L. Langevin (Dorchester), and J. C. Chapais (Kamouraska) and two English-speaking members from Canada East: A. T. Galt (Sherbrooke) and T. D. McGee (Montreal West). It represented the several geographical regions and combined both old campaigners and representatives of newer currents of opinion. The appearance of maintaining a coalition of Conservatives and Reformers from Canada West was by now not very convincing, for Foley was rejected by his constituents (following the earlier fate of Spence, J. C. Morrison, and Sydney Smith), and Isaac Buchanan was hardly a significant figure politically. In Canada East, the team of Cartier, Langevin, and Chapais, who were to lead the Bleu group into the first era after Confederation, made their first appearance together at this time.

The much discussed policy of representation by population, so strongly urged by George Brown and the Clear Grit element in the Liberal party of Canada West, was a very potent factor in effecting the popular support of political groups and in regulating party loyalty in that section of the province. But it was a sectional issue which by its very nature could not appeal to Canada East. It is interesting to note that all Upper Canadian Liberals voted for the principle of representation by population in at least one division in 1863 and 1864, except J. S. Macdonald, E. B. Wood, A. Rankin, and A. N. Richards. Ten Conservatives[10] and two Coalition Reformers[11] also supported representation by population. From Canada East, the lone voice of R. B. Somerville (Huntingdon) supported this principle as it had in previous sessions. While the importance of this theme in influencing provincial politics is very apparent in any reading of the history of this period, the alignment of political groups as late as the year 1864 was still not governed exclusively by this issue.

It was quite clear by the late spring of 1864 that the several major political groups represented in the Legislative Assembly had reached a point where the typical manœuvres of Liberal-Conservatives, combining major elements from both sections of the province in opposition to a co-ordinated union of Liberal elements from the two sections, could give little hope of stable purposeful government. A new sense of direction was furnished on June 30, 1864. On that day the leaders of the Bleu, Upper Canadian Liberal, and Conservative groups agreed to combine their forces in order to alter the frame of the Canadian constitution and provide, in the federal principle, a new field in which the legitimate aspirations of Upper and Lower Canada, and Canada as a whole, might be worked out by the normal interplay of political parties. This was the birth of the "Great Coalition of 1864."

In some respects the coalition of 1864 is very similar to that of 1854. The manœuvre used as its base an existing administration which held the support of the largest French-Canadian group in alliance with a major Upper Canadian group. The necessary additional reinforcement for the administration was found from among moderate Upper Canadian Liberals (Reformers). As in 1854, the new coalition secured an initial large preponderance of votes in the Legislative Assembly, leaving to the opposition a hard core of left-wing members from both sections of the province and an extreme right-wing Conservative position among Upper Canadians. But here the similarity ends. The 1864 coalition was formed for a limited time to enact a specific body of legislation; it was not destined to leave a lasting impression on party alignment. Again, proportions of the numbers of members in the several groups were different. Following the rearrangement of groups in 1854, it was the Upper Canadian radicals who had formed the larger part of the new opposition, and these "Clear Grit" reformers had tended to set the pattern and tone of opposition advocacy. Following the coalition of 1864, the Rouges from Canada East formed the greater part of the opposition, and the voice and viewpoint of A. A. Dorion and his close associates were strong in anti-Confederation activity.

In the coalition of 1854, the rearrangement of groups had taken place at the opening stages of the first session of the fifth parliament. The implications of the new alignment were then worked out during the course of the session. In June 1864, following on the agreement to form a coalition, a breathing spell was needed to formulate the newly agreed legislative policy. Thus, the closing stages of the second session in 1864 do not reflect divisions bearing upon the alignment of parties. The session was concluded speedily, concentrating on money bills, arrangements for the militia, and a number of private measures. The opposition was not homogeneous at this time, though the Rouge members seemed generally to be the principal critics.

In 1865, two sessions of parliament were held. The third session of the eighth parliament met from January to March and was largely occupied by the debates which culminated in the passing of an address in favour of Confederation and the departure of a ministerial delegation to England. A further session, the fourth, met in August and September in order to complete the necessary routine money business for the year and report on the progress of the Confederation project. During both these sessions, the minds of members were quite preoccupied by the constitutional issues, and the lines drawn by the coalition of parties in 1864 held good throughout both of them.

When the Taché-Macdonald cabinet was converted into a coalition government on June 30, 1864, the Lower Canadian membership remained unchanged. As for the Upper Canadian half, I. Buchanan and M. H. Foley, the two ostensibly Reform members, were dismissed, and J. Simpson, a Conservative, was given public employment. George Brown (Oxford South), O. Mowat (Ontario South), and W. McDougall (Ontario North), leading Liberals, were then appointed to office in their stead. This pattern of three Conservatives and three Liberals from Canada West was preserved until Confederation.

There were some eleven changes in the membership of the Legislative Assembly at this time:

July 30, 1864, Ontario North: M. C. Cameron (anti-fed. C.) vice Wm. McDougall (L. cabinet minister) (opposition gain)
August 26, 1864, Jacques Cartier: G. G. Gaucher (Bleu) vice F. Z. Tassé (Bleu) (no change)
September 7, 1864, Niagara: Angus Morrison (Hincks. Ref.) vice J. Simpson (C.) (no change)
September 14, 1864, Peterborough: F. W. Haultain (C.) vice W. S. Conger (C.) (no change)
November 4, 1864, Lanark North: W. McDougall (L.) vice R. Bell (L.) (no change)
January 3, 1865, Chicoutimi & Saguenay: P. A. Tremblay (anti-fed. L.) vice D. E. Price (C.) (oppos. gain)
January 16, 1865, Three Rivers: C. B. de Niverville (Bleu) vice J. E. Turcotte (Bleu) (no change)
January 18, 1865, Ontario South: T. N. Gibbs (C.) vice O. Mowat (L.) (Lib.-Con. gain)
February 21, 1865, Hamilton: C. Magill (C.) vice Isaac Buchanan (Hincks. Ref.) (no change)
December —, 1865, Wentworth North: J. McMonies (L.) vice W. Notman (L.) (no change)
July —, 1866, Oxford North: T. Oliver (L.) vice H. F. MacKenzie (L.) (no change)

Three of these changes represented a change in party alignment of the riding, and these by-elections were much publicized and discussed as indicating the trends in the public view of Confederation. In July 1864, just a month after the House rose, M. C. Cameron, an anti-Confederation Conservative, defeated W. McDougall, a new minister in the coalition government. At the turn of the year, P. A. Tremblay, an anti-Confederation Liberal, was returned from Chicoutimi & Saguenay, replacing D. E. Price, a Lower Canadian Conservative, and in mid-January 1865, T. N. Gibbs, a Confederation Conservative, captured Oliver Mowat's traditionally Liberal riding, Ontario South, when the latter retired to the bench. Except for Cameron and Tremblay, all the new members were in favour of Confederation. The cases of Cameron and Gibbs, however, are significant evidence that the coalition of 1864 was but a temporary parliamentary manœuvre, and that party rivalry, even between different parties to the coalition, continued in the ridings themselves.

IV

The coalition of 1864 immediately broke the deadlock in the Legislative Assembly. A certain degree of autonomy was exercised by many members in reorienting themselves in the face of the new all-absorbing problem of Confederation. The principal example of the new temporary alignment of groups is, of course, the division on March 11, 1865,[12] on the question that an address be presented to the Queen, praying for imperial legislation to bring about British North American Confederation. An extensive sampling of divisions, both before and after this event, substantiates the fact that the lines drawn between sponsors and opponents of this measure held good for nearly every public question. One hundred and twenty-four members voted on the measure, ninety-one in its support and thirty-three in opposition. The members whose votes were not recorded were L. Wallbridge, speaker;

Munro (Durham West) and Notman (Wentworth North), both staunch Liberals and likely supporters; C. Duncan (Brome), an outspoken opponent; and J. B. Daoust (Two Mountains) and J. J. C. Abbott (Argenteuil), whose positions are conjectural. Twenty-nine Liberals and twenty-five Conservatives (and Coalition Reformers) from Canada West, and twenty-four Bleus and ten Conservatives from Canada East, supported the resolution. In addition, P. G. Huot (Quebec City East), E. Rémillard (Bellechasse), and R. B. Somerville (Huntingdon), who had supported the Liberal cause before the coalition, now voted for Confederation and supported the coalition government in day-to-day business. The centre of opposition to Confederation, and to the general working policies of the coalition government, lay with twenty-two Rouges.[13] But each of the principal political groups in the House did provide one member, or a group of members, who opposed Confederation and the coalition government. Seven Upper Canadian Liberals, Biggar (Northumberland East), D. A. Macdonald (Glengarry), J. Macdonald (Toronto West), J. Sandfield Macdonald (Cornwall), Rymal (Wentworth South), Scatcherd (Middlesex West), and T. C. Wallbridge (Hastings North), seceded from the major Liberal group and constituted the second largest segment of the opposition. M. C. Cameron (Ontario North), C. Dunkin (Brome)[14] and Duckett (Soulanges) were Conservatives during other phases of their careers, but distrusted Confederation. And finally, among the Bleu group, Pinsonneault (Laprairie) and Taschereau (Beause) left their party on the isuue, though the former returned quite soon to voting as a Bleu.

v

The fifth session of the eighth parliament, in 1866, witnessed the final episode in the party battle before Confederation. The relative calm and sense of direction that had prevailed while the principle of Confederation was still at issue now began to give place to partisan skirmishing, though an opening move by Dorion (Hochelaga) and Holton (Châteauguay) requesting that the people be consulted before the proclamation of Confederation,[15] was rebuffed by the supporters of the ruling coalition by 19 to 79.

The most obvious departure from the coalition alignment, when the division lists of the session are examined, was the new ferment within the ranks of Upper Canadian Liberals. George Brown, in the coalition cabinet, was quick to sense the approaching difficulty for Liberals. To remain in the coalition government was to remain tied to the Conservatives: to cast free from the coalition was the Liberals' only hope for independent action, however "disloyal" to Confederation this might appear to be. He resigned from office on December 21, 1865, and appeared in the House in 1866 as a critic of many government policies (save that of Confederation) and voted generally with the newly emerging group of advanced, anti-coalition Liberals. On August 9, 10, and 13, he moved resolutions criticizing a government currency measure and objecting to the indemnifying of seigniors for loss of their rights from the common funds of the province, to which Canada West contributed its share; and he sought to institute an investigation into the reasons for confusion in the Crown Lands Department in dealing with the McKay estate[16] In all these questions he was supported by a good proportion of Liberals and some Conservative members.

A. A. Dorion and Holton introduced a number of opposition resolutions, paring away at the budget, favouring settlers, seeking to render the new provincial constitutions of Ontario and Quebec (still called Upper and Lower Canada at this time) more democratic by avoiding a second chamber, by electing it, or at least by electing its speaker, and seeking to secure some amendments to the law concerning weights and measures.[17] Cauchon and Dorion proposed a resolution that would have removed from the Quebec constitution the provisions that were to safeguard the English-speaking ridings.[18] Another cross-current in this session was provided by a bill to authorize the purchase of the Buffalo and Lake Huron Railway by the Grand Trunk. The lines dividing supporters and opponents of the Grand Trunk Railway cut right across the usual party divisions in the House.[19]

Some generalizations appear to follow from a consideration of these and other divisions in the 1866 session. Of the seven Upper Canadian Liberals who had opposed Confederation, J. Macdonald (Toronto West) and T. C. Wallbridge (Hastings North) seemed to be drawing back to a moderate Liberal position. Meanwhile, the remaining five, now joined by George Brown, were attracting a growing number of rank-and-file Liberals into a new advancing liberal policy. L. Burwell (Elgin East), A. MacKenzie (Lambton), A. McKellar (Kent), H. Munro (Durham West), T. Oliver (Oxford North), T. S. Parker (Wellington North), W. Ross (Prince Edward), and J. P. Wells (York North) appeared to be those most affected among the Liberal membership in the House. The remainder of the Liberals tended to vote more moderately according to the example of their cabinet members, Howland and McDougall.

F. W. Haultain (Peterborough) and C. Magill (Hamilton) supported the coalition government and appeared to be Conservatives, but they did tend to favour the new liberal propositions that were advanced by opposition Liberals. They were, perhaps, latter-day Hincksite Reformers. T. N. Gibbs (Ontario South), J. S. Ross (Dundas), and M. C. Cameron (Ontario North) also steered a somewhat liberal course, though they were Conservatives.

In general, the members from Canada East hewed more closely to the party lines. Among the Bleus, Gaudet (Nicolet), Pinsonneault (Laprairie) and to a lesser extent Cornellier (Joliette) departed on a few occasions from the standard voting of their fellows. Huot (Quebec City Centre), Rémillard (Bellechasse), and Somerville (Huntingdon) who had been Liberals, if not Rouges, in the early sessions of the eighth parliament, now voted reasonably consistently for the coalition government.

While there are several exceptions and modifications to the generalization, there was a tendency in the 1866 session for Bleus and Liberal-Conservatives to vote together on the same basis that had prevailed during the Cartier-Macdonald era down to 1862. About half of the Upper Canadian Liberals continued to support the coalition ministry on virtually every occasion. Meanwhile the opposition was now not nearly so confined to Rouge strength, but was coming to enjoy at times approximately fifteen Upper Canadian Liberal votes. The opposition had still not found a unity in its viewpoint, however. There was a large measure of sectional interest in the voting of both Rouge and opposition Liberals. The opposition was still composed of an Upper and a Lower Canadian wing though on occasion they found common ground.

CHAPTER SIX

POLARITY

IN THE POLITICAL CONTESTS during the period of the Union, six major groups comprised the great bulk of members of the Legislative Assembly. The French-Canadian (Liberal)[1] group of 1841, which evolved first through alliance with Baldwin Reformers and later with Conservatives of Canada West into the Bleu tradition, was present in large and significant force in all parliaments. The reformers of Canada West came largely to follow the leadership of Baldwin and his associates by the close of the first parliament, and until 1854 were the second significant group in the House. After the Liberal-Conservative coalition of 1854, representatives of this group and this tradition continued to sit in parliament, but in numbers and influence it declined and had virtually disappeared by the election of 1863. A third major political tradition stemmed from Family Compact Toryism. In the first parliament, only six members represented this viewpoint. However, new associates continued to join the Tory, right wing of Upper Canadian politics and progressively diluted the exclusive Toryism of the group. By 1854, conservative elements were beginning to predominate in the group, and in the last stages of party rivalry before confederation it had become a Conservative group, beset still, however, by a right wing that continued to express something of the old Toryism. In Canada East, the pre-rebellion British-Tory-Commercial group returned in great force to the first parliament. But at each succeeding general election its numbers and its significance as a principal political entity declined. After 1854, it disappeared altogether as a principal group in the House. English-speaking conservative members acted thereafter in concert with the Liberal-Conservative elements in the Assembly.

Two new radical traditions, one from each section of the province, appeared in the Assembly in 1849-50. The Clear Grit movement in Canada West, including some pre-rebellion radicals and also an increasing number of new recruits and others attracted from Baldwin's camp, began to criticize sharply the policies of the Baldwin-Lafontaine and Hincks-Morin governments, and to oppose them. After the realignment of groups in 1854, this Clear Grit tradition was the central core around which the Liberal party of the 1860's and succeeding decades was formed. The Rouge party of Canada East, the sixth and last major political group, emerged concurrently with the Clear Grit movement; and while L. J. Papineau was a major influence in its launching and DeWitt and other veteran politicians immediately joined in its activity, yet it was, in great part, a new mid-nineteenth century party, largely composed of "new" men. The Rouge group, at times, attracted significant numbers of liberal and anti-Bleu votes and was the basis for the emergence of a new Liberal party in Lower Canada. Yet it did not succeed at any time, before 1867, in gaining predominance in its section of the province.*

---

* Figure V is intended to give a graphic representation of the theme of this chapter.

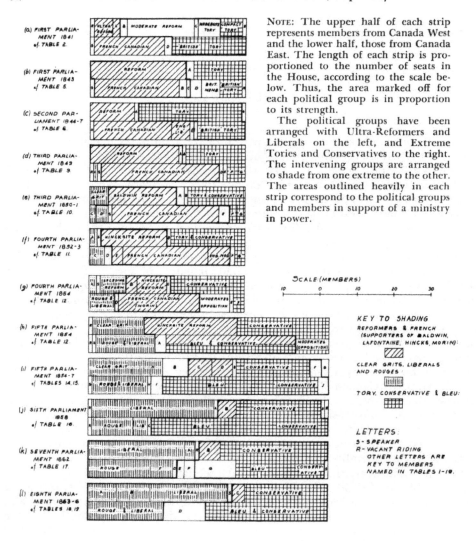

NOTE: The upper half of each strip represents members from Canada West and the lower half, those from Canada East. The length of each strip is proportioned to the number of seats in the House, according to the scale below. Thus, the area marked off for each political group is in proportion to its strength.

The political groups have been arranged with Ultra-Reformers and Liberals on the left, and Extreme Tories and Conservatives to the right. The intervening groups are arranged to shade from one extreme to the other. The areas outlined heavily in each strip correspond to the political groups and members in support of a ministry in power.

FIGURE V. Membership in the Legislative Assembly of Canada, 1841-66.

I

In terms of size and continuity of influence, the record of the French-Canadian (later Bleu) group is most significant. Except in the year 1841, this group had the majority of Lower Canadian members. Only for limited periods under Sydenham in 1841, under Metcalfe and his successors from 1844 to early 1848, and during J. Sandfield Macdonald's administration from May 1862 to March 1864 was government carried on without their active support, and these periods were characterized by much tension and uneasiness on the part of those in power. The major French-Canadian group, throughout the period, was an essential basis upon which to form a government and a principal key to the alignment of parties.

No political group from Canada West enjoyed the same record for continuity in control of its own section of the province. From the late 1820's onward, each succeeding general election in Upper Canada had witnessed an alternating majority for the left and right elements in the Assembly. Although this rhythm was somewhat disrupted in the period of the Union, due to the schisms that characterized the history of the Reform movement, yet the same influences were at work and witnessed major changes in the relative strength of the groups from Canada West in the House. Thus the Baldwin Reformers enjoyed an absolute majority in Canada West in the first and third parliaments, and the Liberals (Clear Grit Reformers) in the sixth and eighth. The Tories predominated in the second parliament. But in the fourth, fifth, and seventh parliaments, the three elements — Clear Grit Reformers, Hincksite (Coalition) Reformers and Conservatives — found themselves so adjusted that they were within one or two votes of deadlock.

In the period before 1854, three principal schemes of alignment were effected in striving to secure a consistent majority in the Assembly. Sydenham chose to base his hopes upon the British-Tory party from Canada East, combined with the moderate centre elements, both Reform and Tory, from Canada West. By 1842 this scheme was considered to be unworkable, and a new arrangement sanctioned by Bagot incorporated French Canadians and Upper Canadian Reformers in support of the government. It was incidental to this arrangement that about half of the British-Tory party also joined with the majority. The Lafontaine-Baldwin ministry, appointed in March 1848, continued this basis of alignment, though without the "British-Tory" support. The third scheme, worked out by Metcalfe, was based upon Tories from both sections of the province and a hope of including some French-Canadian members in the arrangement. Of these three designs, only the one built on the alliance of French Canadians and Reformers seemed to have the characteristics of stability; for the Sydenham arrangement required "management," and the Metcalfe scheme disclosed violent strains within the Upper Canadian Tory group and hostility in Canada East, which then was represented in the executive government almost entirely by the English minority.

The new manifestation of liberalism in 1849 and 1850 had begun to undermine the stability of the alliance of French Canadians and Reformers almost as soon as it was established in power and recognized. Yet from March 1848 to June 1854, the new threat from this left-wing radicalism was not sufficient to upset the alliance, and it enjoyed over six years of authority.

In the nine years from 1841 to 1850, the truly radical elements of the left had remained out of the public eye as a consequence of the rebellions of 1837 and

1838. The re-assertion of a distinctly radical viewpoint, starting in 1850, emphasized the fact that the Baldwin-Lafontaine and Hincks-Morin governments were moderate in outlook and belonged to the centre. From 1850 onward, the Canadian political horizon extended from Rouge and Grit on the left to the Tory fringe of Conservatism on the right. The Reform Ministries from 1850 to 1854 had to contend with opposition from both the right and the left.

II

In June 1854 in the closing session of the fourth parliament, and in September of the same year at the opening of the fifth parliament, the Hincks-Morin government found itself outnumbered by the combined opposition from radicals and Conservatives, yet the opposition from neither the left nor the right was strong enough to command a majority of the Assembly.

The Liberal-Conservative coalition which assumed power in late September 1854 introduced a new alignment of political groups based frankly on the tendency of members to gravitate to either a left or right pole in the political scene. In Canada West, this had the effect of splitting the Hincksite Reformers, half joining the Clear Grits and the other half working with the Conservatives. In Canada East, the French-Canadian group under Morin continued to support the reconstructed ministry and, in effect, thereafter acted as the party of the right. There was now little but fragments left of the old British-Tory-Commercial group and these acted with the Liberal-Conservative ministry.[2] The crisis of 1854 and the formation of the Liberal-Conservative coalition virtually eliminated the centre from the political scene. It followed, as a consequence, that the opposition to the Liberal-Conservatives, and the potential source for an alternative government, lay in co-ordinated action among the Liberal elements on the left.

The sixth parliament, elected in the late days of 1857, saw the Bleus returned in great strength from Canada East and the Liberals (Clear Grit Reformers) with a clear majority in Canada West. The continuing survivors of the Hincksite Reform viewpoint were reduced to five in number. In the first session of the parliament, in late July 1858, the Liberals seized an opportunity to try to form a Liberal government. The Brown-Dorion administration was defeated within a few hours of its formation, but yet demonstrated that the dynamic elements in the Legislative Assembly were now reduced to two in number, the Liberal-Conservatives from both sections of the province on the right and the Liberals and Rouges on the left. This state of alignment remained unaltered through the seventh and until June 1864 in the eighth parliaments, and was again the basic alignment from 1866 on into the period after Confederation.

The real strength of the Liberal and Conservative elements changed little in the general elections of 1861 and 1863. While the Upper Canadian Conservatives and the Lower Canadian Liberals were strengthened in 1861, these two groups lost ground in 1863. The balance of power came to lie with a smaller and smaller group of politically less stable men until a state of deadlock was reached. Then on June 30, 1864, virtually all members from Canada West joined with the Bleu group from Canada East in the coalition which was to bring in Confederation.

III

The first Liberal-Conservative cabinet formed in September 1854 had been composed of three Conservatives, two Coalition Reformers, four French Canadians, and one Lower Canadian "English" member, and had drawn support initially from twenty-five Conservatives, nineteen Reformers, thirty-two French Canadians, and twelve English-speaking Lower Canadians. After the short interlude of Liberal government in August 1858, the basic pattern of the Liberal-Conservative cabinet evolved to twelve members, four each of Conservatives and French Canadians, and two each of Coalition Reformers and Lower Canadian English. These four elements continued to support the Liberal-Conservative governments until 1864. In the ten-year period after 1854, the dwindling group of Hincksite Reformers who supported the Liberal-Conservative cause assumed an importance quite out of proportion to their numbers. During the late sessions of the fifth parliament, many of these members were attracted back to the Liberal alignment, and in ensuing elections others withdrew from public life. Yet from 1861 onward, those Reformers who continued to support the Liberal-Conservative cause added the necessary margin of strength which allowed the Cartier and Macdonald governments to remain in office. In 1863-4, only Jackson (Grey) and Buchanan (Hamilton) represented this tradition, while M. H. Foley was a new recruit on leaving the Liberal ranks. Yet so clearly were these votes essential to the maintenance of the Liberal-Conservative cause that two of these men were included in the cabinet in 1864.

The question of cohesion within the several principal political groups is dealt with more fully in a later chapter.[3] But the over-all evidence of alignment would seem to show that the early efforts to unite members for joint action in the first and second parliaments were subject to internal strains within major political groups. Neither reformers nor tories of either section of the province displayed more than moderate consistency in their voting. While a measure of discipline was obtained in 1848 and 1849 among the supporters of the Lafontaine-Baldwin government, the new ferment generated by Clear Grits and Rouges began again to destroy the parties' unity. After the fifth parliament, however, there are signs of growing discipline. Fewer members are missing from the division rolls on questions involving the life of a government, and larger portions of the membership of the Legislative Assembly can be clearly identified as belonging to a particular group. In earlier parliaments, parties tended to erode away at the edges, while in the sixth, and particularly in the seventh and eighth parliaments, the fluid element in the House was narrowed down to but a few moderates and independents floating in the centre between the major groups.

The last major testings of the solidarity of parties lay in May 1862 on the formation of J. S. Macdonald's Liberal government, in August 1863 at the testing of reaction to the reorganization of the Liberal government, and in March 1864 on the formation of the Taché-Macdonald government. While there was a looseness to party alignment in the early parliaments under the Union, the balance of power came to rest with but a handful of members in the last two parliaments. The deadlock of early 1864 is excellent evidence of the firmness of party discipline by that time.

After 1854, the existence of a continuing Hincksite Reformer group provided an acknowledged middle ground for moderates between the Clear Grit and the Conservative positions. On the formation of the Liberal government in May 1862, a number of moderates did cross the House to support the new government, and some returned in August 1863 to the Liberal-Conservative camp.

The alignment of members of the Legislative Assembly from Canada East was constantly moulded by the overriding influence of French-Canadian nationalism. The two sections of the province continued to react quite differently in politics to each new situation, despite the fact of their legislative union. While the pendulum of political fortune favoured first one and then another group in Canada West, just one moderate French-Canadian group appeared, again and again comprising a majority of members from Canada East. And the members of this French-Canadian group demonstrated a remarkable unanimity of view as they voted throughout the period. The desire to unite in defence of their heritage was stronger, apparently, than transitory influences that tended to divide them. In part, too, their tendency to vote together as a bloc was the result of long tutelage in the province of Lower Canada before 1837. Thus in 1841, all French-Canadian members with the exception of DeSalaberry voted together in opposition to Sydenham's Executive Council, and in 1843-4, when the pressure of circumstance might have suggested the breaking away of a French-Canadian right-wing group, only Barthe, Cuvillier, Noel, D. B. Papineau, J. E. Turcotte, and D. B. Viger seem to have responded. While Lafontaine was in office, loyalty to the French-Canadian tradition was reinforced by the attractions of association with an administration in power.

The return of L. J. Papineau and the appearance of a new liberal viewpoint sponsored within Canada East by French Canadians provided a second and competing centre of attraction for French-Canadian politicians. Thenceforward, there were two major French-Canadian political parties. The Rouge group appeared to revive the liberalism of the Patriot cause of 1837-8, while the more moderate group, always the more numerous, continued to represent conservative, less dynamic, French-Canadianism. In 1854, when the dictates of purely political considerations forced French-Canadian members to choose between left and right, the great majority adhered to the right and thereafter, to the Bleu position. In contrast to the idea of a centre party kept alive by the Hincksite Reform group in Upper Canada, the sense of racial solidarity carried all moderate French-Canadian members into the Bleu camp in the fifth parliament. But almost immediately, the process of consolidating the Bleu party turned up individual moderate members who did not seem to be wholly in sympathy with either the Bleu or the Rouge positions. Thus in 1858 and in 1862, on the formation of Liberal governments, a small number of French Canadians who had not adhered to the Rouge group consistently turned from their Bleu allegiance to support the Liberals and to join the Executive Council. In examining the contests in Canada East ridings during the general elections after 1851, one gains the impression that in addition to Rouge and Bleu candidates, there were a few French-Canadian moderates who would seek to preserve a certain degree of autonomy, though most of their voting would be with the majority of their fellow French Canadians.

In the years between 1854 and Confederation, the Rouge and Bleu groups came more and more to divide the representatives of Canada East exclusively into two camps, the moderates of Lower Canada thus appearing in alignment as a right wing of Rouge supporters. With the emergence of both a right and a left French-Canadian position in politics, most English-speaking members from Canada East tended to drop any pretensions toward separate political tactics and to divide consistently with one or other of the major political groups on the right or left of the House.

CHAPTER SEVEN

IN SEARCH OF "LOOSE FISH"

WHEN THE COURSE of the political battles of the Union period is traced in the contemporary press and in political histories written at different eras since Confederation, the great differences in party nomenclature cause doubts about the consistency of members in their political allegiance and much confusion about the continuity of various groups. An examination of the behaviour of individual members through the whole course of their careers in the Legislative Assembly of the Province of Canada does disclose a very large degree of consistency and continuity on the part both of individual members, and of the groups of members acting as political parties.

Six main traditions in the parliamentary life of the province have already been mentioned. With a mere handful of exceptions, all the members who sat in at least two parliaments may be classified within them, or else in one or another of two lesser and more indefinite "moderate" groupings. The list is as follows:

1. French-Canadian Bleu: the followers of Lafontaine and Morin in the first four parliaments who ended in the ranks of the Parti Bleu under Cartier in the later years. Some English-speaking members acted with this group at all times. By external evidence, it is difficult to distinguish after 1854 between English members who are an integral part of the party and those who are Lower Canadian Conservatives.

2. The British-Commercial-Tory tradition: the remnants of the supporters of the "Chateau Clique" with newly recruited English-speaking members. These were supporters of Sydenham and Metcalfe and opponents of the Lafontaine group. The group dwindled in numbers and significance in the late 1840's and early 1850's.

3. The Rouge party: associates and followers of L. J. Papineau and A. A. Dorion. They were almost entirely recruited from new members appearing after the third parliament, and were distinguished from moderate Liberals by their consistent advocacy of principle and avoidance of association or coalition with the Bleu group.

4. Moderate Liberals of Canada East. Drummond, Lemieux, and Sicotte are the chief examples. Individual members, their careers lay between groups (1) and (3), and paralleled in many ways the Baldwin-Hincks reformers of Canada West who turned Liberal (7).

5. Baldwin-Hincks reformers of Canada West who consistently supported the Liberal-Conservative coalition after 1854.

6. "Clear Grit" tradition: comparable in some respects to the Rouges. These were staunch liberals who beginning in 1850 opposed Baldwin and Hincks and emerged after 1860 in conjunction with group (7) as a Liberal party in Canada West.

7. Reformers who, like J. S. Macdonald, had supported Baldwin before 1854, but progressed into association with the Clear Grits.

8. The Upper Canadian Tory-Conservative tradition.

I

The major French-Canadian political party entered the first parliament in 1841 as the inheritor of the French-Canadian political tradition of the years before the rebellions of 1837-8. Many of the more advanced members of the earlier era were so closely involved in the rebellions that they were not in public life and, as a result, the radical wing of the party was missing from the House. In 1841, the political leaders of French Canada steered clear of advocating republicanism and the more positive themes of L. J. Papineau and sought to unite their people in opposing the Act of Union in all its aspects. This was sound strategy which avoided any taint of "disloyalty" while still appealing very broadly to their people. Although the presentation of anti-Union resolutions in the session of 1841 failed to secure large Upper Canadian support, it did provide a working basis of unity and marked out Baldwin and his small group of Upper Canadian followers as staunch allies.

The political situation in 1842 already showed changes from that in the previous year. By-elections began to whittle away British Tory strength in Canada East as new French-Canadian members were elected. In Canada West, some Moderate Reformers began to join Baldwin's small group of "Ultras," who wished to further co-operation with the French-Canadian group in the House. While Sydenham had been able to carry on his administration without the French Canadians in 1841, Bagot found it essential to include French Canadians and their "Ultra" reform allies in the Executive Council if a stable working majority was to be created in the Legislative Assembly. Thus in mid-September 1842, Lafontaine was appointed to the Executive Council, where Aylwin and A. N. Morin presently joined him as men in the confidence of the French-Canadian group.

The anti-Union policy presently disappeared as a principal theme for the French group because participation in the administration presented new possibilities for positive action in maintaining the interests of French Canada. Throughout the remaining course of government in the Province of Canada, the basic consider-ations governing the French-Canadian group seem to have amounted to preserving unity in order to present a united front in parliament in defence of the French-Canadian way of life.

The crisis that arose between Metcalfe and his Executive Council presented the first major test of French-Canadian unity. The case in favour of the governor's viewpoint was theoretically quite plausible and appealed instinctively to D. B. Viger and his small group of associates.[1] But to support the governor was to sur-render all the gains made in the first parliament in collaboration with reformers from Canada West, and meant a breakdown in French-Canadian political unity. Thus the deviation of D. B. Viger and his associates made no general appeal to French Canada in 1844, and the great majority of Lower Canadian electoral contests in that year returned supporters of Lafontaine. At the next general election, in 1847, the trend again favoured French-Canadian gains from "British" Tories.

The return of L. J. Papineau to Canada and to parliament in 1848 galvanized the more liberal French Canadians to new action. There had been examples of French-Canadian members voting out of unison with the majority of their fellows in a few divisions during the second parliament, but coinciding with the debate on the Rebellion Losses Bill, the liberal element of French Canada began to take on new life and to dispute the monopoly of the political influence of Lafontaine's group in Canada East. Most of the members who voted for the new liberalism were new members of the Legislative Assembly who had not been followers of Lafontaine in the first two parliaments. But there were soms veterans of the French-Canadian group in the earlier parliaments who now turned to give general support to much of the Rouge advocacy in the House (see Tables 10, 11, and 12). J. DeWitt (an American by birth), Holmes, La Terrière, Letellier, Marchildon, and Sicotte were of this group. And in later sessions, Drummond, Lemieux, Evanturel, and J. E. Thibaudeau ceased to vote consistently with the French-Canadian bloc and took up a more advanced liberal position. But these cases hardly constitute a major break in the unity of the French-Canadian party of the 1840's. This older French-Canadian group passed largely unscathed through the era in alliance with major Upper Canadian groups.

By June 1854 the moderate French-Canadian group was faced by another great test of its unity. The atmosphere of the last session of the fourth parliament in this year was charged with excitement and general discontent with the existing régime, and in the last of the three divisions of that session the government was defeated. While La Terrière, Marchildon, and Sicotte appear to have broken with the major group at this point, Cauchon, Dubord, Gouin, Lacoste, LeBlanc, Polette, and Tessier were also among the opposition (see Table 12). Since Gouin, LeBlanc, and Tessier did not return to the House in a later parliament, it is not possible to estimate exactly their viewpoint in 1854. But Cauchon, Dubord, Lacoste, and Polette did return to later parliaments to support the major French-Canadian group. The early divisions of the fifth parliament disclosed the same strains within the French-Canadian representation (see Table 13). While the great majority of the moderate French-Canadian group continued to support the Hincks-Morin ministry, Casault, Cauchon, Dostaler, J. Dufresne, Guévremont and Polette were in opposition until the formation of the Liberal-Conservative coalition, when they returned to join their fellows in its support. Whatever the motives of these members may have been, their action constituted a temporary break in the unity of the group.

From 1854 on to Confederation the course of this party was reasonably straight-forward. As it had now come into alliance with the Conservatives of Canada West and was opposed by the Rouge party in French Canada, it lost much of its earlier claim to be a liberal group. In the late 1850's, the older generation of members who had known the struggles of the early parliaments of the Union were fast disappearing from its ranks in the House, and the new leadership of Cartier was transforming the group into a right-wing party. By 1858, only Cartier, Cauchon, Fournier, Lacoste, Mongenais, and Turcotte were left of the old group that had sat in the third or earlier parliaments. It was in the period after 1854 that the group took up the designation "Bleu" to mark itself off from "Rouge"; though in direct succession to the French party of 1841, the Bleus were somehow altered in their emphasis and outlook. The Bleu cause continued to prosper in Canada East and with but few exceptions its members sponsored Confederation. It was to be the core of the Liberal-Conservative party in Quebec after Confederation.

II

An immediate result of the rebellions of 1837-8 was the elimination of a radical left wing from public life for a decade. The problem of survival in the early days of the Union had held most French Canadians within one political group. The return of L. J. Papineau to public life in 1848, after a sojourn in Europe, coincided with a general resurgence of militant liberalism throughout the western world. In Canada East he found a new generation of French-Canadian intellectuals who where enthusiastic about the new liberalism then current in Europe, and who were reading, discussing, and debating the new ideas. The Institut Canadien of Montreal became a centre for these men. By 1851 they became organized for political action as the Parti Rouge, were nominating candidates in elections, and recruiting a public following with their own periodical press. This movement was not simply a transplanted offshoot of the European liberal movement, though it did draw inspiration from Papineau himself and from the European press. But equally strong in its origins was the patriot tradition of the 1830's which had contained much that was liberal and anti-clerical. In later years, the Rouges were able, with some truth, to represent themselves as the true heirs of the patriot cause of 1837.

Within a few years the Parti Rouge had established itself as the left pole in French-Canadian political life and was seriously challenging the older moderate French-Canadian group which was led by A. N. Morin and then by G. E. Cartier. From studying the division lists in the Legislative Assembly it becomes clear that the great majority of Rouge members of the legislature were new men who started their public life as Rouges. Some more moderate members of parliament were attracted away from the Bleu group; however, these men did not seem to belong whole-heartedly with the Rouges, but simply formed a group of "anti-Bleus" in the House. By June 1854, some seven members of the Assembly seemed to belong to the Rouge group, and they were sixteen strong at the commencement of the fifth parliament. The electoral platform constructed in their earlier days included strong anti-clerical ideas which militated against their general acceptance by French Canada as a whole.

Jacob DeWitt, who had voted with Papineau in pre-rebellion days and had been a supporter of Lafontaine early in the Union, joined with the Rouges in parliament. While Papineau had virtually launched the new party in the House in 1850, A. A. Dorion and the members of the Institut Canadien were the first real nucleus of its strength.

But the Rouge group, while representing the liberal pole of politics in Canada East, were not for many years the only liberals in that section of the province. On three occasions, in August 1858, in May 1862, and in May 1863, there were major efforts to construct or reconstruct Liberal governments for the province. On the two earlier occasions, there was a tacit admission of the existence in Lower Canada of various shades of liberalism; for though A. A. Dorion was included both times, other more moderate men—L. T. Drummond, F. Lemieux, and J. E. Thibaudeau in 1858, and Sicotte, Tessier, McGee, Evanturel, and Abbott in 1862, who were not the original Rouge tradition—made up the majority of the Lower Canadians in the cabinets. When, in May 1863, there was a major reconstruction of the Lower Canadian section of the cabinet, the inclusion of the Rouge partisans, A. A. Dorion,

I. Thibaudeau, Letellier, Huntington, and Laframboise, was the signal for great resentment on the part of the excluded "moderate liberal" ministers, who immediately went into opposition. As late as 1863, then, there were significant distinctions which prevented unity in the liberal ranks in Quebec, and marked out the Rouges as but the left-wing portion of Lower Canadian liberalism.

While the choosing of men for Liberal cabinets emphasized the distinctions between one group of French-Canadian liberals and another, the election contests in the ridings do not reflect these differences. In surveying the electoral contests in the general elections of 1857, 1861, and 1863, we find few occasions when a Rouge, a Moderate Liberal, and a Bleu fought a three-cornered dual in a riding. Much more usual was the type of contest where two candidates, one of the right and one of the left (whether Rouge or Moderate Liberal) fought for the seats.

III

In Canada East, a number of predominantly English-speaking ridings as well as some largely French-Canadian ridings sent Anglo-Saxon members to parliament. These English-speaking members provided further variations and additions to the political alignment in Canada East. In the first parliament in 1841, nearly half the representatives from Canada East voted as a group of English members in support of Lord Sydenham's policies. By continuity in membership and in viewpoint, this "British" Tory group of 1841 perpetuated much of the tradition of the British-Commercial-Tory party of pre-rebellion days. Its membership included elements from the urban ridings of Montreal, Quebec, and Three Rivers, representatives of the English and some French-Canadian seignorial families, Eastern Township members, and government office holders. They continued the basic alignment, between race and race, that had originated in earlier days. With the realignment of groups in the Legislative Assembly in 1842, following the inclusion of Baldwin and Lafontaine in the Executive Council, the long exclusive association of the English-speaking group with the executive was broken, and English Tory and French-Canadian nationalist now joined in support of the government and in influence at the Council board. From September 1842 to late November 1843, the English-Tory group was divided in its allegiance. Slightly more than half of its members gave fairly consistent support to the Executive Council, while some five or six[2] went into opposition. Even at the onset of the crisis of Metcalfe with his Executive Council in November 1843, the whole group did not immediately reunite in the governor's support, but some of its members continued to vote with the Executive Council.

The circumstances that had fostered an exclusively "English" party down to 1841 disappeared progressively in the next few years. In the general election of 1844, while Canada West was swept by a positive response to the governor's appeal, the "English" group in Canada East fell to about thirteen members, and in succeeding elections hovered around a strength of five or less. At the same time, the French-Canadian party had never been without its English element of sympathizers, although in the second parliament (1844-7) their numbers fell to five.[3] Commencing with 1848, when executive government was in the hands of an alliance of Reformers of Canada West with the group of French Canadians in Canada East, ten or more English members of Lower Canada voted with the Reform government.

The whole problem of interpreting the voting of English-speaking members from Canada East in the period after 1854 presents difficulties. As late as 1866, when the constitutional framework for the new province of Quebec was being worked out, the twelve ridings of Pontiac, Ottawa County, Argenteuil, Huntingdon, Missisquoi, Brome, Shefford, Stanstead, Compton, Richmond & Wolfe, Megantic, and Sherbrooke Town were being protected as English-speaking ridings.[4] Throughout the Union period the elections in these ridings had usually followed the Upper Canadian pattern of Reformer opposed to Tory, or Liberal opposed to Conservative. Only in the periods when Sydenham's and Metcalfe's policies were operating did the members from these English-speaking ridings tend to support the governor and oppose his French-Canadian opponents, thus lending a racial flavour to their voting.

As has been noted, the sense of political polarity which operated throughout in Canada West also operated in the English-speaking ridings of Canada East and after 1849 became apparent in the French-Canadian political field as well. The English-speaking ridings of Canada East, though in a minority in their half of the province, did not have an exclusively Tory or Conservative flavour about them. Whether these members did, in fact, attend caucus with Upper Canadian Conservatives or Liberals, or with French-Canadian Bleus and Rouges, is not known, but in the House their votes appeared as additional support to major groups of the right and the left.

It was to be expected, also, that English members of Lower Canada should find their way into the moderate Liberal and Rouge groups in the House. Of these, L. T. Drummond, R. B. Somerville, T. D. McGee, Henry Starnes, and Abbott seemed to vote largely with their French-Canadian Liberal counterparts, and L. H. Holton, John Young, and L. S. Huntington seemed to be active associates of the Rouges. A few careers of Lower Canadian members seem to be unusual or inconsistent, but they do not affect the general trend of the great majority of political lives discussed here.[5]

IV

In Canada West, too, the members returned to the first parliament were strongly influenced by the political traditions that had been brought down from the pre-Union period. A great majority of members thought of themselves as reformers, successors to the opponents of the Family Compact; yet only Robert Baldwin was to emerge as a principal leader from the pre-rebellion reform group. Much speculation and correspondence had been undertaken in 1841 to try to focus the efforts of reformers on a unified plan of action, but during the first session only a handful of men followed Baldwin's lead in seeking a working arrangement with the French-Canadian party. In the second and third sessions in 1842 and 1843, considerable progress was made in constructing a unified reform party, the process being aided by the presence of Baldwin, Hincks, and Small in offices of influence in the Executive Council.

The Metcalfe crisis and the public debate leading up to the 1844 general election imposed great strain upon the new-found unity of the reformers, but the occasion was used to strengthen the ties of unity through mass meetings, dinners, and picnics. The general election of 1844 was a disaster for the reformers, cutting down their numbers to only twelve members, but the defeat helped to further consolidate reform loyalty. In 1848 the reform group was returned in strength, and by the following year, in conjunction with its Lower Canadian associates, was in control of the executive government and implementing a vigorous programme of legislation.

With the session of 1849 a new radical spirit began to stir the left wing of the reform movement and within a year or two was seriously disrupting its unity. By 1850 a group of five[6] had left the ranks of Baldwin reformers and were leading in spirited criticism of the government and advocating further reforms beyond the administration's current policy.

From 1850 until about 1858, the reform movement was rent by severe stresses which disrupted its cohesion and threatened to break it up into a number of warring groups. In the late fall of 1851, Baldwin withdrew from leadership and his mantle passed to Hincks. In an effort to secure some measure of unity, Hincks attempted to meet the demands of the Clear Grit radicals for a more progressive policy and brought Malcolm Cameron and John Rolph, advanced reformers, into his cabinet as a surety of his good faith. In the general election of 1851, there was no great change from the situation at the end of the third parliament in the relative strength of conservatives and reformers. But the differences that divided one group of reformers from another rendered about half of the reformers unreliable as supporters of the Hincks ministry. W. L. Mackenzie continued to plow a lone furrow in the sessions of the fourth parliament and the first appearance of George Brown in the House in 1851 marked the beginning of a "Brownite" form of reform advocacy which was at first in competition with other groups. In addition to George Brown, David Christie, Joseph Hartman, Roderick McDonald, and John White entered upon their important parliamentary careers as "Clear Grit" reformers. The radical reform members in 1852-3 had a strength of eleven.[7] The efforts of Hincks did succeed in retaining the adhesion of most of these men in support of his cabinet until June 1854, but in that short session it was clear that their confidence had been lost. The general election of 1854 hardly altered the relative strength of conservatives and reformers in the House. But, within the reform group itself, the moderate followers of Hincks had increased in proportion to the radicals. Although J. Sandfield Macdonald and Merritt were now voting with the opposition, and Aikins, Ferrie, Lumsden, McKerlie, and J. Scatcherd were new recruits for the Ultra-Reform group, the followers of Hincks at the opening of the session numbered twenty-five to the radicals' fourteen.

The concerted opposition to the ministry by Conservatives, Rouges, and a further miscellaneous group from Lower Canada, as well as the Ultra-Reformers of Canada West, brought down the Hincks-Morin ministry and led to the coalition of Hincksite Reformers with the Conservatives, and the majority of Lower Canadians in support of the new MacNab-Morin (Liberal-Conservative) cabinet. This new Liberal-Conservative alliance appeared to confirm the worst fears of the Ultra-Reformers that Hincks was unscrupulous. They had already predicted, in scathing terms, just such a "combination,"[8] "composed of the odds and ends of all parties, and not actuated by patriotic feelings or honest principles which must come into power..."[9] Immediately following the formation of the new coalition in 1854, a trend began which saw a parade of former supporters of Hincks into the opposition ranks. By September 11, 1854, six additional reformers had joined the opposition (see Table 14) and in the course of the remainder of the first session and in the second, a further seven reform members (see Table 15) joined in the movement. The degree of unity achieved by Baldwin and his aides in 1848 was now broken beyond repair.

In 1857, a reform convention was held in Toronto[10] to seek agreement on a new concerted reform policy for all the groups of reformers who stood in opposition to the Liberal-Conservative government. In effect, this convention did launch a new, more co-ordinated movement which was to be the Liberal party in Canada West and in Ontario after 1867. Meanwhile, some reform members chose to remain in support of the Liberal-Conservative arrangement, seeing the necessity for a coalition and its accompanying necessary sacrifices of principle.[11]

The reformers who turned to oppose the Liberal-Conservative coalition during the course of the fifth parliament represent the main current of the reform tradition at this time. The reformers who continued to support the MacNab-Morin and Taché-Macdonald governments were a continuing but minor current of the reform movement which grew less and less meaningful; yet the continuing Hinck-site Reformers, of whom R. Spence, Sydney Smith, A. Morrison, I. Buchanan and G. Jackson are specific examples, were not without significance in later political alignment. In the last three parliaments under the Union they added a small margin of support to the Liberal-Conservative cause in the Legislative Assembly which, in the approaching deadlock, was quite out of proportion to the actual number of members involved.

V

A last important political tradition that continued to draw the adherence of significant numbers in the Legislative Assembly throughout the period from 1841 to 1867 was the Tory-Conservative group. As in the case of the other main political groups, its roots went back into the pre-rebellion period. Brothers, sons, and other family connections of the Family Compact leaders of the 1820's appeared again and again in the Conservative ranks in Canada West.

In 1841 a small group in the first parliament including J. S. Cartwright (Lennox & Addington), S. Y. Chesley (Cornwall), J. Johnston (Carleton), A. N. MacNab (Hamilton), G. Sherwood (Brockville), and J. Woods (Kent) were recognized by Sydenham as Compact Tories. In the first session of the first parliament they preserved a consistent opposition to Sydenham's arrangements and legislation. In 1842, they formed a nucleus in opposition to the newly reconstructed Executive Council sponsored by Sir Charles Bagot, and as the force of political polarity began to arrange members in larger political groupings in the second and third sessions, they were joined by some four or five moderate Tories (see Tables 3 and 4) who had previously given some support to Sydenham.

Up to late November 1843, this Tory group was a forward projection of the Family Compact viewpoint. The events of late 1843 and 1844, which saw Sir Charles Metcalfe actively sponsoring political action to oppose the reformers of the late Executive Council, resulted in a major victory for the Tory cause in Canada West and introduced some new members of more moderate views into its parliamentary ranks. At the general election, or in subsequent by-elections, J. H. Cameron, William Cayley, W. H. Dickson, J. A. Macdonald, A. H. Meyers, and B. Seymour joined the party ranks; Cameron, Cayley, and Macdonald being destined to play leading roles in the evolution of the party from Compact Toryism to the more moderate conservatism of later years. But in the 1840's the older tradition was still very strong.

W. H. Draper was singled out by Metcalfe, as the most talented available member in the Tory connection, to head the ordering of business in both the Executive Council and the Legislative Assembly. Since Draper's views were moderate and since he did not belong to the Compact Tory group, his choice was calculated to bring some measure of unity to the Tory ranks. Yet the political stresses of the era were not sufficient to attract all Tory members of the House into a unified, manageable group. Again, Metcalfe had originally hoped to avoid partisanship in erecting his system of power and tried to secure the adhesion of moderate reformers to his cause during the early summer of 1844. The resulting government from 1844 to 1848 was "rightist" and almost exclusively Tory in its makeup; yet its unity was disturbed by the inherent clash between the exclusiveness of the right-wing Tories and the aspirations of both Metcalfe and Draper to broaden the basis and the policy of the group in power.

As late as the spring of 1847, the moderate tendencies of Draper were still in the ascendent, and a cabinet of new young men, Cayley, J. A. Macdonald, and J. H. Cameron, was in power. But on Draper's retirement, Henry Sherwood's appointment as attorney-general (Upper Canada) seemed to imply the resurgence of Compact Tory influence. The Tory era of government from 1844 to 1848 had disclosed great stresses within the group as a whole, but it had also been a time of experimentation, and indicated clearly the problems of unity which were to be faced in the future.

From 1848 to 1851 the Tory cause was at low ebb; the explosion of frustration in the burning of the Montreal parliament buildings and the episode of the annexation manifesto have long been recognized as its finale. But the dictates of political polarity indicated a place for a political group of the right from Canada West, and in spite of the crushing defeat in the elections of 1847, J. P. Crysler, Malloch, and Stevenson had been returned to augment the Conservative element in the Tory group. In this parliament the Toronto-centred Tories were out-numbered by the non-Toronto group, over half being from the eastern district from Trenton to Bytown.

In the fourth parliament and thereafter the term "Conservative" appears more frequently in the press in referring to the party, and moderate influences are more in evidence. But at no time, during the pre-Confederation period, were the Conservatives free from considerable influence from a reactionary right wing. In 1854, MacNab, a somewhat chastened Compact Tory, became titular head of the new coalition cabinet—a proof that conservatism still needed the support of Tory opinion—and in 1856, when MacNab was "unloaded," J. H. Cameron was prepared to carry on the advocacy of staunch partisanship and aloofness from mediating policies. But the conclusion of a political alliance between the moderate French Canadians and the Tory-Conservative group in 1854 set the stage for a new era in which a premium was placed upon compromise in the everdy-day course of political business, and the exclusiveness of old traditional Toryism had to respond by conciliation, in times of crisis at least, or give up any hope of future victory.

As John A. Macdonald came into acknowledged leadership of the Conservatives, the possibility of creating a broad-based moderate party of the right in Canada West, first explored by W. H. Draper, grew to be a reality. To some extent, both in its ability to work with the major French-Canadian party and in its striving to incorporate within its support the moderate, middle-of-the-road opinion of Canada West, the Conservative party after 1854 is comparable to Baldwin's reform party from 1842 to 1851. Yet both Baldwin reformers and Macdonald conservatives had followed the dictates of political polarity, and had campaigned, respectively, as partisans of the "left" and partisans of the "right." During the period from 1854 to 1867, and beyond that date for some decades, the Conservative party, through this characteristic ability to compromise, continued to attract to its own support moderate adherents of the liberal cause.

In the early 1860's, however, the general appeal of political platforms asserting the particular viewpoint of one or other of the major sections of Canada and the popularity of clearly stated political doctrines worked against the Conservative party at the polls, and it was falling behind the Liberal party.

As in Canada East, a number of Upper Canadian members of the Legislative Assembly did not follow closely any of the major political traditions. Colonel John Prince, member for Essex from 1841 to 1854, was one of these individualists, and the careers of J. P. Roblin, G. B. Lyon (Fellows), J. W. Gamble, and J. Y. Bown are also unusual.

Although it is true, as a generalization, that the two streams of political life flowed on apart in their separate fields of Canada East and Canada West; yet, some hints do come to light to imply a connection between the "English" members of Canada East and the parties of Canada West. The analysis of voting in the House gives no clear evidence in this connection, and, in any case, the broad interpretations arrived at in this study are not radically affected by such considerations. Nevertheless, it is worth noting why one might entertain them in the first place.

The founding of the Montreal *Pilot* by Hincks to meet the need for a reform journal in English in Canada East is plain evidence of Lower Canadian interest in Upper Canadian party strife. The unique support of representation by population by R. B. Somerville of Huntingdon and the status of John Rose as a Lower Canadian yet a representative of conservatism in the Executive Council from August 1858 to June 1861 are further evidence of Upper Canadian politics impinging upon the Lower Canadian field. It was J. A. Macdonald, moreover, who wrote to A. T. Galt of Sherbrooke soliciting his support for the Bleu cause in 1858. In fact, the connections between the political life of the English-speaking minority in Canada East and that of Canada West were natural developments anticipated by the framers of the Union. But the techniques of research used here do not produce new conclusive data in this regard.

CHAPTER EIGHT

THE FACE OF THE LAND

THERE WAS no legal requirement in the Province of Canada that a member of the Legislative Assembly had to be a resident of the constituency he represented in the House. In a number of cases candidates came down to their ridings from the cities, towns, or distant parts of the province. Thus some of the more famous political leaders, for example, A. N. Morin, L. T. Drummond, Francis Hincks, and Malcolm Cameron, were returned to the Assembly from at least three different ridings at various stages of their careers. And there are a number of examples of members being returned by two different constituencies at the same general election. It follows, then, that in addition to an appreciation of the strength and composition of political groups, there remains for analysis the further field of the political complexion of the ridings themselves. Although most ridings cannot be described as being consistently of one political loyalty or another throughout the whole period, yet an examination of the evidence does disclose a basis for generalization. The evidence is consolidated in two forms: in tabular form in Figure VI, and in map form in Maps A, B, and C. When the material presented in Figure VI, showing the political complexion of members as they were returned from each riding in successive general elections, was plotted on maps of the province, some interesting conclusions became apparent. Though readers will come to these charts with slightly different backgrounds of information, and each will appreciate the visual detail in his own way, a brief commentary on them is offered here as a general guide.

I

In the whole period of the Union, from 1841 to 1867, there was only one redistribution of seats that made major changes in the boundaries of the electoral districts. This redistribution was made law by the statute 16 Victoria, chapter 152, passed by the parliament of the Province of Canada in 1853. The new ridings were used for the first time in the general elections of 1854, which returned the fifth parliament of the Province of Canada and increased the number of members elected from eighty-four to one hundred and thirty.[1]

Apart from major changes, however, for anyone following the course of politics from one parliament to another in this era, there are a sufficient number of minor alterations in the naming of ridings to cause confusion. A first key to resolving these difficulties may be found in the arrangement of Figure VI. Each geographical area is kept, where possible, in the same horizontal line, and the major changes in name are indicated. Several extreme cases should be noted. They are as follows:

The townships of Albion, Caledon, Chingacousy, Toronto, and Toronto Gore were a single riding returning one member to each parliament; yet the name of the riding changed twice. For the general elections of 1841 and 1844, they constituted the Second Riding of York; for the general elections of 1847-8 and 1851, they were the West Riding of York; while in 1854 and thereafter they were the County of Peel. In Figure VI these several designations of the one area are assembled on the line for Peel. The examples of Sherbrooke County and Saguenay in Canada East are complicated not only by a change of name, but also by a change in area and boundaries. In the simpler case, that of Sherbrooke, there was one change in boundary: in the redistribution of 1853 the area of the riding was reduced. The name Sherbrooke County was used from 1841 to 1853, and was then changed to Sherbrooke & Wolfe. In the general elections for the sixth, seventh, and eighth parliaments, the riding was designated Richmond & Wolfe, and it appears under this name in Figure VI. The name Saguenay, from 1841 to 1853, referred to the riding on the north shore of the St. Lawrence River to the east of Montmorency and astride the Saguenay River. In the redistribution of 1853 the area was divided into two ridings, the one along the Saguenay River being denominated Chicoutimi & Tadoussac, while the second one along the St. Lawrence shore to Montmorency was called Saguenay. Both these ridings were renamed in 1855,[2] the one along the Saguenay River becoming Chicoutimi & Saguenay, while the St. Lawrence shore riding became Charlevoix. Figure VI assembles the data under Charlevoix and Chicoutimi & Saguenay.

While most of the other changes in nomenclature follow the conventions explained above, the following may be useful as a quick reference:

Between the second and third parliaments:

Northumberland North became Peterborough
Halton West became Waterloo
Lincoln South became Welland
York First became York South
York Second became York West
York Third became York East
York Fourth became York North

Between the fourth and fifth parliaments areas and boundaries were altered, but there is general continuity between:

York West (4th parl.) and Peel (5th parl.)
York South (4th parl.) and York West (5th parl.)
Leinster (4th parl.) and L'Assomption (5th parl.)
Montreal County (4th parl.) and Jacques Cartier and Hochelaga (5th parl.)
Missisquoi (4th parl.) and Missisquoi and Brome (6th parl.)

Maps A, B, and C were drawn using modern maps to supply the outline of physical features, and the various statutes of Upper and Lower Canada, the Province of Canada, and the Imperial parliament to designate the boundaries. Where minor changes in limits occurred, liberty has been taken in drawing the boundary, to make the work of map production easier. In the preliminary work on mapping a number of maps produced in the period 1843-70 were consulted, but the problems arising from different systems of projection, and the discrepancies between the political boundaries as laid down by the different authorities, left the impression that no one map was a suitable authority for reproduction here.

II

Map A shows the general nature of the politics of the province in the period from

FIGURE VI. Members of the Union Parliaments by Constituencies.

NOTES: (1) The political viewpoint of the member at the time of the election is shown; no attempt is made to represent changes of view between elections. (2) The ridings have been numbered arbitrarily, 1-65 in Canada West, 66-135 in Canada East, corresponding to the numbering on the maps. The table is arranged to show the changes of name of some ridings, and the relationship between ridings at the redistribution for the fifth parliament.

Column headers (sessions):

FIRST 1841–44 · SECOND 1844–47 · THIRD 1848–51 · FOURTH 1853–54 · FIFTH 1854–57 · SIXTH 1858–61 · SEVENTH 1861–63 · EIGHTH 1863–67

1. BRANT EAST
2. BRANT WEST
3. BROCKVILLE
4. CARLETON
5. CORNWALL
6. DUNDAS
7. DURHAM EAST
8. DURHAM WEST
9. ELGIN EAST
10. ELGIN WEST
11. ESSEX
12. FRONTENAC
13. GLENGARRY
14. GRENVILLE SOUTH
15. GREY
16. HALDIMAND
17. HALTON
18. HAMILTON
19. HASTINGS NORTH
20. HASTINGS SOUTH
21. HURON and BRUCE
22. KENT
23. KINGSTON
24. LAMBTON
25. LANARK NORTH
26. LANARK SOUTH
27. LEEDS and GRENVILLE N.
28. LEEDS SOUTH
29. LENNOX and ADDINGTON
30. LINCOLN
31. LONDON
32. MIDDLESEX EAST
33. MIDDLESEX WEST
34. NIAGARA
35. NORFOLK
36. NORTHUMBERLAND EAST
37. NORTHUMBERLAND WEST
38. ONTARIO NORTH
39. ONTARIO SOUTH
40. OTTAWA
41. OXFORD NORTH
42. OXFORD SOUTH
43. PEEL
44. PETERBOROUGH
45. PRESCOTT
46. PRINCE EDWARD
47. RENFREW
48. RUSSELL
49. SIMCOE NORTH
50. SIMCOE SOUTH
51. STORMONT
52. TORONTO EAST
53. TORONTO WEST
54. VICTORIA
55. WATERLOO NORTH
56. WATERLOO SOUTH
57. WELLAND
58. WELLINGTON NORTH
59. WELLINGTON SOUTH
60. WENTWORTH NORTH
61. WENTWORTH SOUTH
62. YORK EAST
63. YORK WEST

No.	Constituency
67.	EGAN
68.	BEAUCE
69.	BEAUHARNOIS
70.	BELLECHASSE
71.	BERTHIER
72.	BONAVENTURE
73.	BROME
74.	CHAMBLY
75.	CHAMPLAIN
76.	CHARLEVOIX
77.	CHATEAUGUAY
78.	CHICOUTIMI and SAGUENAY
79.	COMPTON
80.	DORCHESTER
81.	DRUMMOND and ARTHABASKA
82.	GASPÉ
83.	HOCHELAGA
84.	HUNTINGDON
85.	IBERVILLE
86.	JACQUES CARTIER
87.	JOLIETTE
88.	KAMOURASKA
89.	LAPRAIRIE
90.	L'ASSOMPTION
91.	LAVAL
92.	LEVIS
93.	LOTBINIÈRE
94.	MASKINONGÉ
95.	MÉGANTIC
96.	MISSISQUOI
97.	MONTCALM
98.	MONTMAGNY
99.	MONTMORENCY
100.	MONTMORENCY
101.	MONTREAL EAST
102.	MONTREAL CENTRE
103.	MONTREAL WEST
104.	NAPIERVILLE
105.	NICOLET
106.	OTTAWA COUNTY
107.	PONTIAC
108.	PORTNEUF
109.	QUEBEC EAST
110.	QUEBEC CENTRE
111.	QUEBEC WEST
112.	QUEBEC COUNTY
113.	RICHMOND and WOLFE
114.	RICHELIEU
115.	RIMOUSKI
116.	ROUVILLE
117.	ST. HYACINTHE
118.	ST. JOHNS
119.	ST. MAURICE
120.	SHEFFORD
121.	SHERBROOKE
122.	SOULANGES
123.	STANSTEAD
124.	TEMISCOUATA
125.	TERREBONNE
126.	THREE RIVERS
127.	TWO MOUNTAINS
128.	VAUDREUIL
129.	VERCHERES
130.	YAMASKA

KEY: * Earlier name of constituency; (?) Exact alignment of member in doubt (or unusual); ——— Tory, Conservatives, Bleu; —— Baldwin - Lafontaine - Hincks Reformer, Moderate; ..... Clear Grit, Rouge, Liberal

1841 to 1854. During this period the meaningful divisions in political warfare were between tories and reformers in Canada West, and between the French party of Lafontaine and Morin and the disintegrating tory group in Canada East. Because the reformers and French group commonly shared the same political viewpoint from 1842 to 1854, these two groups have been similarly shaded in the map. The tory groups, also, share a tory shading. This is not to imply, of course, that in either case there was but one unified party with ramifications throughout the two parts of the province. It was only from about 1850 that the "Clear Grit departure" and the Rouge movement in Canada East began to have a significance that could be plotted on the map. The ridings that produced overt radicals of the Rouge or Clear Grit type in the 1850's thus are differentiated. It is clear in Map A that the French group in the House represented virtually all the rural ridings bordering on the St. Lawrence and Richelieu rivers. This near-monopoly was broken in the Eastern Townships, on the Ottawa River, in Beauharnois in the southwest, and in the frontier ridings of the Gulf of St. Lawrence, Gaspé, and Bonaventure. In Canada West the reform movement had several areas of power. The hinterland behind Toronto and Hamilton provided a stretch of rural ridings that had responded to reforming currents of thought in the 1830's, and still provided the backbone of reform strength. In the far west, Kent was an outpost of the movement. In the hinterland behind Brockville the counties of Leeds, Grenville, and Lanark were strong in their liberalism; and likewise at the far east of Upper Canada, in Glengarry and Prescott, there was notable reform strength.

In Canada West the tory cause was strong in most of the towns, except Bytown, and in the rural scene there were the several tory areas: around Kingston; in Carleton and Russell in the Ottawa Valley; West York and Simcoe, west and northwest of Toronto; and Huron, the frontier county north of London. Toryism did not remain entrenched in the towns and cities of Canada East, Sherbrooke Town being alone in its consistency. Megantic, Stanstead, Missisquoi, and Sherbrooke County were the last rural strongholds of tory power. Gaspé and Bonaventure presented a special case, for the settlements there were atypical and subject to patriarchal control by "merchant princes." The effect of Robert Christie of Gaspé and the several members from Bonaventure was usually to augment tory-conservative strength in the Legislative Assembly.

The special radical indication in Kamouraska refers to the support given Luc Letellier in famous political duels with J. C. Chapais, though he sat only briefly in the third parliament after being returned in a by-election. The other radicals were elected to the fourth parliament, L. J. Papineau being returned for Two Mountains at a by-election.

III

Because the Hincksite Reformers represented a middle position in politics between tories on one extreme and Clear Grits on the other, and because their numbers dwindled in the sixth, seventh, and eighth parliaments, they do not show up in their true proportions in Map A just described, or in Map B, which shows the generalized political situation in the period 1854-67. At the opening of the fifth parliament in September 1854, before it was clear that the Hincks-Morin ministry had lost its majority, the Moderate Reformers were present in significant strength. It is this situation, showing the result of the 1854 election and prior to the erection of a Liberal-Conservative coalition, that is shown in the small sectional Map C.

The Clear Grit and opposition reformers held a crescent in the hinterland about the west end of Lake Ontario, extending from Ontario South to Lincoln. In the west, they held Lambton and Middlesex West; in the east, Hastings South and the three ridings about Cornwall. The reformers who supported Hincks held a significant section of ridings north of Lake Erie and across the northern frontier north of Toronto, from Grey to Victoria. In the east they held the three Leeds and Grenville ridings, Lanark North, and Renfrew. Other scattered ridings from Essex to Lennox & Addington completed their strength. The conservatives filled the remaining spaces. Already, in 1854, they had established a continuous bridge of ridings from Kingston on the upper St. Lawrence through to Carleton, Russell, and Prescott on the Ottawa River. This bridge was to remain characteristic in the next general elections. Within a few weeks of the general election of 1854, which is represented in Map C, the whole nature of the situation had changed, and the map becomes invalid. On the formation of the coalition government in late September, the Hincksite Reformers began to move to the support of either Ultra-Reformers or Conservatives.

IV

Map B is a companion to Map A and carries the general pattern of political geography through the four parliaments from 1854 to 1867. During this later period the alignment of political groups had changed. The Conservatives of Canada West were allied with the "Bleu" group of French Canadians from Canada East, and the same code of shading is used for these two groups. In Canada West, it is clear that the Conservatives had lost ground considerably from the situation of 1854 as shown in Map C, and they had not fallen heir to many of the former Hincksite Reform ridings except in the Niagara peninsula and Middlesex East.

In Canada East, on the other hand, the major French group had continued to hold the larger proportion of the rural ridings along the St. Lawrence River. The Conservative members returned from the English-speaking Eastern Townships were additional strength for the Conservative-Bleu forces in parliament. Compton, Brome, Stanstead, Richmond & Wolfe, and the town of Sherbrooke stand out in Map B a paler reflection of the tory bloc in Map A.

The Clear Grit, Rouge, and Liberal cause during the period 1854-67 was subject to great internal tensions. It will be clear from the analysis in previous chapters that Sandfield Macdonald Liberals and Clear Grits followed different courses, and that all Liberals in Canada East were not Rouges. Yet, in mapping the over-all political scene, it is not a distortion of the truth to use one code of shading to designate this whole company of Liberals.

In Map B it is apparent that the Liberals' strength was consolidated in the southwestern peninsula of Canada West, and all about Toronto and the Lake Ontario shore to the east. In the far east, around Cornwall and in Lanark North, they continued to hold the ground. In Canada East, the Liberal cause flourished in the Richelieu Valley, as in 1837, and in the southwest. The borderland where new French settlements were beginning to take up land in the Eastern Townships was a fertile area for Rouge enthusiasm. And north of Montreal, in Joliette and Terrebonne, Liberalism made progress.

There is no single generalization to be made about urban ridings; for in the

KEY TO THE NUMBERS
IDENTIFYING RIDINGS

1	BRANT EAST	66	ARGENTEUIL
2	BRANT WEST	67	BAGOT
3	BROCKVILLE	68	BEAUCE
4	CARLETON	69	BEAUHARNOIS
5	CORNWALL	70	BELLECHASSE
6	DUNDAS	71	BERTHIER
7	DURHAM (EAST)	72	BONAVENTURE
8	DURHAM (WEST)	73	BROME (formerly MISSISQUOI EAST)
9	ELGIN EAST	74	CHAMBLY
10	ELGIN WEST	75	CHAMPLAIN
11	ESSEX	76	CHARLEVOIX (formerly SAGUENAY)
12	FRONTENAC	77	CHATEAUGUAY
13	GLENGARRY	78	CHICOUTIMI & SAGUENAY (formerly SAGU., CHICO & TADOUSSAC)
14	GRENVILLE (SOUTH)	79	COMPTON
15	GREY	80	DORCHESTER
16	HALDIMAND	81	DRUMMOND (& ARTHABASKA)
17	HALTON	82	GASPÉ
18	HAMILTON	83	HOCHELAGA
19	HASTINGS (NORTH)	84	HUNTINGDON
20	HASTINGS (SOUTH)	85	IBERVILLE
21	HURON (& BRUCE)	86	JACQUES CARTIER (formerly MONTREAL COUNTY)
22	KENT	87	JOLIETTE
23	KINGSTON	88	KAMOURASKA
24	LAMBTON	89	LAPRAIRIE
25	LANARK (NORTH)	90	L'ASSOMPTION (formerly LEINSTER)
26	LANARK SOUTH	91	LAVAL
27	LEEDS & GRENVILLE NORTH	92	L'ISLET
28	LEEDS (SOUTH)	93	LEVIS
29	LENNOX & ADDINGTON	94	LOTBINIÈRE
30	LINCOLN	95	MASKINONGÉ
31	LONDON	96	MEGANTIC
32	MIDDLESEX (EAST)	97	MISSISQUOI (1854-7 WEST)
33	MIDDLESEX WEST	98	MONTCALM
34	NIAGARA	99	MONTMAGNY
35	NORFOLK	100	MONTMORENCY
36	NORTHUMBERLAND (EAST)	101	MONTREAL (EAST)
37	NORTHUMBERLAND WEST	102	MONTREAL (CENTRE)
38	ONTARIO NORTH	103	MONTREAL (WEST)
39	ONTARIO SOUTH	104	NAPIERVILLE
40	OTTAWA (formerly BYTOWN)	105	NICOLET
41	OXFORD (NORTH)	106	OTTAWA COUNTY
42	OXFORD (SOUTH)	107	PONTIAC
43	PEEL (formerly YORK SECOND, YORK WEST)	108	PORTNEUF
44	PERTH	109	QUEBEC (EAST)
45	PETERBOROUGH (formerly NORTHUMBERLAND N.)	110	QUEBEC (CENTRE)
46	PRESCOTT	111	QUEBEC (WEST)
47	PRINCE EDWARD	112	QUEBEBEC COUNTY
48	RENFREW	113	RICHMOND & WOLFE (formerly SHERBROOKE CO., SHERBROOKE & WOLFE)
49	RUSSELL	114	RICHELIEU
50	SIMCOE (NORTH)	115	RIMOUSKI
51	SIMCOE (SOUTH)	116	ROUVILLE
52	STORMONT	117	ST HYACINTHE
53	TORONTO (EAST)	118	ST JOHNS
54	TORONTO (WEST)	119	ST MAURICE
55	VICTORIA	120	SHEFFORD
56	WATERLOO (NORTH) (formerly HALTON WEST)	121	SHERBROOKE TOWN
57	WATERLOO SOUTH	122	SOULANGES
58	WELLAND (formerly LINCOLN SOUTH)	123	STANSTEAD
59	WELLINGTON NORTH	124	TEMISCOUATA
60	WELLINGTON SOUTH	125	TERREBONNE
61	WENTWORTH (NORTH)	126	THREE RIVERS
62	WENTWORTH SOUTH	127	TWO MOUNTAINS
63	YORK NORTH (formerly YORK FOURTH)	128	VAUDREUIL
64	YORK EAST (formerly YORK THIRD)	129	VERCHERES
65	YORK WEST (formerly YORK FIRST, YORK SOUTH)	130	YAMASKA

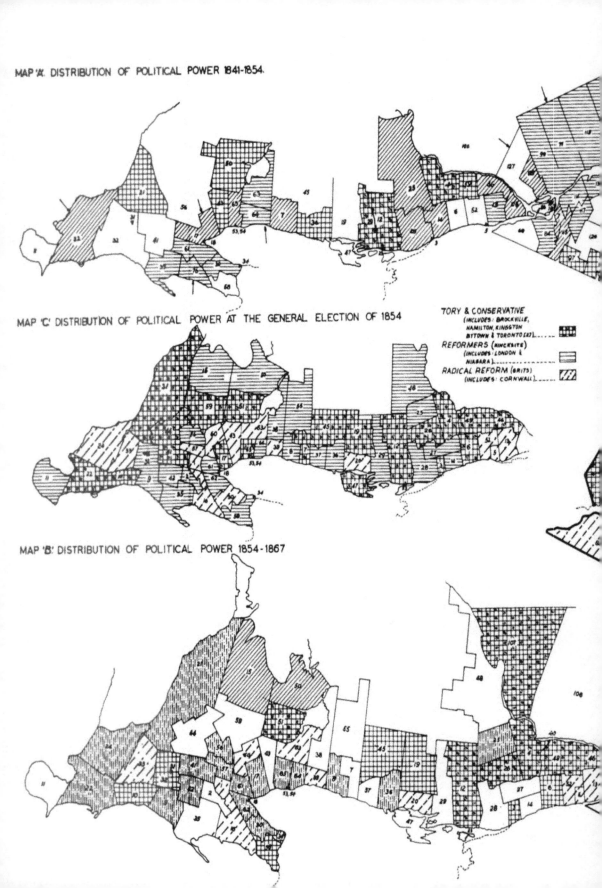

MAP 'A'. DISTRIBUTION OF POLITICAL POWER 1841-1854.

MAP 'C' DISTRIBUTION OF POLITICAL POWER AT THE GENERAL ELECTION OF 1854

MAP 'B'. DISTRIBUTION OF POLITICAL POWER 1854-1867

TORY & CONSERVATIVE
(INCLUDES: BROCKVILLE,
HAMILTON, KINGSTON
BYTOWN & TORONTO [2])......

REFORMERS (HINCKSITE)
(INCLUDES: LONDON &
NIAGARA).........

RADICAL REFORM (GRITS)
(INCLUDES: CORNWALL)......

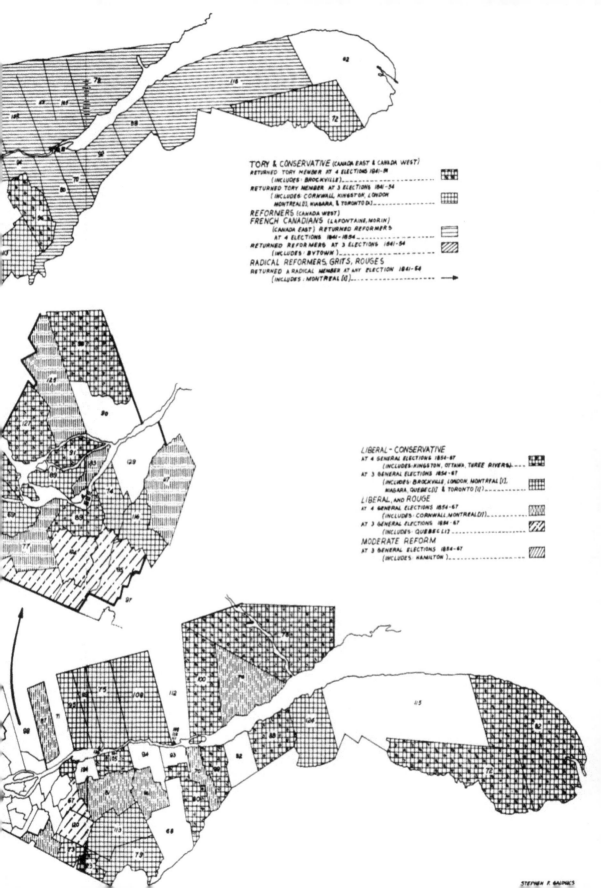

TORY & CONSERVATIVE (CANADA EAST & CANADA WEST)
RETURNED TORY MEMBER AT 4 ELECTIONS 1841-54
(INCLUDES: BROCKVILLE)
RETURNED TORY MEMBER AT 3 ELECTIONS 1841-54
(INCLUDES: CORNWALL, KINGSTON, LONDON
MONTREAL[1], NIAGARA, & TORONTO D.)
REFORMERS (CANADA WEST)
FRENCH CANADIANS (LAFONTAINE, MORIN)
(CANADA EAST) RETURNED REFORMERS
AT 4 ELECTIONS 1841-1854
RETURNED REFORMERS AT 3 ELECTIONS 1841-54
(INCLUDES: BYTOWN)
RADICAL REFORMERS, GRITS, ROUGES
RETURNED A RADICAL MEMBER AT ANY ELECTION 1841-54
(INCLUDES: MONTREAL [1])

LIBERAL-CONSERVATIVE
AT 4 GENERAL ELECTIONS 1854-67
(INCLUDES: KINGSTON, OTTAWA, THREE RIVERS)
AT 3 GENERAL ELECTIONS 1854-67
(INCLUDES: BROCKVILLE, LONDON, MONTREAL [1],
NIAGARA, QUEBEC[1] & TORONTO [1])
LIBERAL, AND ROUGE
AT 4 GENERAL ELECTIONS 1854-67
(INCLUDES: CORNWALL, MONTREAL[1])
AT 3 GENERAL ELECTIONS 1854-67
(INCLUDES: QUEBEC L1)
MODERATE REFORM
AT 3 GENERAL ELECTIONS 1854-67
(INCLUDES: HAMILTON)

STEPHEN F. GALDINES

state of economic development of Canada in the period dealt with here, there was no one system of forces equally at work on all non-rural ridings. It might be supposed too, that "frontier" ridings would respond similarly in the political battle; yet Conservatism retained a hold in the "western frontier" in Simcoe South, and in the counties of Peterborough and Hastings North. The pioneer ridings of Canada East gave the same mixed response in politics.

Although political maps are an aid to generalization, it should be remembered that conservative ridings did not contain conservatives exclusively, nor radical ridings nothing but radicals. In fact, all ridings were the scene of conflicting political groups. At general elections polling took place at from four to more than a dozen polling places in different parts of the ridings. When the material is available[3] and the results of the polling in each township and local area is prepared in map form, a most complicated checker-board effect is obtained.

CHAPTER NINE

CONCLUSIONS

SINCE THE TECHNIQUE employed in this research was designed to concentrate upon the identification of the personnel who composed political groups in the period 1841-67 and to deal with the alignment of the groups identified, it would be wrong to embark upon large general speculations that do not arise exclusively from the material dealt with. Yet, within this limited field, a number of conclusions do emerge which are in some measure new.

The term "party" was used quite generally during the period of the Union, and has been used consistently by historians since, to describe various political groups. But to what extent were political groups permanent, and to what extent were they *ad hoc* arrangements constructed from time to time to meet changing circumstances? There is always the suggestion that the term "party" is a misnomer unless it implied a consistent group of men working in a continuing organization from one decade to another. It would now appear, on the basis of the foregoing evidence, that there was a large measure of consistency in the political behaviour of most members of the Legislative Assembly, and that political groups did preserve their identity as they faced new situations from year to year. There was, necessarily, an interrelation between the form and practice of party life and the constitutional framework of the era in which they operated. The conventions governing the actions of Monarch, Cabinet, and Houses of Parliament at Westminster were constantly in Canadian minds as models that should and could be approximated in the provincial government. The procedures and forms of the House of Commons had evolved in the course of long experiment, seeking means to control the executive organs of government in England. During the earlier years of the Union, the precedents established at Westminster were called into use in working out conventions to govern the relationship between Legislative Assembly, Executive Council, and governor. Political party groupings had been emerging to meet various situations in Upper and Lower Canada for some two decades before the Union. But as the nature of the Executive Council evolved, under the guidance of Durham, Sydenham, and Bagot, toward the prototype of the English cabinet, its membership became a legitimate prize to be sought after by political groups.

Not only was it true that the final steps in its evolution toward cabinet status required the pressure of united, disciplined, political parties, but the converse also holds, that the evolving status of the Executive Council called forth more unified party activity to secure control of it. With the disappearance of Sydenham from the scene, there was an increasing awareness of a sense of political polarity in the Legislative Assembly, and by 1844 one principal theme dominated the general election: support or opposition to "the late executive councillors." From this time forward, members of the Legislative Assembly were broadly grouped as Ministerialists and Opposition, as those "in" power or those "out." But the mere sense of polarity does not imply, necessarily, that the "ins" and "outs" of one era will retain their grouping through varying fortunes from one decade to another.

Many jokes and innuendoes have emerged on the theme of "loose fish," a term applied to members who were thought to be without strong party affiliation and willing to pursue the more attractive bait. Undoubtedly, in the limited period of single sessions and in connection with specific measures, some votes were "sold." But in tracing the broad course of political careers and the composition of political groups from year to year, no list of "loose fish" appears. Ambitious or unusually independent men did "cross the House" from time to time, but the cases of a second crossing to return to the original loyalty are very few in number. The term "loose fish" was most useful in political journalism in the heat of election campaigns, but does not appear as a pattern of behaviour for any noticeable number of members.

If loyalty to party is measured in terms of consistent support of major party policies and consistent support in divisions having the force of votes of confidence, then the evidence points to a surprisingly large measure of stability on the part of the great majority of members. It can be concluded then, in spite of the gradual evolution of political groups and the tendency to apply different names to the same political group as it progressed from era to era, that there were permanent political parties during the whole Union period and that these parties were largely consistent in membership, viewpoint, and policy.

While political parties antedated the Union of 1841, and continued to be a major preoccupation of public men from that time forward, yet several experiences during the period covered by this present research might imply that an alternative scheme without the idiom of "party" might have been possible, and might even have been preferable. Lord Sydenham's dealings with Canada West seem to have implied a denial of the reality of political partisanship. He consistently discouraged the recognition of parties as corporate groups with which the governor would work, and in Canada East his selections of associates to assist in government were based on a choice of race, excluding the French Canadians, rather than on the political basis of sponsoring Tories. His analysis of Canadian problems assured him that good practical measures of government would win support from the majority of moderate men. Again in 1842-3, and from 1848 to 1854, the administrations of Lafontaine and Baldwin and of Hincks and Morin, although presented in partisan terms, proved in retrospect to have been moderate governments of the "centre" opposed by extremists on both the "right" and the "left." Although the considerable readjustments of 1854 relegated political rivalry to duels between right and left, yet there is much in the Liberal-Conservative administrations of 1854-62 that smacks of practical moderate government, and certainly strong opposition was forthcoming from the right wing of the party at various times, as well as from the Liberal opposition on the left. One seeks in vain to find any dynamic matter of principle that distinguished the enactments or administration of the J. Sandfield Macdonald governments of 1862-4 from the Liberal-Conservative governments that preceded and succeeded them. And finally, at the end of the Union period, only a coalition to form a strong government "of the centre" was capable of working out the project of Confederation.

These experiences seem to lead to the conclusion that the party rivalry between right and left did not represent any deep and fundamental division among Canadians, and that there were large areas of government business that admitted of only a moderate compromise solution. It follows, then, that Sydenham's insight may have been fundamentally sound; that is, if party rivalry could be side-tracked as superfluous, effective government could be conducted by non-partisan moderates.

On the other hand, the need for political parties in order to advocate and win responsible government and a recognized status for French Canada revived the partisan system in 1842. When the original goals of the Reform alliance had been won, the realignment of groups in 1854 gave a new impetus to party life and, by eliminating the centre grouping, precluded any hope for a moderate non-party government.

The principle of the double majority advocated at various stages of the Union— namely, that legitimate stable government under the Union should be conducted only by those having the confidence of a majority of members from both Canada East and Canada West—is associated with the idea of non-partisan government. In a sense, Canada East was always prepared for the double majority scheme, for it did, in every general election from 1844 onward, return the same majority party fully competent to represent the views of the great majority of Lower Canadians. When this Lower Canadian majority was allied with Upper Canadian Reformers, it had the aspect of a party of the "left." Later, after 1854, in alliance with Upper Canadian Conservatives, it had the aspect of a party of the "right." Yet this French-Canadian majority, down to the early 1860's, was actually a moderate centre group. It was the instability of Upper Canadian politics, which sent delegations of first one and then another political complexion to Parliament, that virtually nullified the efforts of first the Reform alliance and then the Liberal-Conservative coalition to realize' the double majority principle.

The fact that the major French-Canadian group was returned consistently, and usually in such strength that it was the largest group in the Legislative Assembly, was most important. All stable government during the Union was based upon this French-Canadian group, with other appropriate and available elements added to it. It should be noted, however, that this major party from Canada East was at no time exclusively French Canadian. In the election campaign of 1841, John Neilson, a Quebec journalist, was a principal organizer of the French-Canadian anti-Unionist group and, together with Armstrong, Aylwin, Holmes, and Leslie, sat and acted with this group in the Assembly. At no time during the Union did this party, or for that matter the Rouge party, fail to have an English-speaking element in its ranks.

The charting of data on the political parties on maps of the province has presented a comprehensive graphic representation of the political battles. While little that is entirely new has emerged, the historian's generalizations can now be a good deal more specific. The consistent strength of the moderate French-Canadian party along the St. Lawrence, the solidly Conservative bloc from Kingston to the Ottawa River, the growth of Reform and presently of Liberal strength through much, though not all, of southwestern Upper Canada, the radicalism of the southern Richelieu Valley, and the earlier distribution of British-Tory strength in the Montreal district and Eastern Townships—all stand out clearly.

Main trends through the course of the parliamentary history of the Province of Canada now become clear cut. On the one side, the continuing strength of the Bleu party right down to the 1863 election plainly showed no sign of abatement so long as Lower Canadians were defending their way of life in the same arena with Anglo-Saxons. Although the Liberal party made rapid strides in Quebec after 1867, it was in changed circumstances; the arena was then predominantly French Canadian.

On the other side, in Canada West the trend was progressively in favour of the Liberal party through the Union period. The Conservative (Tory) party did not secure a majority in Canada West at any election after that in 1844, although it had great strength as late as 1851 and 1854. But if the Reformers and their Liberal successors on the left did outreach their Conservative opponents, their chronic lack of cohesion was also characteristic down to the 1860's. The continuing major influence of the Conservative party in Canada West was due in part to the fragments of the Reform group which from time to time broke away from their fellows to align themselves with the Conservatives. With the tendency to stronger discipline generally growing within party ranks, the prospects for continued Liberal ascendency in a ninth and tenth parliament under the Union were thus very bright indeed.

Without a doubt, the internal discipline and cohesion of parties and political groups strengthened perceptibly during the experience of the Union. The techniques of analysis used throughout this research posed very difficult problems of interpretation in the first parliament (1841-3), and, when applied for the sake of a test to the later parliaments of Upper and Lower Canada, disclosed much greater autonomy then in the voting of individual members than appeared in the late 1850's and 1860's. By 1848 and 1849, in fact, the behaviour of the great majority of members was consistent; but in the sessions 1850 to 1858 the effect of the new radical movements was noticeable in the "fraying" of the left wings of the moderate groups. After 1858, when the effects of the readjustments of 1854 had become apparent to most men, the solidarity of groups was notably strengthened. On the eve of Confederation, in 1866, there was another manifestation of blurred party lines as some Liberals ceased to give full support to the coalition government and began to vote for characteristically Liberal motions. It is questionable, however, whether a searching analysis of the divisions in the Canadian House of Commons is necessary after 1867, except in well-known periods of political crisis, so well were the boundaries of parties and political groups marked out.

When, in 1867, the principal Canadian political arena was shifted to the federal House of Commons, a number of important traditions and habits of mind and action were passed on from the preceding provincial Legislative Assemblies. Though the members from Nova Scotia and New Brunswick made weighty contributions, we must here confine ourselves to the experience of the Province of Canada.

An effort was made by Sir John A. Macdonald to carry forward into post-Confederation politics the proposition that a coalition of moderate men, both Liberal and Conservative, who had been in the forefront in implementing the plan of federation, was now a general moderate party of the centre prepared to man and direct the operations of the new government. And, indeed, there were a number of outstanding Liberals, comparable to the Hincksite Reformers of 1854 and subsequent years, who supported the Liberal-Conservative government after 1867 and gave colour to the idea. But, in actual fact, the political polarity that had grown up in the Province of Canada in the late 1850's and early 1860's had not disappeared and was quite apparent in the general election that chose the first members of the Dominion parliament. In 1861 and 1863, the Liberal-Conservative cause had depended upon the strength of the Bleu party in Canada East, with significant added support from Conservatives and Moderate Reformers from Canada West. The strength of the Liberal party in the same elections had lain with the Clear Grit Liberals of Canada West, with added Rouge and Liberal support from Canada East. In the first parliament of the Dominion of Canada, these nuclei of Liberal and of Liberal-Conservative power were still the same, although additional forces were now recruited from the Maritime Provinces.

The Upper Canadian political rivalry between Tories and Reformers, and the Lower Canadian rivalry between French-Canadian nationalists and "British" Tories had been carried forward down to 1854 in the United Province. The rise of the Rouge and Clear Grit radical movements had so strained this earlier traditional alignment that by 1854 it had become meaningless. Soon after 1854 it was clear that a new alignment had developed in both sections of the province. In Canada East, both political poles were predominantly French Canadian, the Rouges standing on the left and the Bleus on the right. English-speaking members of Canada East associated themselves with the one or the other. In Canada West, the new Liberal cause stemmed directly from the Clear Grit movement of the early 1850's; all more moderate shades of opinion after 1854 were included in the (Liberal-)Conservative camp. The same traditions and loyalties that had prevented government by the centre under the Union then continued to act after 1867, and fostered the political battle between Liberals and Liberal-Conservatives. Thus the readjustment in the alignment of political groups that occurred in 1854 constituted a watershed in Canadian political history with a significance that extended far beyond 1867, and the end of the old United Province.

During the period from 1841 to 1867, however, the total public life of French Canada and English-speaking Canada was thrown together in one governmental system, combined in one Legislative Assembly. It was a unique occurrence in Canadian history. It is a stimulating and enlightening experience to come to grips with the workings of the two historical traditions under these special circumstances.

NOTES

CHAPTER ONE

1. D. Daly, C. D. Day, C. R. Ogden, R. Baldwin, W. H. Draper, J. H. Dunn, S. B. Harrison, and R. B. Sullivan.

2. The names of some constituencies of Canada West were changed before the 1847 elections. In several cases the changes are not self-evident. To avoid confusion in the readers' minds, the later name is given in brackets, where it is thought to be useful.

3. G. P. Scrope, *Memoir of the Life of the Right Honourable Charles Lord Sydenham, G.C.B.* (London, 2nd ed., 1843), p. 217.

4. June 23, 1841, pp. 65, 65-6, 67. Footnotes which refer to specific divisions quote the date and the page reference in the appropriate volume of the *Journals of the Legislative Assembly*.

5. July 29, concerning a Board of Works Bill, p. 250; August 5, August 18, and August 19, concerning an Upper Canadian Municipal Bill, pp. 295, 373, 384-5; September 3, concerning the "Harrison Resolutions," pp. 481-2; September 6, concerning a revision of the Customs Law, p. 499; and September 11, at the passing of the Loan Bill, with its Imperial guarantee, pp. 569-70.

6. It should be noted that in mid-August 1841, W. Dunlop (Tory) was seated in the place of J. M. Strachan (Reformer), Huron.

7. Cartwright (Lennox & Addington), Johnston (Carleton), MacNab (Hamilton), Moffatt (Montreal), and Neilson (Quebec County) were the minority.

8. October 31, p. 86; November 3, p. 91; and November 16, p. 133.

9. In Table 4, five Moderate Tories, Dunlop, A. McLean, Murney, Henry Smith, and W. Stuart, are identified. Black, Forbes, McCulloch, Hale, and Watts are the Tories in opposition in Canada East, while Wakefield, Simpson, Child, Jones, Moore, and Hamilton join Daly in continued support of the reconstructed Executive Council.

10. W. H. Merritt to E. Ryerson, January 25, 1844: "Most of the present members will feel themselves committed by the recent vote; they will all be pressing for a new election; and shape their course to the prevailing opinion." Quoted in Egerton Ryerson, *The Story of My Life*, J. George Hodgins, ed., (Toronto, 1883), p. 317.

11. Higginson to Ryerson, September 8, 1844: "Dissolution or no dissolution, still undetermined. Thorburn declines office. We must have an Inspector-General, and from Upper Canada Liberals. Where are we to find one fit for the duties?" Quoted in Hodgins, *Ryerson*, p. 339.

12. *Montreal Pilot,* September 30, 1844.

13. *Montreal Pilot,* September 28, 1844.

14. November 28, 1844, pp. 1-2.

15. December 6, 1844, p. 20.

16. December 9, 1844, p. 29.

17. From the *Montreal Transcript*, November 9, 1844: "According to calculation, the members returned, up to the present moment, are divided as follows:

Conservatives:		*Radicals:*	
Upper Canada	28	Upper Canada	13
Lower Canada	15	Lower Canada	25
	43		38

Add to these the three unreturned constituencies, and we have the full number (84) of which the House is composed."

18. The three members not voting are the speaker, MacNab, and LeBoutillier of Bonaventure, who had not yet taken his seat; and the riding of Saguenay was vacant, due to the double return of A. N. Morin from Saguenay and Bellechasse.

19. Till November 25, 1845.

20. Cummings (Lincoln South), Hale (Northumberland South), Seymour (Lennox & Addington), and Munro (York 3) from Canada West, and Scott (Two Mountains) and Watts (Drummond) from Canada East, each cast more than one vote that seemed to be "out of line."

21. June 11, 1847: Baldwin-Lafontaine amendment to the address in reply to the speech from

the throne, p. 26; June 23, 1847: Scott-Chabot motion for an address requesting the governor to form "a strong and efficient administration," p. 68; July 7, 1847: M. Cameron-Baldwin objection to the competence of the commissioner of Crown Lands (D. B. Papineau), pp. 112-13; July 19, 1847: Cayley-Badgley motion for the House in Committee of Supply, pp. 163-4; July 17, 1847: Baldwin-Price moving an address to the governor regretting the lack of vigour in carrying out the works programme at Windsor Harbour, p. 208.

22. Cf. correspondence between W. H. Draper and Hon. R. E. Caron, and between Hon. R. E. Caron and L. H. Lafontaine and A. N. Morin (Montreal, 1846?).

23. J. E. Turcotte was first elected for St. Maurice in 1841, and seemed to be a stalwart French-Canadian party man in the first parliament down to the Metcalfe crisis; on December 1, the day preceding the definitive division on the crisis, in which he divided with his compatriots, he associated himself with Tories from both sections of the province and with D. B. Viger and Noel in dividing in favour of postponing the debate on the resignation of the Executive Council. In the general elections of 1844 he was defeated in St. Maurice by Desaulniers, and in 1847 in both Champlain and St. Maurice by Guillet and L. J. Papineau, respectively. It was not until 1851 that he was again returned to the House.

CHAPTER TWO

1. Their platform included electoral reform, free trade, free navigation of the St. Lawrence, reform in the Post Office Department, cheaper Crown land sales, and the institution of responsible government. Louis P. Turcotte, *Le Canada sous l'Union, 1841-1867,* 2e partie (Quebec, 1882), chap. I, p. 33.

2. Francis Hincks' *Pilot* published in Montreal, did much to point up the contest in these "Anglo-Saxon" areas.

3. February 25, 1848, p. 1.

4. March 3, 1848, p. 17.

5. March 3, 1848, p. 21.

6. Two seats, Three Rivers and Terrebonne, were vacant; speaker not voting.

7. January 22, 1849, p. 14; March 2, 1849, p. 122; March 4, 1849, p. 142.

8. March 27, 1849, p. 184; May 15, 1849, pp. 303-4.

9. May 11, 1849, p. 293; May 11, 1849, p. 294; May 18, 1849, p. 310.

10. January 24, 1849, p. 24.

11. January 24, 1849, p. 24.

12. May 15, 1850, p. 9. Baldwin and Malloch moved that a petition including these propositions be not received. The members mentioned, in dividing against the motion, were not, technically, advocating the principle. Yet in the circumstances, these members were going out of their way to make some point regarding the subject matter of the petition.

13. May 22, 1850, p. 20.

14. July 18, 1850, pp. 159-60.

15. Divisions May 22, 1850, p. 20; and June 26, 1851, p. 117.

16. Division July 27, 1850, p. 202.

17. Division July 27, 1850, p. 202.

18. Division August 4, 1851, p. 232.

19. Bell (Lanark), Burritt (Grenville), Fergusson (Waterloo), Flint (Hastings), Hall (Peterborough), Lyon (Russell), Merritt (Lincoln), McFarland (Welland), J. C. Morrison (York West), Notman (Middlesex), Price (York South), W. B. Richards (Leeds), J. Scott (Bytown), Hermanus Smith (Wentworth) — all Upper Canadian reformers; and Fourquin dit Leveille (Yamaska), Guillet (Champlain), Laurin (Lotbinière), and W. H. Scott (Two Mountains) — Lower Canadian supporters of the administration.

20. July 15, 1851, p. 162.

21. August 13, 1851, p. 276; August 16, 1851, p. 289; August 20, 1851, p. 301; August 26, 1851, p. 327.

22. June 21, 1850, pp. 84-9; June 28, 1850, pp. 103-5; July 1, 1851, pp. 129-30.

23. July 26, 1850, p. 197.

24. August 1, 1850, p. 223; August 6, 1850, p. 257; August 1, 1851, p. 224.

25. July 30, 1850, p. 211; July 31, 1850, p. 216; August 1, 1850, p. 222.

26. June 28, 1850, p. 107; July 29, 1851, p. 205.

27. August 19, 1852, p. 2.

28. On August 30, 1852 (p. 55), and September 17, 1852 (p. 164), Langton (Peterborough, "left-

wing" Conservative) supported the government's programme, while Stuart (Quebec City), Le-Boutillier (Bonaventure), J. McDougall (Drummond), and L. M. Viger (Leinster), together with the remaining Conservatives of Canada West, opposed the policy.

29. November 2, 1852, p. 373.

30. M. Cameron (Huron), D. Christie (Wentworth), Fergusson (Waterloo), Hincks (Oxford), Richards (Leeds), and Rolph (Norfolk).

31. April 4, 1853, p. 518.

32. April 6, 1853 (p. 689) — motion by A. N. Richards and Morin giving "hoist" to the second reading of the Bill to Abolish Rectories. The following reformers voted "nay," supporting the principle of the bill: D. Christie (Wentworth), Fergusson (Waterloo), Hartman (York North), R. McDonald (Cornwall), W. L. Mackenzie (Haldimand), Mattice (Stormont), White (Halton), and Amos Wright (York East).

33. June 19, 1854, p. 22.

34. June 20, 1854, p. 28.

35. June 20, 1854, p. 29.

36. D. Christie (Wentworth) was, at this time, among the more radical reformers; L. J. Papineau would undoubtedly have opposed the ministry as a left-wing critic; while Henry Smith was throughout the era a consistent Conservative, and L. M. Viger a consistent Ministerialist. Some slight doubt in each case prevents a prediction of the position of the other six members.

CHAPTER THREE

1. The newly erected ridings in Canada West were: Brant East, Brant West, Elgin East, Elgin West, Grey, Lambton, Leeds & Grenville North, Ontario North, Perth, Renfrew, Victoria, Wellington North, Wellington South (13); the following ridings were split into two: Durham, Hastings, Lanark, Middlesex, Northumberland, Oxford, Simcoe, Waterloo, Wentworth (9); in adjusting the hinterland around Toronto, York West became Peel, York South disappeared in York West, and York East was divided to create Ontario South (1); in Canada East the following new names appeared: Argenteuil, Bagot, Beauce, Châteauguay, Chicoutimi & Tadoussac, Compton, Iberville, Joliette, Laprairie, Laval, Levis, Maskinongé, Montcalm, Montmagny, Napierville, Pontiac, St. John's, Soulanges, Temiscouata (19); Missisquoi was divided into two, Montreal County divided into Hochelaga and Jacques Cartier, and the cities of Montreal and Quebec each received one additional seat (4). Leinster was renamed L'Assomption. These notes do not indicate exact geographical readjustments, but are only useful in accounting for the names of ridings. It is impossible to analyse the 1854 election in strict terms of gain and loss, for the principal protagonists from the past followed no pattern in either staying in the ridings whose names were perpetuated, or in contesting the newly named ones. By 1857, a few further adjustments were made, chiefly in the names of constituencies. The riding along the Saguenay River and to the north was renamed Chicoutimi & Saguenay, while the former Saguenay riding to the south, on the St. Lawrence, became Charlevoix. Sherbrooke & Wolfe became Richmond & Wolfe, Missisquoi East became Brome.

2. September 5, 1854, pp. 2-3 and 3.

3. September 7, 1854, pp. 11-12.

4. September 20, 1854, pp. 75-6, 79.

5. Cauchon had opposed the Hincks-Morin ministry in 1854, and was said at about this period to have a personal following of eighteen members; cf. Dent II, p. 337. It has not been possible to identify this group in the present study. L. O. David in *Canada sous l'Union*, p. 57, says of him in part: "... apres la retraite de [Lafontaine] il alla d'un camp a l'autre, servit sous tous les drapeaux, obligea tous les governements a compter avec lui. . . ."

6. May 30, 1856, pp. 554-5. See Table 15. The division on the "Corrigan Affair" on March 10, and the various divisions concerning the seat of government question show the House divided in terms of religious affiliation and local sectional interest, but do not give any clear identification of "party lines."

7. It is possible that B. R. Church, J. C. Morrison, D. Roblin, and Sydney Smith were purposely abstaining from this division, and should be included with E. Cook and five other reformers who were temporarily unsympathetic toward the reconstructed ministry. Had they voted with the opposition they would have brought the ministry to within one or two votes of defeat.

CHAPTER FOUR

1. Beginning with the general election of 1857 the alignment of major political groups was reasonably clear, and the details of the contests are easily available in parliamentary papers, e.g.,

Appendix 28, *Legislative Assembly Journals*, 1858; *Sessional Papers*, no. 24, 1862, and *Sessional Papers*, no. 48, 1863 (August session). It has not been considered necessary to rehearse the details of these general elections here.

2.   Elgin East: Burwell (L.) vs. Southwick (R.); Hamilton: I. Buchanan (R.) vs. Baker (L.); Lambton: M. Cameron (R.) vs. H. F. MacKenzie (R.); Ontario South: Mowat (L.) vs. J. C. Morrison (R.); and Wentworth North: Notman (L.) vs. R. Spence (R.). It was about this time that the political press began to call opposition reformers of Upper Canada "Liberals."

3.   All five voted with the Liberal-Conservatives in favour of Henry Smith as speaker at the beginning of the session, and though some of them voted on June 2 in favour of unseating G. B. L. Fellows, the Conservative from Russell, and in favour of some small items advocated by Liberals, there is no clear-cut break from the voting of the large majority of fellow Lower Canadians until the "Ottawa Crisis" arose in July. Dawson (Three Rivers) did not appear on the division lists, but presumably belonged among the government supporters.

4.   On August 2, 1858, Lotbinière, Middlesex West, and Wellington North were vacant, and H. Smith (Frontenac) was speaker. The total voting membership of the House was thus 126, and not 130.

5.   J. E. Turcotte (Three Rivers, Liberal-Conservative) and L. V. Sicotte (St. Hyacinthe, Liberal), were candidates for the speakership; the seven government supporters were: I. Buchanan (Hamilton), M. C. Cameron (Ontario North), W. Clarke (Wellington North), J. Crawford (Toronto East), F. W. Haultain (Peterborough), A. F. Hooper (Lennox & Addington), and J. H. Pope (Compton); R. B. Somerville (Huntingdon) was at this time an Independent Liberal; and the riding of Perth was vacant due to the double return of M. H. Foley for both Perth and Waterloo North.

6.   Anderson (Prince Edward), J. H. Cameron (Peel), M. C. Cameron (Ontario North), Carling (London), Clarke (Wellington), J. Crawford (Toronto East), Haultain (Peterborough), Hooper (Lennox & Addington), A. Morris (Lanark South), W. Ryerson (Brant West), G. Sherwood (Brockville), T. C. Street (Welland), Walsh (Norfolk), Conservatives; Dunsford (Victoria), Jackson (Grey), and A. Morrison (Simcoe North), Coalition Reformers; and R. B. Somerville (Huntingdon), Independent Liberal. This listing is based upon divisions on April 1, 1862 (p. 35), and February 20, 1863 (p. 32). On the latter occasion B. Tett (Leeds South) changed to favour "representation by population," and T. M. Daly, newly returned for Perth, also supported the principle.

7.   Legislative councillor, who had opposed the Hincks-Morin ministry in 1854 while a member of the Legislative Assembly.

CHAPTER FIVE

1.   E. P. Taché was titular head of the ministry.

2.   Foley subsequently voted in support of the Liberal government until its resignation in March 1864, but was then admitted to the newly formed Liberal-Conservative Taché-Macdonald government. But, failing of re-election, he was dropped from the Executive Council on June 29, 1864, on the formation of the "Great Coalition." Sicotte's appointment as a judge, September 5, 1863, was the occasion for further strong protest against the J. Sandfield Macdonald-Dorion government. Evanturel, McGee, and Abbott opposed the Macdonald-Dorion administration and supported the Taché-J. A. Macdonald government after March 30, 1864, McGee being admitted to the cabinet on that date as minister of agriculture.

3.   *The Canadian Parliamentary Companion*, Henry J. Morgan, ed. (3rd ed.; Montreal 1864), shows Bown and Buchanan as "British Constitutionalists," with the explanation that "this party is composed of nearly the whole of the supporters of the late Cartier-McDonald [*sic*] Administration with others who have joined them under the above name."

4.   August 13, 1863, p. 20.

5.   August 29, 1863, pp. 57-8.

6.   September 18, 1863, pp. 143-4.

7.   October 8, 1863, pp. 250-1.

8.   May 17, 1864, p. 217.

9.   June 14, 1864, p. 388.

10.   J. Carling (London), R. J. Cartwright (Lennox & Addington), J. Cockburn (Northumberland West), T. R. Ferguson (Simcoe South), T. Higginson (Prescott), A. Morris (Lanark South), W. F. Powell (Carleton), T. C. Street (Welland), A. Walsh (Norfolk), and C. Willson (Middlesex East).

11.   I. Buchanan (Hamilton) and G. Jackson (Grey).

12.   March 11, 1865, pp.192-3.

13.   P. A. Tremblay (Chicoutimi & Saguenay) is included in this number, but soon thereafter voted as a Bleu.

14.   C. Dunkin did not divide on March 11, but had delivered a long and closely reasoned

address condemning Confederation during the debate on the measure.
15. June 11, 1866, p. 13.
16. August 9 and 10, pp. 331-2; August 10, pp. 349-50; August 13, p. 371.
17. July 25, pp. 208, 210-11; August 2, pp. 275, 277, 279; August 10, p. 343.
18. August 2, p. 280.
19. July 9, pp. 118-19; July 22, p. 196; July 30, p. 241.

CHAPTER SIX

1. In French-Canadian nomenclature the term "Libereau" is used very extensively. In 1841, it included all the French-Canadian members who followed Lafontaine and Morin, together with several Anglo-Saxon associates, e.g., Neilson, DeWitt, Leslie, Aylwin, etc. At later stages, adjectives such as *democratique* were used to differentiate the new growing radical tradition. The protagonists of both "Rouge" and "Bleu" viewpoints in the late 1850's used "liberaux" as a general designation of their own people.
2. It is at this point that the French-Canadian group in support of the ministry can properly be designated as "Bleu." Some years were needed to adjust the leadership and viewpoint of the group before they emerged as a homogeneous party under Cartier.
3. See chap. VII.

CHAPTER SEVEN

1. See chap. I, p. 17.
2. H. Black (Quebec City), C. J. Forbes (Two Mountains), E. Hale (Sherbrooke Town), M. McCulloch (Terrebonne), and R. N. Watts (Drummond), and to some extent S. S. Foster (Shefford).
3. D. M. Armstrong (Berthier), T. C. Aylwin (Quebec City), J. DeWitt (Leinster), L. T. Drummond (Portneuf), and J. Leslie (Verchères).
4. Journals of the Legislative Assembly, 1866, p. 258.
5. Note the careers of W. H. Scott, R. N. Watts, J. S. Sanborn, J. O'Farrell, C. Sylvain, R. Christie, and A. T. Galt.
6. H. J. Boulton (Norfolk), M. Cameron (Kent), C. Hopkins (Halton), P. Perry (York East), and W. L. Mackenzie (Haldimand).
7. See Table 11 — nine normally supporting the government, and two in opposition.
8. Ontario Archives, Clark Papers, William McDougall to C. Clark, February 2, 1853.
9. *North American*, February 1, 1853, leading article entitled "McKenzie's Message — The Reform Party."
10. See J. M. S. Careless, *Brown of the Globe* (Toronto, 1959), vol. I, pp. 233-7.
11. Ontario Archives, Kirby Papers, J. C. Morrison to William Kirby, April 15, 1855: ". . . in common with many others I am supporting men for whom I have no peculiar regard and whose measures under other circumstances I should have endeavoured to have modified, but when I took into account that these men by accepting the coalition were sacrificing in a much greater degree their principles, . . . and that no other government could have been formed. . . ."

CHAPTER EIGHT

1. Some minor changes in the boundaries between one riding and another did occur from time to time, but they are not important to the political analysis undertaken here, and have not been reflected in the mapping.
2. Statute of Canada, 18 Vic., c 76, 1855.
3. For example: Province of Canada Legislative Assembly, vol. XXII, 1863, Sessional Papers No. 48, gives a breakdown of the voting in the various subdivisions, in tabular form. In the riding of Carleton, as a random example, the conservative candidate W. F. Powell led in Nepean, March, Goulburn, Huntley, and Marlborough, while the liberal candidate D. McLachlan led in Fitzroy, North Gower, Torbolton, and Richmond Village. The final count returned Powell with 1,011 votes, to the opponent's 856. Yet Carleton had been consistently a tory and conservative riding from 1841 to 1867.

BIBLIOGRAPHICAL NOTE

THIS BOOK is based, principally, on an exhaustive examination of the twenty-six volumes of the *Journals of the Legislative Assembly of the Province of Canada*, together with the appropriate Sessional Papers. The journals of the Upper Canadian and Lower Canadian legislative assemblies before 1841, and those of the Canadian House of Commons immediately after Confederation were examined, to ensure continuity of treatment.

The published *Confederation Debates* and the fragmentary sections of a *Mirror of Parliament* for 1841, 1846, and 1860 augmented an extensive search of the contemporary political press. The details of election contests in the ridings down to 1854 have been gleaned almost entirely from newspapers, and newspapers have supplemented the findings from the journals of the legislature at all general elections and political crises.

In addition to the many published biographies of Canadian members of parliament, the collected papers of John A. Macdonald (before 1867), John Sandfield Macdonald, Robert Baldwin, A. N. Buell, Colonel Charles Clarke, William Kirby, D. B. Stevenson, and Colonel Samuel Street have been examined in the Public Archives of Canada, the Ontario Archives, and the Toronto Public Reference Library.

No political maps published during the union or immediately after Confederation seemed to fulfill the needs of this book. The maps published here have used the outlines of modern government maps. The political subdivisions are based on a careful study of the statutes of Great Britain, Lower Canada, Upper Canada, and the Province of Canada which from time to time fixed and altered the names and the boundaries of ridings.

The work of a generation of Canadian scholars reflected largely in the *Reports* of the Canadian Historical Association and in the *Canadian Historical Review* is the invaluable background for any work in this field.

TABLE 1
First Parliament, 1st Session, 1841: Divisions on the Principle of the Act of Union, June 23

OPPONENTS OF UNION	SUPPORTERS OF UNION [1]

Ultra-Reformers (Canada West):
- R. Baldwin, Hastings
- J. Durand, Halton West
- F. Hincks, Oxford
- C. Hopkins, Halton East
- J. H. Price, York First
- J. F. Small, York Third

6

Government Members and Moderates (Canada West):
- G. M. Boswell, Northumberland South
- I. Buchanan, Toronto
- M. Cameron, Lanark
- J. Cook, Dundas
- S. Crane, Grenville
- S. Derbishire, Bytown
- *J. H. Dunn*, Toronto
- J. Gilchrist, Northumberland North
- *H. H. Killaly*, London
- J. S. Macdonald, Glengarry
- D. McDonald, Prescott
- W. H. Merritt, Lincoln North
- J. Morris, Leeds
- I. W. Powell, Norfolk
- J. P. Roblin, Prince Edward
- Hermanus Smith, Wentworth
- E. Steele, Simcoe
- J. M. Strachan, Huron
- D. Thorburn, Lincoln South
- D. Thompson, Haldimand
- J. T. Williams, Durham

21

Compact Party and Moderate Tories (Canada West):
- E. C. Campbell, Niagara
- J. S. Cartwright, Lennox & Addington
- S. Y. Chesley, Cornwall
- *W. H. Draper*, Russell
- G. Duggan, York, Second
- Jas. Johnston, Carleton
- A. McLean, Stormont
- A. N. MacNab, Hamilton
- G. Sherwood, Brockville
- Henry Smith, Frontenac
- J. Woods, Kent

11

Independent (Canada West):
- J. Prince, Essex

1

French-Canadian Group (Canada East):
- D. M. Armstrong, Berthier
- T. C. Aylwin, Portneuf
- J. G. Barthe, Yamaska
- A. Berthelot, Kamouraska
- T. Boutillier, St. Hyacinthe
- H. Desriviers, Verchères
- R. J. Kimber, Champlain
- A. N. Morin, Nicolet
- J. Neilson, Quebec County
- J. B. J. Noel, Lotbinière
- E. Parent, Saguenay
- F. A. Quesnel, Montmorency
- J. M. Raymond, Leinster
- A. G. Ruel, Bellechasse
- A. C. Taschereau, Dorchester
- J. E. Turcotte, St. Maurice
- D. B. Viger, Richelieu

17

Government Members (Canada East):
- H. Black, Quebec City
- M. Child, Stanstead
- *D. Daly*, Megantic
- *C. D. Day*, Ottawa County
- A. M. Delisle, Montreal County
- M. A. DeSalaberry, Rouville
- J. W. Dunscomb, Beauharnois
- S. S. Foster, Shefford
- E. Hale, Sherbrooke Town
- B. Holmes, Montreal City
- R. Jones, Missisquoi
- M. McCulloch, Terrebonne
- G. Moffatt, Montreal City
- J. Moore, Sherbrooke County
- *C. R. Ogden*, Three Rivers
- C. Robertson, Two Mountains
- J. Simpson, Vaudreuil
- R. N. Watts, Drummond
- J. Yule, Chambly

19

Independents (Canada East):
- R. Christie, Gaspé
- J. R. Hamilton, Bonaventure

2

Independent (Canada East):
- D. Burnet, Quebec City

1

Speaker: A. Cuvillier, Huntingdon
Absent: M. Borne, Rimouski
    T. Parke, Middlesex
    E. P. Taché, L'Islet
Vacant: Kingston
    York Fourth

6

Note:
[1] Names of executive councillors in italic.

[93]

TABLE 2

TABLE 2
First Parliament, 1st Session, 1841 : Basic Alignment

OPPONENTS OF SYDENHAM		SUPPORTERS OF SYDENHAM	
Ultra-Reformers (Canada West):		*Ultra-Reformers* (Canada West) (B, Fig. Va):	
R. Baldwin, Hastings [4]		J. E. Small, York Third	
J. Cook, Dundas [4]		F. *Hincks*, Oxford	
J. Durand, Halton West [4]			
C. Hopkins, Halton East			2
J. H. Price, York First [4]			
	5		
		Government Members and Moderates (Canada West):	
		G. M. Boswell, Northumberland South	
		I. Buchanan, Toronto	
Reformers (Canada West) (A, Fig. Va):		M. Cameron, Lanark [3]	
W. H. Merritt, Lincoln North		S. Crane, Grenville [2]	
J. Morris, Leeds		S. Derbishire, Bytown [3]	
		J. H. Dunn, Toronto [3]	
	2	J. Gilchrist, Northumberland North [3]	
		S. B. Harrison, Kingston [3]	
		H. H. Killaly, London [3]	
		J. S. Macdonald, Glengarry	
Compact Tories (Canada West):		D. McDonald, Prescott	
J. S. Cartwright, Lennox & Addington [4]		T. *Parke*, Middlesex [3]	
S. Y. Chesley, Cornwall [4]		I. W. Powell, Norfolk	
Jas. Johnston, Carleton		J. P. Roblin, Prince Edward	
A. N. MacNab, Hamilton		Hermanus Smith, Wentworth	
G. Sherwood, Brockville [4]		E. Steele, Simcoe [3]	
J. Woods, Kent		D. Thorburn, Lincoln South	
		D. Thompson, Haldimand	
	6	J. T. Williams, Durham [3]	
			19
French-Canadian Group (Canada East):		*Sydenham Tories* (Canada West):	
D. M. Armstrong, Berthier [4]		E. C. Campbell, Niagara [2]	
T. C. Aylwin, Portneuf [4]		W. H. Draper, Russell [3]	
J. G. Barthe, Yamaska [4]		W. Dunlop, Huron [3]	
A. Berthelot, Kamouraska [4]		A. McLean, Stormont	
M. Borne, Rimouski [2]		Henry Smith, Frontenac	
T. Boutillier, St. Hyacinthe [4]			
H. Desriviers, Verchères [4]			5
R. J. Kimber, Champlain [2]			
A. N. Morin, Nicolet [4]		*Independent* (Canada West) (C, Fig. Va):	
J. Neilson, Quebec County [4]		J. Prince, Essex	
J. B. J. Noel, Lotbinière [4]			
E. Parent, Saguenay			1
F. A. Quesnel, Montmorency			
J. M. Raymond, Leinster			
A. G. Ruel, Bellechasse [2]		*Government Members* (Canada East):	
E. P. Taché, L'Islet [4]		H. Black, Quebec City	
A. C. Taschereau, Dorchester		M. Child, Stanstead	
J. E. Turcotte, St. Maurice [4]		*D. Daly*, Megantic [3]	
D. B. Viger, Richelieu [4]		*C. D. Day*, Ottawa County [3]	
		A. M. Delisle, Montreal County [3]	
	19	M. A. DeSalaberry, Rouville [3]	
		J. W. Dunscomb, Beauharnois [3]	
		S. S. Foster, Shefford [3]	
Independents (Canada East) (D, Fig. Va):		E. Hale, Sherbrooke Town	
R. Christie, Gaspé [4]		J. R. Hamilton, Bonaventure	
D. Burnet, Quebec City		B. Holmes, Montreal City	
		R. Jones, Missisquoi	
	2	M. McCulloch, Terrebonne	
		G. Moffatt, Montreal City	
		J. Moore, Sherbrooke County	
		C. R. Ogden, Three Rivers [3]	
Speaker: A. Cuvillier, Huntingdon		C. Robertson, Two Mountains [3]	
		J. Simpson, Vaudreuil [3]	
Vacant: York Fourth		R. N. Watts, Drummond	
		J. Yule, Chambly	
Disputed: York Second			
	3		20

Notes:
[1] Names of executive councillors in italic.
[2] Much absent, exact position not confirmed.
[3] Consistent supporter of Sydenham.
[4] Consistent opponent of Sydenham.

TABLE 3

FIRST PARLIAMENT, 2ND SESSION, 1842: PROBABLE ALIGNMENT OF MEMBERS AT SESSION OPENING [1]

LEFT	MODERATE	RIGHT
Ultra-Reformers (Canada West):	*Moderate Reformers* (Canada West):	*Compact Tories* (Canada West):
R. Baldwin, Hastings [2]	G. M. Boswell, Northumberland South	J. S. Cartwright, Lennox &
H. J. Boulton, Niagara	I. Buchanan, Toronto	Addington
J. Durand, Halton West	M. Cameron, Lanark	S. Y. Chesley, Cornwall
C. Hopkins, Halton East	J. Cook, Dundas	Jas. Johnston, Carleton
W. H. Merritt, Lincoln North	S. Crane, Grenville	A. N. MacNab, Hamilton
J. Morris, Leeds	S. Derbishire, Bytown	G. Sherwood, Brockville
J. H. Price, York First	*J. H. Dunn*, Toronto [2]	J. Woods, Kent
J. E. Small, York Third [2]	J. Gilchrist, Northumberland North	
	S. B. Harrison, Kingston [2]	6
8	*F. Hincks*, Oxford [2]	
	H. H. Killaly, London [2]	
French-Canadian Group (Canada East):	J. S. Macdonald, Glengarry	*"British" Tory Group* (Canada East):
D. M. Armstrong, Berthier	D. McDonald, Prescott	H. Black, Quebec City
J. G. Barthe, Yamaska	T. Parke, Middlesex	M. Child, Stanstead
A. Berthelot, Kamouraska	I. W. Powell, Norfolk	*D. Daly*, Megantic [2]
M. Borne, Rimouski	J. P. Roblin, Prince Edward	A. M. Delisle, Montreal County
T. Boutillier, St. Hyacinthe	Hermanus Smith, Wentworth	J. W. Dunscomb, Beauharnois
R. J. Kimber, Champlain	E. Steele, Simcoe	C. J. Forbes, Two Mountains
L. H. Lafontaine, York Fourth [2]	D. Thorburn, Lincoln South	S. S. Foster, Shefford
J. B. J. Noel, Lotbinière	D. Thompson, Haldimand	E. Hale, Sherbrooke Town
D. P. Papineau, Ottawa County	J. T. Williams, Durham [3]	R. Jones, Missisquoi
E. Parent, Saguenay		M. McCulloch, Terrebonne
F. A. Quesnel, Montmorency	21	G. Moffatt, Montreal City
E. P. Taché, L'Islet		J. Moore, Sherbrooke County
A. C. Taschereau, Dorchester	*Moderate Tories* (Canada West):	*C. R. Ogden*, Three Rivers
J. E. Turcotte, St. Maurice	*W. H. Draper*, Russell	J. Simpson, Vaudreuil
A. Turgeon, Bellechasse	W. Dunlop, Huron	W. Walker, Rouville
D. B. Viger, Richelieu	A. McLean, Stormont	R. N. Watts, Drummond
L. M. Viger, Nicolet	Henry Smith, Frontenac	J. Yule, Chambly
T. C. Aylwin, Portneuf [2]	4	17
J. DeWitt, Leinster		
J. Leslie, Verchères	*Independent* (Canada West):	
J. Neilson, Quebec County	J. Prince, Essex	
21	1	
	Independents and Moderates (Canada East):	
	R. Christie, Gaspé	
	D. Burnet, Quebec City	
	J. R. Hamilton, Bonaventure	
	B. Holmes, Montreal City	
	4	

Speaker: A. Cuvillier, Huntingdon

Disputed: York Second

2

Notes:
[1] Names of executive councillors on Sept. 8, 1842 in italic.
[2] Executive councillors who held office at any time between Sept. 15, 1842 and Sept. 30, 1843.
[3] Williams was soon to join Tory ranks.

TABLE 4

FIRST PARLIAMENT, 3RD SESSION, 1843: MID-SESSION ALIGNMENT

OPPOSITION		GOVERNMENT [1]

Compact Tories (Canada West):
J. S. Cartwright, Lennox & Addington
S. Y. Chesley, Cornwall
G. Duggan, York Second
Jas. Johnston, Carleton
A. N. MacNab, Hamilton
G. Sherwood, Brockville
H. Sherwood, Toronto
J. Woods, Kent

8

Independents (Canada West):
J. P. Roblin, Prince Edward
E. Steele, Simcoe
J. T. Williams, Durham

3

Reformers (Canada West):
R. Baldwin, Rimouski
G. M. Boswell, Northumberland South
H. J. Boulton, Niagara
M. Cameron, Lanark
J. Cook, Dundas
S. Crane, Grenville [2]
S. Derbishire, Bytown
J. H. Dunn, Toronto
J. Durand, Halton West
J. Gilchrist, Northumberland North
S. B. Harrison, Kingston
F. Hincks, Oxford
C. Hopkins, Halton East
H. H. Killaly, London
J. S. Macdonald, Glengarry
D. McDonald, Prescott
W. H. Merritt, Lincoln
J. Morris, Leeds
T. Parke, Middlesex
I. W. Powell, Norfolk
J. H. Price, York First
J. E. Small, York Third
Hermanus Smith, Wentworth
D. Thompson, Haldimand
D. Thorburn, Lincoln South

25

Moderate Tories (Canada West):
W. Dunlop, Huron
A. McLean, Stormont
E. Murney, Hastings
Henry Smith, Frontenac
W. Stuart, Russell

5

Independent (Canada West):
J. Prince, Essex

1

"British" Tory Group (Canada East):
H. Black, Quebec City
C. J. Forbes, Two Mountains
E. Hale, Sherbrooke Town
M. McCulloch, Terrebonne [2]
R. N. Watts, Drummond [2]

5

Independents (Canada East):
S. S. Foster, Shefford
J. Neilson, Quebec County

2

French-Canadian Group (Canada East):
D. M. Armstrong, Berthier
J. G. Barthe, Yamaska
P. Beaubien, Montreal City [2]
A. Berthelot, Kamouraska
T. Boutillier, St. Hyacinthe
J. Chabot, Quebec City
T. Franchère, Rouville
A. Jobin, Montreal County
H. Judah, Champlain
L. Lacoste, Chambly
L. H. Lafontaine, York Fourth
A. N. Morin, Saguenay
J. B. J. Noel, Lotbinière
D. B. Papineau, Ottawa County
F. A. Quesnel, Montmorency
E. P. Taché, L'Islet
A. C. Taschereau, Dorchester
J. E. Turcotte, St. Maurice
A. Turgeon, Bellechasse
D. B. Viger, Richelieu
L. M. Viger, Nicolet
T. C. Aylwin, Portneuf
J. DeWitt, Leinster
B. Holmes, Montreal City
J. Leslie, Verchères

25

Speaker: A. Cuvillier, Huntingdon

Vacant: Three Rivers

2

"British" Group (Canada East):
M. Child, Stanstead
D. Daly, Megantic
R. Jones, Missisquoi [2]
J. R. Hamilton, Bonaventure
J. Moore, Sherbrooke County
J. Simpson, Vaudreuil
E. G. Wakefield, Beauharnois

7

Notes:
[1] Names of executive councillors in italic.
[2] Members who did not attend the session.

Independent (Canada East):
R. Christie, Gaspé

1

TABLE 5
FIRST PARLIAMENT, 3RD SESSION, 1843: DIVISIONS ON THE RESIGNATION OF
THE EXECUTIVE COUNCILLORS, DEC. 2

SUPPORTERS OF THE LATE COUNCIL	SUPPORTERS OF THE GOVERNOR
Reformers (Canada West):	*Tories* (Canada West):
R. Baldwin, Rimouski	J. S. Cartwright, Lennox & Addington
G. M. Boswell, Northumberland South	S. Y. Chesley, Cornwall
H. J. Boulton, Niagara	W. Dunlop, Huron
M. Cameron, Lanark	Jas. Johnston, Carleton
S. Crane, Grenville	E. Murney, Hastings
S. Derbishire, Bytown	A. N. MacNab, Hamilton
J. H. Dunn, Toronto	A. McLean, Stormont
J. Durand, Halton West	H. Sherwood, Toronto
J. Gilchrist, Northumberland North	Henry Smith, Frontenac
S. B. Harrison, Kingston	W. Stuart, Russell
F. Hincks, Oxford	J. Woods, Kent
C. Hopkins, Halton East	
J. S. Macdonald, Glengarry	11
D. McDonald, Prescott	
W. H. Merritt, Lincoln	
J. Morris, Leeds	
T. Parke, Middlesex	
I. W. Powell, Norfolk	
J. H. Price, York First	
J. E. Small, York Third	
Hermanus Smith, Wentworth	
E. Steele, Simcoe	
D. Thompson, Haldimand	
D. Thorburn, Lincoln South	
24	
Independent (Canada West):	*Independents* (Canada West) (A, Fig. V*b*):
J. Prince, Essex	J. P. Roblin, Prince Edward
	J. T. Williams, Durham
1	
	2
French-Canadian Group (Canada East):	*"British Tory" Group* (Canada East):
D. M. Armstrong, Berthier	H. Black, Quebec City
J. G. Barthe, Yamaska	C. J. Forbes, Two Mountains
P. Beaubien, Montreal City	E. Hale, Sherbrooke Town
A. Berthelot, Kamouraska	
T. Boutillier, St. Hyacinthe	3
J. Chabot, Quebec City	
A. Jobin, Montreal County	
L. Lacoste, Chambly	
L. H. Lafontaine, York Fourth	
A. N. Morin, Saguenay	
D. B. Papineau, Ottawa County	*"British" Members* (Canada East):
F. A. Quesnel, Montmorency	S. S. Foster, Shefford
E. P. Taché, L'Islet	J. R. Hamilton, Bonaventure
J. E. Turcotte, St. Maurice	J. Simpson, Vaudreuil
L. M. Viger, Nicolet	E. G. Wakefield, Beauharnois
T. C. Aylwin, Portneuf	
J. DeWitt, Leinster	4
J. Leslie, Verchères	
18	
"British" Members (Canada East) 1(B, Fig. V*b*):	
M. Child, Stanstead	
J. Moore, Sherbrooke County	*French-Canadian Members* (Canada East) (D, Fig. V*b*):
2	J. Neilson, Quebec County
	J. B. J. Noel, Lotbinière
Independent (Canada East) (C, Fig. V*b*):	D. B. Viger, Richelieu
R. Christie, Gaspé	
	3
1	

Speaker:	A. Cuvillier, Huntingdon	
Vacant:	Three Rivers	
Absent:	J. Cook, Dundas, Opponent of Metcalfe	
	T. Franchère, Rouville,	–do–
	B. Holmes, Montreal City,	–do–
	H. Judah, Champlain,	–do–
	H. H. Killaly, London,	–do–
	A. C. Taschereau, Dorchester,	–do–
	A. Turgeon, Bellechasse,	–do–
	D. Daly, Megantic, Supporter of Metcalfe	
	G. Duggan, York Second,	–do–
	R. Jones, Missisquoi,	–do–
	M. McCulloch, Terrebonne,	–do–
	G. Sherwood, Brockville,	–do–
	R. N. Watts, Drummond,	–do–
	15	

TABLE 6
Second Parliament, 1st Session, 1844: Alignment for November, December

OPPOSITION	GOVERNMENT SUPPORTERS [1]
Reformers (Canada West):	*Tories and Conservatives* (Canada West):
R. Baldwin, York Fourth [3]	W. H. Boulton, Toronto
M. Cameron, Lanark [3]	G. Chambers, Halton East
S. B. Harrison, Kent [2]	J. Cummings, Lincoln South
J. S. Macdonald, Glengarry [3]	W. H. Dickson, Niagara
D. A. Macdonell, Stormont	G. Duggan, York Second [3]
W. H. Merritt, Lincoln [2,3]	W. Dunlop, Huron [3]
I. W. Powell, Norfolk [3]	E. Ermatinger, Middlesex
J. H. Price, York First [3]	O. R. Gowan, Leeds
J. P. Roblin, Prince Edward	G. B. Hall, Northumberland South
J. E. Small, York Third [3]	H. D. Jessup, Grenville
Hermanus Smith, Wentworth [3]	Jas. Johnston, Carleton [3]
D. Thompson, Haldimand [3]	L. Lawrason, London
	J. A. Macdonald, Kingston
12	Rolland Macdonald, Cornwall
	G. MacDonell, Dundas
Independent (Canada West) (A, Fig. V*c*):	A. H. Meyers, Northumberland North
J. Prince, Essex [3]	E. Murney, Hastings [3]
	A. Petrie, Russell
1	R. Riddell, Oxford
	W. B. Robinson, Simcoe
French-Canadian Group (Canada East):	B. Seymour, Lennox & Addington
D. M. Armstrong, Berthier [3]	G. Sherwood, Brockville [3]
A. Berthelot, Kamouraska [3]	H. Sherwood, Toronto [3]
L. Bertrand, Rimouski	Henry Smith, Frontenac [3]
T. Boutillier, St. Hyacinthe [3]	N. Stewart, Prescott
J. Cauchon, Montmorency	W. Stewart, Bytown [3]
J. Chabot, Quebec City [3]	J. Webster, Halton West
P. J. O. Chauveau, Quebec County	J. T. Williams, Durham [3]
F. Desaulniers, St. Maurice	
T. Franchère, Rouville [3]	28
A. Jobin, Montreal County [3]	
L. Lacoste, Chambly [3]	*"British" Tory Group* (Canada East):
L. H. Lafontaine, Terrebonne [3]	S. Brooks, Sherbrooke County
J. P. Lantier, Vaudreuil	E. Colville, Beauharnois
J. Laurin, Lotbinière	*D. Daly*, Megantic [3]
B. H. LeMoine, Huntingdon	C. C. S. DeBleury, Montreal City
A. P. Méthot, Nicolet	S. S. Foster, Shefford [3]
A. N. Morin, Bellechasse [3]	E. Grieve, Three Rivers
L. Rousseau, Yamaska	E. Hale, Sherbrooke Town [3]
E. P. Taché, L'Islet [3]	J. McConnell, Stanstead
P. E. Taschereau, Dorchester [3]	G. Moffatt, Montreal City
	D. B. Papineau, Ottawa County
20	W. H. Scott, Two Mountains
	Jas. Smith, Missisquoi
Divided apart from the French-Canadian Group Dec. 6:	R. N. Watts, Drummond [3] 13
L. Guillet, Champlain	
1	
"English" Liberals (Canada East):	Speaker: A. N. MacNab, Hamilton
T. C. Aylwin, Quebec City [3]	
J. DeWitt, Leinster [3]	Absent: J. LeBoutillier (B, Fig. V*c*)
L. T. Drummond, Portneuf	
J. Leslie, Verchères [3]	Vacant: Saguenay
W. Nelson, Richelieu	
	3
5	
Independent (Canada East) (B, Fig. V*c*):	
R. Christie, Gaspé [3]	
1	

Notes:
[1] Names of executive councillors in italic.
[2] Did not divide.
[3] Member in same alignment in closing stages of the first parliament.

TABLE 7

SECOND PARLIAMENT, 3RD SESSION, 1847: ALIGNMENT FOR JUNE, JULY

OPPOSITION		GOVERNMENT SUPPORTERS [1]

OPPOSITION

Reformers (Canada West):
R. Baldwin, York Fourth
M. Cameron, Lanark
R. B. Conger, Prince Edward
J. S. Macdonald, Glengarry
D. A. Macdonell, Stormont
W. H. Merritt, Lincoln
I. W. Powell, Norfolk
J. H. Price, York First
Hermanus Smith, Wentworth
D. Thompson, Haldimand

10

French-Canadian Group (Canada East):
D. M. Armstrong, Berthier
A. Berthelot, Kamouraska
L. Bertrand, Rimouski
T. Boutillier, St. Hyacinthe
J. Cauchon, Montmorency
J. Chabot, Quebec City
P. J. O. Chauveau, Quebec County
F. Desaulniers, St. Maurice
C. F. Fournier, L'Islet
T. Franchère, Rouville
L. Guillet, Champlain
A. Jobin, Montreal County
L. Lacoste, Chambly
L. H. Lafontaine, Terrebonne
M. P. D. LaTerrière, Saguenay
J. P. Lantier, Vaudreuil
J. Laurin, Lotbinière
F. Lemieux, Dorchester
B. H. LeMoine, Huntingdon
A. P. Méthot, Nicolet
A. N. Morin, Bellechasse
L. Rousseau, Yamaska

22

"English" Liberals (Canada East):
T. C. Aylwin, Quebec City
J. DeWitt, Leinster
L. T. Drummond, Portneuf
J. Leslie, Verchères
W. Nelson, Richelieu

Crossed to join Liberals March 27, 1846:
W. H. Scott, Two Mountains
R. N. Watts, Drummond

7

Independent (Canada West); crossed to
support Government in July 1847:

J. Prince, Essex

1

Conservative (Canada West); divided
against Government July 19, 1847:

E. Ermatinger, Middlesex

1

Tories (Canada West); divided against
Government July 27, 1847:

O. R. Gowan, Leeds
G. Monro, York Third

2

Speaker: A. N. MacNab, Hamilton

1

GOVERNMENT SUPPORTERS [1]

Tories and Conservatives (Canada West):
W. H. Boulton, Toronto
J. H. Cameron, Cornwall
W. Cayley, Huron
G. Chambers, Halton East
J. Cummings, Lincoln South
W. H. Dickson, Niagara
G. Duggan, York Second
G. B. Hall, Northumberland South
H. D. Jessup, Grenville
G. Lyon, Carleton
J. A. Macdonald, Kingston
G. MacDonell, Dundas
A. H. Meyers, Northumberland North
E. Murney, Hastings
A. Petrie, Russell
R. Riddell, Oxford
W. B. Robinson, Simcoe
B. Seymour, Lennox & Addington
G. Sherwood, Brockville
H. Sherwood, Toronto
Henry Smith, Frontenac
N. Stewart, Prescott
W. Stewart, Bytown
J. Webster, Halton West
J. T. Williams, Durham
J. Wilson, London
J. Woods, Kent

27

"British" Tory Group (Canada East):
W. Badgley, Missisquoi
S. Brooks, Sherbrooke County
E. Colville, Beauharnois
D. Daly, Megantic
C. C. S. DeBleury, Montreal City
S. S. Foster, Shefford
E. Hale, Sherbrooke Town
J. LeBoutillier, Bonaventure
J. McConnell, Stanstead
G. Moffatt, Montreal City
D. B. Papineau, Ottawa County
D. B. Viger, Three Rivers

12

Independent (Canada East); crossed to
support Government Mar. 23, 1846:
R. Christie, Gaspé

1

Note:
[1] Names of executive councillors in italic.

TABLE 8

THIRD PARLIAMENT, 1st SESSION, 1848: BASIC ALIGNMENT

OPPOSITION	GOVERNMENT SUPPORTERS [1]

Reformers (Canada West):
R. Baldwin, York North [2]
R. Bell, Lanark
W. H. Blake, York East [3]
H. J. Boulton, Norfolk
R. Burritt, Grenville
M. Cameron, Kent [2]
B. Flint, Hastings
J. Hall, Peterborough
F. Hincks, Oxford (after March 3) [4]
T. H. Johnson, Prescott
G. B. Lyon, Russell
J. S. Macdonald, Glengarry [2]
W. H. Merritt, Lincoln [2]
D. McFarland, Welland
J. C. Morrison, York West
W. Notman, Middlesex
J. H. Price, York South [2]
W. B. Richards, Leeds
J. Scott, Bytown
Hermanus Smith, Wentworth [2]
Jas. Smith, Durham
D. Thompson, Haldimand [2]
J. Wetenhall, Halton

23

French-Canadian Group (Canada East):
D. M. Armstrong, Berthier [2]
P. Beaubien, Chambly
T. Boutillier, St. Hyacinthe [2]
J. Cauchon, Montmorency [2]
J. Chabot, Quebec City [2]
P. J. O. Chauveau, Quebec County [2]
P. Davignon, Rouville
A. J. Duchesnay, Portneuf
N. Dumas, Leinster
T. Fortier, Nicolet
C. F. Fournier, L'Islet [2]
M. Fourquin dit Leveille, Yamaska
L. Guillet, Champlain [2]
A. Jobin, Montreal County [2]
L. H. Lafontaine, Montreal City [2]
M. P. D. Laterrière, Saguenay [2]
J. Laurin, Lotbinière [2]
F. Lemieux, Dorchester [2]
P. C. Marquis, Kamouraska
J. B. Mongenais, Vaudreuil
L. J. Papineau, St. Maurice
T. Sauvageau, Huntingdon
J. C. Taché, Rimouski

23

"English" Liberals (Canada East):
T. C. Aylwin, Quebec City [2]
J. DeWitt, Beauharnois [2]
L. T. Drummond, Shefford [2]
J. Egan, Ottawa County
B. Holmes, Montreal City
J. Leslie, Verchères [2]
W. Nelson, Richelieu [2]
W. H. Scott, Two Mountains [2]
R. N. Watts, Drummond [2]

9

Independent Tory (Canada East):
B. C. A. Gugy, Sherbrooke Town

1

Speaker: A. N. Morin, Bellechasse
Vacant: Terrebonne
Three Rivers

3

Tories and Conservatives (Canada West):
W. H. Boulton, Toronto [2]
J. H. Cameron, Cornwall [2]
P. Carroll, Oxford (until March 1) [4]
W. Cayley, Huron [2]
J. P. Crysler, Dundas
W. H. Dickson, Niagara [2,3]
J. A. Macdonald, Kingston [2]
A. N. MacNab, Hamilton
E. Malloch, Carleton
A. H. Meyers, Northumberland [2]
A. McLean, Stormont
W. B. Robinson, Simcoe [2]
B. Seymour, Lennox & Addington [2]
G. Sherwood, Brockville [2]
H. Sherwood, Toronto [2]
Henry Smith, Frontenac [2]
D. B. Stevenson, Prince Edward
J. Webster, Waterloo [2]
J. Wilson, London [2]

18

Independent (Canada West):
J. Prince, Essex

1

"British" Tory Group (Canada East):
W. Badgley, Missisquoi [2]
S. Brooks, Sherbrooke County [2]
W. Cuthbert, Bonaventure
D. Daly, Megantic [2]
J. McConnell, Stanstead [2]

5

Independent (Canada East):
R. Christie, Gaspé [2]

1

Notes:
[1] Names of executive councillors in italic.
[2] Member similarly oriented at close of previous parliament.
[3] Did not divide during the Session.
[4] Oxford: Carroll unseated and Hincks declared elected.

TABLE 9

THIRD PARLIAMENT, 2ND SESSION, 1849: ERA OF THE REBELLION LOSSES BILL

OPPOSITION	SUPPORTERS OF REFORM GOVERNMENT [1]
Tories (Canada West):	*Reformers* (Canada West):
W. H. Boulton, Toronto [2]	R. Baldwin, York North
W. Cayley, Huron [2]	R. Bell, Lanark
J. P. Crysler, Dundas [2]	W. J. Blake, York East
W. H. Dickson, Niagara [2]	H. J. Boulton, Norfolk
J. A. Macdonald, Kingston [2]	R. Burritt, Grenville [3]
A. N. MacNab, Hamilton [2]	*M. Cameron*, Kent
E. Malloch, Carleton [2]	A. J. Fergusson, Waterloo
A. H. Meyers, Northumberland [2]	B. Flint, Hastings
A. McLean, Stormont [2]	J. Hall, Peterborough
W. B. Robinson, Simcoe [2]	*F. Hincks*, Oxford
B. Seymour, Lennox & Addington [2]	T. H. Johnson, Prescott [2]
G. Sherwood, Brockville [3]	G. B. Lyon, Russell [3]
H. Sherwood, Toronto [3]	J. S. Macdonald, Glengarry [3]
Henry Smith, Frontenac [2]	*W. H. Merritt*, Lincoln
D. B. Stevenson, Prince Edward [2]	D. McFarland, Welland
	J. C. Morrison, York West
15	W. Notman, Middlesex
	J. H. Price, York South
	W. B. Richards, Leeds
	J. Scott, Bytown
	Hermanus Smith, Wentworth
	Jas. Smith, Durham [2]
	D. Thompson, Haldimand
	J. Wetenhall, Halton [3]
	24
Independent (Canada West) (B, Fig. V*d*):	
J. Prince, Essex [2]	
1	*Convert to Reform Party* (Canada West);
	Crossed to Reform ranks, Mar. 1849; (A, Fig. V*d*):
	J. Wilson, London (a)
	1
Tories (Canada East) (G, Fig. V*d*):	*French-Canadian Party* (Canada East):
W. Badgley, Missisquoi [2]	D. M. Armstrong, Berthier
S. Brooks, Sherbrooke County [2,4]	P. Beaubien, Chambly
	T. Boutillier, St. Hyacinthe
2	G. E. Cartier, Verchères
	J. Cauchon, Montmorency
	J. Chabot, Quebec City
	P. J. O. Chauveau, Quebec County
	P. Davignon, Rouville
	J. DeWitt, Beauharnois
	L. T. Drummond, Shefford
Conservative Independents (Canada East) (F, Fig. V*d*):	A. J. Duchesnay, Portneuf
R. Christie, Gaspé [2]	N. Dumas, Leinster
B. C. A. Gugy, Sherbrooke Town [2]	T. Fortier, Nicolet
J. McConnell, Stanstead [2]	C. F. Fournier, L'Islet
	M. Fourquin dit Leveille, Yamaska
3	L. Guillet, Champlain
	B. Holmes, Montreal City
	A. Jobin, Montreal County
	L. H. Lafontaine, Montreal City
	M. P. D. LaTerrière, Saguenay
	J. Laurin, Lotbinière
	F. Lemieux, Dorchester
Liberal Independent (Canada East) (C, Fig. V*d*):	P. C. Marquis, Kamouraska
L. J. Papineau, St. Maurice	F. X. Méthot, Quebec City
	J. B. Mongenais, Vaudreuil
	W. Nelson, Richelieu
1	A. Polette, Three Rivers
	T. Sauvageau, Huntingdon
	W. H. Scott, Two Mountains
	J. C. Taché, Rimouski
Speaker: A. N. Morin, Bellechasse	*L. M. Viger*, Terrebonne
	R. N. Watts, Drummond
Vacant: Megantic	
	32
Absent: J. H. Cameron, Cornwall (Tory)	*Moderate Independents* (Canada East) (E, Fig. V*d*):
W. Cuthbert, Bonaventure	J. Egan, Ottawa County (a)
(Moderate, D, Fig. V*d*)	A. T. Galt, Sherbrooke County [4]
4	1

Notes:
[1] Names of executive councillors in italic.
[2] Voted against Rebellion Losses Bill.
[3] Absent from division on Rebellion Losses Bill.
[4] Sherbrooke County: S. Brooks died Mar. 22, 1849; A. T. Galt elected in his place.

TABLE 10

THIRD PARLIAMENT, 3RD AND 4TH SESSIONS, 1850–1: EMERGENCE OF NEW RADICALISM

OPPOSITION	REFORM GOVERNMENT [1]
Conservatives (Canada West):	**Reformers (Canada West):**
W. H. Boulton, Toronto [2,3]	R. Baldwin, York North
J. H. Cameron, Cornwall [3]	R. Bell, Lanark [7]
W. Cayley, Huron [3]	R. Burritt, Grenville [7]
J. P. Crysler, Dundas [3]	A. J. Fergusson, Waterloo [7]
W. H. Dickson, Niagara [3]	B. Flint, Hastings [7]
J. A. Macdonald, Kingston	J. Hall, Peterborough [3,7]
A. N. MacNab, Hamilton [3]	*F. Hincks*, Oxford
E. Malloch, Carleton [3]	J. S. Macdonald, Glengarry
A. H. Meyers, Northumberland [3]	*W. H. Merritt*, Lincoln [7]
A. McLean, Stormont [3]	D. McFarland, Welland [3,7]
W. B. Robinson, Simcoe [3]	J. C. Morrison, York West
B. Seymour, Lennox & Addington [3]	W. Notman, Middlesex [7]
G. Sherwood, Brockville [3]	*J. H. Price*, York South
H. Sherwood, Toronto [3]	W. B. Richards, Leeds
Henry Smith, Frontenac [3]	J. Scott, Bytown [3,7]
D. B. Stevenson, Prince Edward [3]	Hermanus Smith, Wentworth [3,7]
	J. Smith, Durham [7]
16	D. Thompson, Haldimand [4,7]
	J. Wilson, London
	18
Clear Grits and Ultra-Reformers (Canada West):	**Ministerialists (Canada East):**
H. J. Boulton, Norfolk [2,3]	D. M. Armstrong, Berthier
M. Cameron, Kent [2]	T. Boutillier, St. Hyacinthe
C. Hopkins, Halton [2,3]	G. E. Cartier, Verchères
P. Perry, York East [2]	J. Cauchon, Montmorency
W. L. Mackenzie, Haldimand [2,3,4]	J. Chabot, Quebec City
	P. J. O. Chauveau, Quebec County
5	P. Davignon, Rouville
	L. T. Drummond, Shefford
	A. J. Duchesnay, Portneuf
	N. Dumas, Leinster
	T. Fortier, Nicolet
	C. F. Fournier, L'Islet
Independent (Canada West) (B, Fig. V*e*):	M. Fourquin dit Leveille, Yamaska
J. Prince, Essex [2,3]	L. Guillet, Champlain [7]
	A. Jobin, Montreal County
1	L. Lacoste, Chambly
	L. H. Lafontaine, Montreal City
	M. P. D. LaTerrière, Saguenay [7]
	J. Laurin, Lotbinière [7]
	F. Lemieux, Dorchester
	P. C. Marquis, Kamouraska [5]
	F. X. Méthot, Quebec City
Tories (Canada East) (G, Fig. V*e*):	J. B. Mongenais, Vaudreuil
W. Badgley, Missisquoi [3]	W. Nelson, Richelieu
B. C. A. Gugy, Sherbrooke Town	A. Polette, Three Rivers
	D. Ross, Megantic
2	J. Sauvageau, Huntingdon
	J. C. Taché, Rimouski
	L. M. Viger, Terrebonne
	R. N. Watts, Drummond
	29
Conservative Independent (Canada East) (F, Fig. V*e*):	
R. Christie, Gaspé [2,3]	
J. McConnell, Stanstead [2,3]	**Liberals (Canada East) (D, Fig. V*e*):**
	J. De Witt, Beauharnois [6]
2	B. Holmes, Montreal City [6]
	L. Letellier, Kamouraska [6,5]
	3
Liberal Independents (Canada East) (C, Fig. V*e*):	**Moderates (Canada East); much absent from House, exact viewpoint difficult to interpret (E, Fig. V*e*):**
L. J. Papineau, St. Maurice [2]	W. Cuthbert, Bonaventure
J. S. Sanborn, Sherbrooke County [2,3]	J. Egan, Ottawa County
	W. H. Scott, Two Mountains [3,7]
2	3
	Moderate Independents (Canada West) (A, Fig. V*e*):
	T. H. Johnson, Prescott (c)
Speaker: A. N. Morin, Bellechasse	G. B. Lyon, Russell (c)
1	2

Notes:
[1] Names of executive councillors in italic.
[2] Leaders in agitation for constitutional reform.
[3] Voted to abolish Court of Chancery, June 26, 1851.
[4] Haldimand: W. L. Mackenzie vice D. Thompson, April 21, 1851.
[5] Kamouraska: L. Letellier vice P. C. Marquis, Feb. 1, 1851.
[6] Decidedly liberal viewpoint.
[7] Several votes implying liberal tendencies beyond government policy.

TABLE 11

FOURTH PARLIAMENT, 1ST SESSION, 1852–3: BASIC ALIGNMENT

OPPOSITION		REFORM GOVERNMENT [1]	
Conservatives (Canada West):		*Reformers* (Canada West):	
W. H. Boulton, Toronto [3,6]			
A. A. Burnham, Northumberland		ADVANCED REFORMERS	
G. Crawford, Brockville		*M. Cameron*, Huron [6]	
T. C. Dixon, London		D. Christie, Wentworth	
J. W. Gamble, York South		A. J. Fergusson, Waterloo [6]	
J. Langton, Peterborough		J. Hartman, York North	
G. B. Lyon, Russell [6]		R. McDonald, Cornwall	
E. Malloch, Carleton [6]		*J. Rolph*, Norfolk [6]	
E. Murney, Hastings		J. W. Rose, Dundas	
J. A. Macdonald, Kingston [6]		J. White, Halton	
A. N. MacNab, Hamilton [6]		A. Wright, York East	
G. P. Ridout, Toronto			
W. B. Robinson, Simcoe [6]			
B. Seymour, Lennox & Addington [6]		MODERATE REFORMERS	
J. Shaw, Lanark		J. DeLong, Leeds [4]	
H. Sherwood, Toronto [3,6]		*F. Hincks*, Oxford [6]	
Henry Smith, Frontenac [6]		T. H. Johnson, Prescott [6]	
D. B. Stevenson, Prince Edward [6]		W. Mattice, Stormont	
T. C. Street, Welland		W. H. Merritt, Lincoln [6]	
C. Willson, Middlesex		J. C. Morrison, Niagara [6]	
G. Wright, York West		D. McLachlin, Bytown	
		W. Patrick, Grenville	
	20	W. B. Richards, Leeds [2,4,6]	
		J. Smith, Durham [6]	
Independent Reformers (Canada West) (A, Fig. Vf):			18
G. Brown, Kent			
W. L. Mackenzie, Haldimand [6]		*Ministerialists* (Canada East):	
		G. E. Cartier, Verchères [6]	
	2	J. Cauchon, Montmorency [6]	
		J. Chabot, Bellechasse [2,6]	
		J. C. Chapais, Kamouraska	
Moderate Independent (Canada West) (B, Fig. Vf):		P. J. O. Chauveau, Quebec County [2,6]	
J. Prince, Essex [6]		P. B. Dumoulin, Yamaska	
		T. Fortier, Nicolet [6]	
	1	C. F. Fournier, L'Islet [6]	
		A. N. Gouin, Richelieu	
		L. Lacoste, Chambly [6]	
Tories (Canada East) (G, Fig. Vf):		J. Laurin, Lotbinière [6]	
W. Badgley, Montreal City [6]		O. LeBlanc, Beauharnois	
J. G. Clapham, Megantic		D. LeBoutillier, Bonaventu	
G. O. Stuart, Quebec City		F. Lemieux, Dorchester [6]	
		J. B. Mongenais, Vaudreuil [6]	
	3	*A. N. Morin*, Terrebonne [6]	
		A. Polette, Three Rivers [6]	
		J. N. Poulin, Rouville	
Rouges (Canada East) (C, Fig. Vf):		J. C. Taché, Rimouski [6]	
J. H. Jobin, Berthier		U. J. Tessier, Portneuf	
L. J. Papineau, Two Mountains [6]		J. E. Turcotte, St. Maurice	
M. F. Valois, Montreal County		J. B. Varin, Huntingdon	
J. Young, Montreal City [2]		L. M. Viger, Leinster [6]	
	4		23
		Liberals (Canada East) (E, Fig. Vf):	
Independents (Canada East) (D, F, Fig. Vf):		*M. P. D. LaTerrière*, Saguenay [6]	
R. Christie, Gaspé [6]		T. Marchildon, Champlain	
J. S. Sanborn, Sherbrooke County [6]		L. V. Sicotte, St. Hyacinthe	
H. Dubord, Quebec City			
	3		3
		"English" Moderates (Canada East):	
		L. T. Drummond, Shefford [6]	
		J. Egan, Ottawa County [6]	
		A. T. Galt, Sherbrooke Town [5]	
Speaker: J. S. Macdonald, Glengarry		J. McDougall, Drummond	
		S. Paige, Missisquoi	
	1	E. Short, Sherbrooke Town [5]	
		T. L. Terrill, Stanstead	
			6

Notes:
[1] Names of executive councillors throughout the session in italic.
[2] Executive councillors for a portion only of the session.
[3] Toronto: S. Sherwood vice W. H. Boulton, April 28, 1853.
[4] Leeds: J. Delong vice W. B. Richards, July 13, 1853.
[5] Sherbrooke Town: A. T. Galt vice E. Short, Mar. 8, 1853.
[6] Members who sat at the close of the third parliament.

TABLE 12
Fourth Parliament, 2nd Session, 1854

OPPOSITION OF THE "LEFT"	GOVERNMENT SUPPORTER [1]	OPPOSITION OF THE "RIGHT"
Seceding Reformers (Canada West): D. Christie, Wentworth [2] A. J. Fergusson, Waterloo J. Hartman, York North R. McDonald, Cornwall W. Mattice, Stormont J. W. Rose, Dundas J. White, Halton 7	*Reformers* (Canada West): *M. Cameron*, Huron J. DeLong, Leeds *F. Hincks*, Oxford J. C. Morrison, Niagara W. Patrick, Grenville *J. Rolph*, Norfolk J. Smith, Durham A. Wright, York East 8	*Conservatives* (Canada West): A. A. Burnham, Northumberland G. Crawford, Brockville T. C. Dixon, London J. W. Gamble, York South J. Langton, Peterborough G. B. Lyon, Russell J. A. Macdonald, Kingston A. N. MacNab, Hamilton E. Malloch, Carleton E. Murney, Hastings G. P. Ridout, Toronto W. B. Robinson, Simcoe B. Seymour, Lennox & Addington J. Shaw, Lanark H. Sherwood, Toronto Henry Smith, Frontenac [2] D. B. Stevenson, Prince Edward T. C. Street, Welland C. Willson, Middlesex G. Wright, York West 20
Opposition Reformers (Canada West) (A, Fig. V*g*): G. Brown, Kent W. L. Mackenzie, Haldimand 2	*Independent* (Canada West) (C, Fig. V*g*): J. Prince, Essex 1	
Rouges and Liberals (Canada East): J. H. Jobin, Berthier M. P. D. LaTerrière, Saguenay T. Marchildon, Champlain L. J. Papineau, Two Mountains [2] L. V. Sicotte, St. Hyacinthe M. F. Valois, Montreal County J. Young, Montreal City 7	*Ministerialists* (Canada East): G. E. Cartier, Verchères *J. Chabot*, Bellechasse J. C. Chapais, Kamouraska *P. J. O. Chauveau*, Quebec County *L. T. Drummond*, Shefford P. B. Dumoulin, Yamaska J. Egan, Ottawa County T. Fortier, Nicolet C. F. Fournier, L'Islet J. Laurin, Lotbinière F. Lemieux, Dorchester J. B. Mongenais, Vaudreuil *A. N. Morin*, Terrebonne S. Paige, Missisquoi J. N. Poulin, Rouville J. S. Sanborn, Sherbrooke County J. C. Taché, Rimouski J. E. Turcotte, St. Maurice J. B. Varin, Huntingdon L. M. Viger, Leinster [2] 20	*Tories, Conservatives* and *Temporary Opponents* (Canada East): W. Badgley, Montreal City (Tory) (F, Fig. V*g*) J. Cauchon, Montmorency (Temporary) J. G. Clapham, Megantic (Tory) (F, Fig. V*g*) H. Dubord, Quebec City (Independent) A. N. Gouin, Richelieu (Temporary) L. Lacoste, Chambly (Temporary) O. LeBlanc, Beauharnois (Temporary) J. McDougall, Drummond (Conservative) A. Polette, Three Rivers (Temporary) U. J. Tessier, Portneuf (?) G. O. Stuart, Quebec City (Tory) (F, Fig. V*g*) 11
Speaker: J. S. Macdonald, Glengarry Absent: (And view-point not well known) Reformers: T. H. Johnson, Prescott D. McLachlin, Bytown W. H. Merritt, Lincoln (B, Fig. V*g*) Moderates: D. LeBoutillier, Bonaventure Independ: R. Christie, Gaspé (E, Fig. V*g*) Liberal: T. L. Terrill, Stanstead 7	*Independent* (Canada East) (D, Fig. V*g*): A. T. Galt, Sherbrooke Town 1	

Notes:
[1] Names of executive councillors in italic.
[2] Absent and viewpoint well known.

TABLE 13
FIFTH PARLIAMENT, 1ST SESSION, 1854: OPENING DIVISIONS

OPPOSITION OF THE "LEFT"	GOVERNMENT SUPPORTERS [1]	OPPOSITION OF THE "RIGHT"
Ultra-Reformers (Clear Grits) (Canada West):	*Moderate (Hincksite) Reformers (Canada West):*	*Conservatives (Canada West):*
J. C. Aikins, Peel	R. Bell, Lanark North	J. G. Bowes, Toronto
G. Brown, Lambton [2]	H. Biggar, Brant West	F. H. Burton, Durham East
A. J. Fergusson, Wellington South [2]	B. R. Church, Leeds & Grenville North	J. H. Cameron, Toronto
R. Ferrie, Waterloo South	J. DeLong, Leeds South [2]	W. Cayley, Huron & Bruce
B. Flint, Hastings South [3]	M. H. Foley, Waterloo North	G. K. Chisholm, Halton
J. Hartman, York North [2]	J. Frazer, Welland	W. Clarke, Wellington North
J. M. Lumsden, Ontario South	S. B. Freeman, Wentworth South	G. Crawford, Brockville [2,3]
J. S. Macdonald, Glengarry	J. Gould, Ontario North	J. P. Crysler, Dundas
R. McDonald, Cornwall [2]	*F. Hincks, Refrew* [2]	T. M. Daly, Perth [3]
W. L. Mackenzie, Haldimand [2]	G. Jackson, Grey	J. W. Gamble, York West [2]
D. McKerlie, Brant East	A. Morrison, Simcoe North	J. Langton, Peterborough [2]
W. Mattice, Stormont [2]	J. C. Morrison, Niagara [2]	E. Larwill, Kent
W. H. Merritt, Lincoln	H. Munro, Durham West	G. B. Lyon (Fellows), Russell [2]
J. Scatcherd, Middlesex West	W. Niles, Middlesex East	G. Macbeth, Elgin West
	W. Patrick, Grenville South [2]	H. W. McCann, Prescott
14	A. Rankin, Essex [3]	J. A. Macdonald, Kingston [2]
	D. Roblin, Lennox & Addington	A. N. MacNab, Hamilton [2]
	J. Rolph, Norfolk [2]	D. Matheson, Oxford North
	J. Ross, Northumberland East	E. Murney, Hastings North [2]
	J. Smith, Victoria [2]	W. F. Powell, Carleton
	S. Smith, Northumberland West	W. B. Robinson, Simcoe South [2]
	G. Southwick, Elgin East	J. Shaw, Lanark South [2]
	R. Spence, Wentworth North	Henry Smith, Frontenac [2]
	J. Wilson, London	D. B. Stevenson, Prince Edward [2]
	A. Wright, York East [2]	A. Yeilding, Bytown
		25
	25	
Rouges and Liberals (Canada East):	*Ministerialists (Canada East):*	*Moderates in Opposition (Canada East):*
F. Bourassa, St. John's	J. Blanchet, Quebec City	N. Casault, Montmagny
J. O. Bureau, Napierville	T. Brodeur, Bagot	J. Cauchon, Montmorency [2]
A. Cooke, Ottawa County	G. E. Cartier, Verchères [2]	P. E. Dostaler, Berthier
N. Darche, Chambly	*J. Chabot, Quebec City* [2]	J. Dufresne, Montcalm
J. DeWitt, Châteauguay	J. C. Chapais, Kamouraska [2]	J. M. Ferris, Missisquoi East
A. A. Dorion, Montreal	*P. J. O. Chauveau, Quebec County* [2]	J. B. Guévremont, Richelieu
J. B. E. Dorion, Drummond & Arthabaska	J. B. Daoust, Two Mountains	J. O'Farrell, Lotbinière
L. H. Holton, Montreal	L. L. Desaulniers, St. Maurice	A. Polette, Three Rivers
J. H. Jobin, Joliette [2]	B. Dionne, Temiscouata	R. B. Somerville, Huntingdon
C. J. Laberge, Iberville	T. Fortier, Nicolet [2]	
T. Marchildon, Champlain [2]	C. F. Fournier, L'Islet [2]	9
J. Papin, L'Assomption	I. Gill, Yamaska	
G. M. Prévost, Terrebonne	P. Labelle, Laval	
M. F. Valois, Jacques Cartier [2]	J. Laporté, Hochelaga	
J. Young, Montreal [2]	J. LeBoutillier, Gaspé [3]	
	F. Lemieux, Levis [2]	
16	T. J. J. Loranger, Laprairie	
	L. H. Masson, Soulanges [3]	
	J. Meagher, Bonaventure	
	J. B. Mongenais, Vaudreuil [2]	
	A. N. Morin, Chicoutimi & Tadoussac [2]	
	J. N. Poulin, Rouville [2]	
	B. Pouliot, Dorchester	
	J. C. Taché, Rimouski [2]	
	J. E. Thibaudeau, Portneuf [2]	
	J. E. Turcotte, Maskinongé [2]	
	ENGLISH MEMBERS	
	C. Alleyn, Quebec City	
	S. Bellingham, Argenteuil	
	L. T. Drummond, Shefford	
	J. Egan, Pontiac	
	W. L. Felton, Sherbrooke & Wolfe	
	W. Rhodes, Megantic	
	D. Ross, Beauce	
	T. L. Terrill, Stanstead	
	H. H. Whitney, Missisquoi West	
	35	
	Independent Liberals (Canada East) (A, Fig. Vh):	
	A. T. Galt, Sherbrooke Town [2]	
	P. G. Huot, Saguenay	
	J. S. Sanborn, Compton [2]	
Speaker: L. V. Sicotte, St. Hyacinthe		
Vacant: Bellechasse		
Oxford South 3	3	

Notes:
[1] Names of executive councillors in italic.
[2] Members in the same alignment at the close of the previous parliament.
[3] Absent Members.

TABLE 14

FIFTH PARLIAMENT, 1ST SESSION, 1854: FORMATION OF THE MORIN-MACNAB MINISTRY, SEPT. 11

OPPOSITION	GOVERNMENT [1]	GOVERNMENT (CONT.) [1]
Ultra-Reformers (Canada West):	*Conservatives* (Canada West) (Includes E, F, G, Fig. Vi):	*Ministerialists* (Canada East) (Includes J, Fig. Vi): [4]
J. C. Aikins, Peel	J. G. Bowes, Toronto	J. Blanchet, Quebec City
G. Brown, Lambton	F. H. Burton, Durham East	T. Brodeur, Bagot
A. J. Fergusson, Wellington South	J. H. Cameron, Toronto	G. E. Cartier, Verchères
R. Ferrie, Waterloo South	*W. Cayley*, Huron & Bruce	*J. Chabot*, Quebec City
B. Flint, Hastings South	G. K. Chisholm, Halton	J. C. Chapais, Kamouraska
J. Hartman, York North	W. Clarke, Wellington North	*P. J. O. Chauveau*, Quebec County
J. M. Lumsden, Ontario South	G. Crawford, Brockville	J. B. Daoust, Two Mountains
J. S. Macdonald, Glengarry	J. P. Crysler, Dundas	L. L. Desaulniers, St. Maurice
R. McDonald, Cornwall	T. M. Daly, Perth	B. Dionne, Temiscouata
W. L. MacKenzie, Haldimand	J. W. Gamble, York West	T. Fortier, Nicolet
D. McKerlie, Brant East	J. Langton, Peterborough	C. F. Fournier, L'Islet
W. Mattice, Stormont	E. Larwill, Kent	I. Gill, Yamaska
W. H. Merritt, Lincoln	G. B. Lyon (Fellows), Russell	P. Labelle, Laval
J. Scatcherd, Middlesex West	G. Macbeth, Elgin West	J. Laporté, Hochelaga
	H. W. McCann, Prescott	J. LeBoutillier, Gaspé
14	*J. A. Macdonald*, Kingston	F. Lemieux, Levis
	A. N. MacNab, Hamilton	T. J. J. Loranger, Laprairie
Seceding Reformers (Canada West) (A, Fig. Vi): [3]	D. Matheson, Oxford North	L. H. Masson, Soulanges
M. H. Foley, Waterloo North	E. Murney, Hastings North	J. Meagher, Bonaventure
J. Frazer, Welland	W. F. Powell, Carleton	J. B. Mongenais, Vaudreuil
S. B. Freeman, Wentworth North	W. B. Robinson, Simcoe South	*A. N. Morin*, Chicoutimi & Tadoussac
J. Rolph, Norfolk	J. Shaw, Lanark South	J. N. Poulin, Rouville
J. Wilson, London	Henry Smith, Frontenac	B. Pouliot, Dorchester
A. Wright, York East	D. B. Stevenson, Prince Edward	J. C. Taché, Rimouski
	A. Yielding, Bytown	J. E. Thibaudeau, Portneuf
6		J. E. Turcotte, Maskinongé
	25	
Rouges and Liberals (Canada East):		
F. Bourassa, St. John's		ENGLISH MEMBERS
J. O. Bureau, Napierville	*Moderate Reformers* (Canada West) (B, C, D, Fig. Vi): [3]	C. Alleyn, Quebec City
A. Cooke, Ottawa County	R. Bell, Lanark North [2]	S. Bellingham, Argenteuil
C. Daoust, Beauharnois	H. Biggar, Brant West [2]	L. T. Drummond, Shefford
N. Darche, Chambly	B. R. Church, Leeds & Grenville North	J. Egan, Pontiac
J. DeWitt, Châteauguay	J. DeLong, Leeds South [2]	W. L. Felton, Sherbrooke & Wolfe
A. A. Dorion, Montreal	J. Gould, Ontario North [2]	W. Rhodes, Megantic
J. B. E. Dorion, Drummond & Arthabaska	F. Hincks, Renfrew	D. Ross, Beauce
L. H. Holton, Montreal	G. Jackson, Grey [2]	T. L. Terrill, Stanstead
J. H. Jobin, Joliette	A. Morrison, Simcoe North	H. H. Whitney, Missisquoi West
C. J. Laberge, Iberville	J. C. Morrison, Niagara	
T. Marchildon, Champlain	H. Munro, Durham West [2]	35
J. Papin, L'Assomption	W. Niles, Middlesex East	
G. M. Prévost, Terrebonne	W. Patrick, Grenville South [2]	*Moderates* (Canada East):
M. F. Valois, Jacques Cartier	A. Rankin, Essex	N. Casault, Montmagny
J. Young, Montreal	D. Roblin, Lennox & Addington	J. Cauchon, Montmorency
	J. Ross, Northumberland East	P. E. Dostaler, Berthier
16	J. Smith, Victoria	J. Dufresne, Montcalm
	S. Smith, Northumberland West	J. M. Ferris, Missisquoi East
Independent Liberals (Canada East) (I, Fig. Vi):	G. Southwick, Elgin East	J. O'Farrell, Lotbinière
A. T. Galt, Sherbrooke Town	*R. Spence*, Wentworth North	J. B. Guévremont, Richelieu
P. G. Huot, Saguenay		A. Polette, Three Rivers
J. S. Sanborn, Compton		R. B. Somerville, Huntingdon
3	19	9

Speaker: L. V. Sicotte, St. Hyacinthe	*Notes:*
	[1] Names of executive councillors in italic.
Vacant: Bellechasse	[2] Members who crossed into opposition at later stages of the fifth parliament (B, Fig. Vi).
Oxford South	[3] Supported Hincks-Morin government Sept. 5, 1854.
3	[4] Supported Hincks-Morin government Sept. 5 and 7, 1854.

TABLE 15
Fifth Parliament, 3rd Session, 1856: The Exclusion of MacNab, May 30

OPPOSITION		GOVERNMENT [1]

OPPOSITION

Ultra-Reformers (Canada West):
J. C. Aikins, Peel
G. Brown, Lambton
D. Christie, Brant East
A. J. Fergusson, Wellington South
R. Ferrie, Waterloo South [3]
B. Flint, Hastings South [3]
M. H. Foley, Waterloo North [2]
J. Frazer, Welland [2]
S. B. Freeman, Wentworth North [2]
J. Hartman, York North
J. M. Lumsden, Ontario South
J. S. Macdonald, Glengarry
R. McDonald, Cornwall
W. L. Mackenzie, Haldimand
W. Mattice, Stormont
W. H. Merritt, Lincoln
J. Rolph, Norfolk [2]
J. Scatcherd, Middlesex West
J. Wilson, London [2]
A. Wright, York East

Crossed into opposition before March, 1855 (B, Fig. Vi):
J. Gould, Ontario North [2]
H. Munro, Durham North [2]

Crossed into opposition April 21, 1856 (B, Fig. Vi):
R. Bell, Lanark North [2]
W. Niles, Middlesex East [2]
W. Patrick, Grenville South [2]

Crossed into opposition May 30, 1856 (B, Fig. Vi):
H. Biggar, Brant West [2]
J. DeLong, Leeds South [2]

27

Conservatives (Canada West); crossed into opposition April 21, 1856 (G, Fig. Vi):
J. H. Cameron, Toronto
E. Murney, Hastings North

2

Rouges and Liberals (Canada East):

ROUGES
F. Bourassa, St. John's
J. O. Bureau, Napierville
A. Cooke, Ottawa County [3]
C. Daoust, Beauharnois
N. Darche, Chambly
J. DeWitt, Châteauguay
A. A. Dorion, Montreal
J. B. E. Dorion, Drummond & Arthabaska
L. H. Holton, Montreal
J. H. Jobin, Joliette
C. J. Laberge, Iberville
J. Papin, L'Assomption
G. M. Prévost, Terrebonne
M. F. Valois, Jacques Cartier [3]
J. Young, Montreal [3]

LIBERALS (I, Fig. Vi)
A. T. Galt, Sherbrooke Town
P. G. Huot, Saguenay
J. S. Sanborn, Compton

18

Speaker: L. V. Sicotte, St. Hyacinthe

1

Conservatives (Canada West); voted against government May 30, subsequently supported it (F, Fig. Vi):
D. Matheson, Oxford North
W. F. Powell, Carleton

voted against government May 30, and did not divide in the House again
A. N. MacNab, Hamilton

3

Conservative (Canada West); passed into opposition and supported Reformers (E, Fig. Vi):
J. W. Gamble, York West

1

Reformers (Canada West); voted against government May 30, subsequently supported it (C, Fig. Vi):
E. Cook, Oxford South
G. Jackson, Grey [2]
A. Rankin, Essex
J. Ross, Northumberland East [2]
James Smith, Victoria [2]
G. Southwick, Elgin East [2]

6

Rouge (Canada East); supported government May 30, subsequently returned to opposition (H, Fig. Vi):
T. Marchildon, Champlain

1

Ministerialists (Canada East); voted against government May 30, subsequently supported it (J, Fig. Vi):
W. L. Felton, Sherbrooke & Wolfe
T. J. J. Loranger, Laprairie
W. Rhodes, Megantic

3

GOVERNMENT [1]

Conservatives (Canada West):
J. G. Bowes, Toronto
F. H. Burton, Durham East
W. Cayley, Huron & Bruce
G. K. Chisholm, Halton [3]
W. Clarke, Wellington North
W. S. Conger, Peterborough
G. Crawford, Brockville
J. P. Crysler, Dundas
T. M. Daly, Perth [3]
E. Larwill, Kent
G. B. Lyon (Fellows), Russell
G. Macbeth, Elgin West
H. W. McCann, Prescott
J. A. Macdonald, Kingston
W. B. Robinson, Simcoe South
J. Shaw, Lanark South
Henry Smith, Frontenac
D. B. Stevenson, Prince Edward
J. Supple, Renfrew
A. Yielding, Bytown

20

Coalition Reformers (Canada West) (D, Fig. Vi):
B. R. Church, Leeds & Grenville North [2,3]
A. Morrison, Simcoe North [2]
J. C. Morrison, Niagara [2,3]
D. Roblin, Lennox & Addington [2,3]
R. Spence, Wentworth North [2]
Sydney Smith, Northumberland West [2,3]

6

Ministerialists (Canada East):

BLEUS
J. Blanchet, Quebec City
T. Brodeur, Bagot
G. E. Cartier, Verchères
N. Casault, Montmagny
J. Cauchon, Montmorency
J. Chabot, Quebec City
J. C. Chapais, Kamouraska
J. B. Daoust, Two Mountains
L. L. L. Desaulniers, St. Maurice
B. Dionne, Temiscouata
P. E. Dostaler, Berthier
J. Dufresne, Montcalm
F. Evanturel, Quebec City
O. C. Fortier, Bellechasse
T. Fortier, Nicolet
C. F. Fournier, L'Islet
I. Gill, Yamaska
J. B. Guévremont, Richelieu
P. Labelle, Laval
J. Laporté, Hochelaga
J. Leboutillier, Gaspé
F. Lemieux, Levis
L. H. Masson, Soulanges
J. Meagher, Bonaventure
J. B. Mongenais, Vaudreuil
A. Polette, Three Rivers
J. N. Poulin, Rouville
B. Pouliot, Dorchester
J. C. Taché, Rimouski
J. E. Thibaudeau, Portneuf
J. E. Turcotte, Maskinongé

CONSERVATIVES
C. Alleyn, Quebec City
S. Bellingham, Argenteuil
L. T. Drummond, Shefford [3]
J. Egan, Pontiac [3]
J. M. Ferris, Missisquoi East
J. O'Farrell, Lotbinière
D. E. Price, Chicoutimi & Tadoussac
D. Ross, Beauce
R. B. Somerville, Huntingdon
T. L. Terrill, Stanstead
H. H. Whitney, Missisquoi West [3]

42

Notes:
[1] Names of executive councillors in italic.
[2] Hincks supporter at opening of fifth parliament.
[3] Absent May 30, 1856.

TABLE 16

SIXTH PARLIAMENT, 1ST SESSION, 1858: THE BROWN-DORION MINISTRY [1]

LIBERALS AND ROUGES		LIBERAL-CONSERVATIVES

Liberals (Canada West):
J. C. Aikins, Peel [6]
R. Bell, Lanark North [6]
H. Biggar, Brant West [6]
G. Brown, Toronto [3, 5, 6]
L. Burwell, Elgin East
D. Christie, Brant East [6]
J. R. Clark, Northumberland East
S. Connor, Oxford South [5]
J. W. Cook, Dundas
W. C. Dorland, Prince Edward
M. H. Foley, Waterloo North [3, 5, 6]
J. Gould, Ontario North [6]
J. Hartman, York North [5, 6]
J. Holmes, Huron & Bruce
W. P. Howland, York West
D. A. Macdonald, Glengarry
J. S. Macdonald, Cornwall [3, 5, 6]
W. McDougall, Oxford North [5]
A. McKellar, Kent
W. L. Mackenzie, Haldimand [6]
W. D. Mattice, Stormont
W. H. Merritt, Lincoln
O. Mowat, Ontario South [3, 5]
H. Munro, Durham West [6]
W. Notman, Wentworth North
W. Patrick, Grenville South [6]
W. Powell, Norfolk
J. Rymal, Wentworth South
T. Short, Peterborough
D. Stirton, Wellington South
L. Wallbridge, Hastings South
J. White, Halton
A. Wright, York East [6]

33

Rouges (Canada East):
F. Bourassa, Jr., St. John's [5]
J. O. Bureau, Napierville [5, 6]
A. A. Dorion, Montreal [2, 5, 6]
N. Hébert, Megantic
J. H. Jobin, Joliette [6]
C. J. Laberge, Iberville [6]
M. Laframboise, Bagot
T. D. McGee, Montreal [5]
D. E. Papineau, Ottawa County
E. U. Piché, Berthier [5]

10

Independent Liberal (Canada West); voted against the Brown-Dorion Government Aug. 2. (A, Fig. Vj):
J. S. Hogan, Grey

1

Independent (Canada East); crossed into support of Liberal-Conservatives, Aug. 2 (C, Fig. Vj):
A. T. Galt, Sherbrooke [4]

1

Liberals (Canada East); crossed into support of Brown-Dorion Government, Aug. 2:
L. T. Drummond, Shefford [3, 5]
F. Lemieux, Levis [5]
D. Ross, Beauce
R. B. Somerville, Huntingdon
J. E. Thibaudeau, Port Neuf [3]

5

Conservatives (Canada West):
G. Benjamin, Hastings North
F. H. Burton, Durham East [6]
J. Cameron, Victoria
J. Carling, London
W. Cayley, Renfrew [2, 6]
T. M. Daly, Perth [6]
G. B. L. Fellows, Russell [6]
T. R. Ferguson, Simcoe South
O. R. Gowan, Leeds & Grenville North
G. Macbeth, Elgin West [6]
H. W. McCann, Prescott [6]
J. A. Macdonald, Kingston [2, 4, 6]
J. MacLeod, Essex
G. McMicken, Welland
A. W. Playfair, Lanark South
W. F. Powell, Carleton [6]
J. B. Robinson, Jr., Toronto
R. W. Scott, Ottawa City
W. Scott, Waterloo South [5]
G. Sherwood, Brockville [4, 5]
J. Simpson, Niagara
M. Talbot, Middlesex East
B. Tett, Leeds South

23

Coalition Reformers (Canada West) (B, Fig. Vj):
I. Buchanan, Hamilton
M. Cameron, Lambton
A. Morrison, Simcoe North [6]
D. Roblin, Lennox & Addington [6]
Sydney Smith, Northumberland West [2, 4, 6]

5

Bleus (Canada East):
L. Archambault, L'Assomption
M. G. Baby, Rimouski [6]
J. O. Beaubien, Montmagny
G. E. Cartier, Verchères [2, 4, 6]
J. Cauchon, Montmorency [6]
J. C. Chapais, Kamouraska [6]
C. Cimon, Charlevoix
D. A. Coutleé, Soulanges
J. B. Daoust, Two Mountains [6]
L. L. L. Desaulniers, St. Maurice [6]
B. Dionne, Temiscouata [6]
H. Dubord, Quebec City
J. Dufresne, Montcalm [6]
O. C. Fortier, Bellechasse [6]
C. F. Fournier, L'Islet [6]
J. Gaudet, Nicolet
L. H. Gauvreau, Maskinongé
I. Gill, Yamaska [5, 6]
P. Labelle, Laval [6]
L. Lacoste, Chambly
H. L. Langevin, Dorchester
J. Laporte, Hochelaga [6]
J. LeBoutillier, Gaspé [6]
T. J. J. Loranger, Laprairie [2, 6]
J. Meagher, Bonaventure [6]
L. S. Morin, Terrebonne
G. Ouimet, Beauharnois
C. Panet, Quebec County
L. V. Sicotte, St. Hyacinthe [2, 4]
G. H. Simard, Quebec City
J. F. Sincennes, Richelieu
F. Z. Tassé, Jacques Cartier
J. E. Turcotte, Champlain [6]

33

Conservatives (Canada East):
C. Alleyn, Quebec City [2, 4, 6]
S. Bellingham, Argenteuil [7]
T. E. Campbell, Rouville
W. M. Dawson, Three Rivers [5]
C. Dunkin, Drummond & Arthabaska
J. M. Ferris, Brome [6]
R. V. Harwood, Vaudreuil
E. Heath, Pontiac
J. H. Pope, Compton
D. E. Price, Chicoutimi & Saguenay
J. Rose, Montreal [4]
H. Starnes, Châteauguay
T. L. Terrill, Stanstead [6]
W. H. Webb, Richmond & Wolfe
H. H. Whitney, Missisquoi [6]

15

Speaker: Henry Smith, Frontenac

Vacant: Lotbinière
Middlesex West
Wellington North

4

Notes:
[1] Names of executive councillors in italic.
[2] Member of Executive Council July 29, 1858.
[3] Member of Executive Council (Brown-Dorion) Aug. 2–4, 1858.
[4] Member of Executive Council from Aug. 7, 1858.
[5] Member who did not divide during the crisis.
[6] Member in the same alignment at close of previous parliament (1857).

TABLE 17
SEVENTH PARLIAMENT, 1ST SESSION, 1862 [1]

LIBERALS		LIBERAL-CONSERVATIVES

Liberals (Canada West):
R. Bell, Lanark North [2]
J. Y. Bown, Brant East
L. Burwell, Elgin East [2]
S. Connor, Oxford South [2]
J. Cowan, Waterloo South
J. Dickson, Huron & Bruce
M. H. Foley, Waterloo North [2]
M. Harcourt, Haldimand [2]
W. P. Howland, York West [2]
D. A. Macdonald, Glengarry [2]
J. S. Macdonald, Cornwall [2]
W. McDougall, Oxford North [2]
A. McKellar, Kent [2]
A. Mackenzie, Lambton
O. Mowat, Ontario South [2]
H. Munro, Durham West [2]
W. Notman, Wentworth North [2]
W. Patrick, Grenville South [2]
A. Rankin, Essex
J. Rymal, Wentworth South [2]
T. Scatcherd, Middlesex West
D. Stirton, Wellington South [2]
L. Wallbridge, Hastings South [2]
J. White, Halton [2]
A. Wilson, York North [2]
A. Wright, York East [2]

26

Liberals (Canada West); voted in favour of the Militia Bill, May 20, 1862 (A, Fig. Vk):
S. Ault, Stormont
J. L. Biggar, Northumberland East
J. S. Smith, Durham East

3

Conservatives (Canada West):
W. Anderson, Prince Edward
R. Bell, Russell
G. Benjamin, Hastings North [2]
J. H. Cameron, Peel
M. C. Cameron, Ontario North
J. Carling, London [2]
W. Clarke, Wellington North
J. Cockburn, Northumberland West
J. Crawford, Toronto East
T. R. Ferguson, Simcoe South [2]
F. W. Haultain, Peterborough
A. F. Hooper, Lennox & Addington
F. Jones, Leeds & Grenville North
G. Macbeth, Elgin West [2]
H. W. McCann, Prescott [2]
J. A. Macdonald, Kingston [2]
A. Morris, Lanark South
J. Morton, Frontenac
M. B. Portman, Middlesex East
W. F. Powell, Carleton [2]
J. B. Robinson, Toronto West [2]
J. S. Ross, Dundas
W. Ryerson, Brant West
R. W. Scott, Ottawa City [2]
G. Sherwood, Brockville [2]
J. Simpson, Niagara [2]
T. C. Street, Welland
B. Tett, Leeds South [2]
A. Walsh, Norfolk

29

Rouges and Liberals (Canada East) (Includes C, Fig. Vk):
J. J. C. Abbott, Argenteuil [2]
A. A. Archambault, L'Assomption
F. Bourassa, St. John's [2]
J. O. Bureau, Napierville [2]
J. B. E. Dorion, Drummond & Arthabaska
L. T. Drummond, Rouville [2]
A. Dufresne, Iberville
F. Evanturel, Quebec County
J. P. Falkner, Hochelaga
M. Fortier, Yamaska
L. S. Huntington, Shefford
N. Hébert, Megantic [2]
P. G. Huot, Quebec City East [2]
J. H. Jobin, Joliette [2]
H. G. Joly, Lotbinière
A. E. Kierskowski, Verchères
L. Labrèche, Terrebonne
M. Laframboise, Bagot [2]
T. D. McGee, Montreal West [2]
J. O'Halloran, Missisquoi
E. Rémillard, Bellechasse
L. V. Sicotte, St. Hyacinthe
H. Starnes, Châteauguay

23

Independent Liberal (Canada East); voted in favour of the Militia Bill, May 20, 1862 (D, Fig. Vk):
R. B. Somerville, Huntingdon [2]

1

Bleus (Canada East); voted against the Militia Bill, May 20, 1862, but subsequently opposed the Liberal Government (G, Fig. Vk):
J. O. Beaubien, Montmagny [2]
J. Beaudreau, Richelieu
J. D. Brousseau, Portneuf
J. B. Daoust, Two Mountains [2]
P. E. Dostaler, Berthier
C. F. Fournier, L'Islet [2]
J. Gaudet, Nicolet [2]
J. B. Mongenais, Vaudreuil [2]
J. J. Ross, Champlain
G. H. Simard, Quebec City West [2]
H. E. Taschereau, Beauce

11

Coalition Reformers (Canada West) (B, Fig. Vk):
I. Buchanan, Hamilton [2]
J. W. Dunsford, Victoria
G. Jackson, Grey
D. McLachlin, Renfrew
A. Morrison, Simcoe North [2]
J. C. Rykert, Lincoln [2]

6

Conservatives (Canada East):
C. Alleyn, Quebec City Centre [2]
C. Dunkin, Brome [2]
A. T. Galt, Sherbrooke [2]
A. Knight, Stanstead
J. H. Pope, Compton [2]
J. Rose, Montreal Centre [2]

Members who later supported the Liberal Government:
W. M. Dawson, Ottawa County [2]
D. E. Price, Chicoutimi & Saguenay [2]

8

Independents (Canada East) (E, Fig. Vk):
C. Boucher de Boucherville, Chambly
T. J. J. Loranger, Laprairie

2

Moderates (Canada East); voted in favour of the Militia Bill, May 20, 1862 (F, Fig. Vk):
A. Gagnon, Charlevoix
J. B. J. Prévost, Soulanges
G. Sylvain, Rimouski

3

Bleus (Canada East):
M. W. Baby, Temiscouata [2]
J. G. Blanchet, Levis
G. Caron, Maskinongé [2]
G. E. Cartier, Montreal East [2]
J. Cauchon, Montmorency [2]
J. C. Chapais, Kamouraska [2]
C. DeCazes, Richmond & Wolfe
P. Denis, Beauharnois
L. L. L. Desaulniers, St. Maurice [2]
J. Dufresne, Montcalm [2]
H. L. Langevin, Dorchester [2]
J. LeBoutillier, Gaspé [2]
L. S. Morin, Laval [2]
J. Poupore, Pontiac
T. Robitaille, Bonaventure
F. Z. Tassé, Jacques Cartier

16

Speaker: J. E. Turcotte, Three Rivers

Vacant: Perth

2

Notes:
[1] Members of the Liberal-Conservative cabinet down to May 23, 1862, and the members of the Liberal cabinet which was formed on May 24 in italic.
[2] Member in same alignment at the close of the sixth parliament.

TABLE 18
EIGHTH PARLIAMENT, 1863–4: BASIC ALIGNMENT [1]

LIBERALS		LIBERAL-CONSERVATIVES

Liberals (Canada West) (Includes A, B, Fig. VI):
S. Ault, Stormont [5,7]
R. Bell, Lanark North [5,7]
J. L. Biggar, Northumberland East [5,7]
I. E. Bowman, Waterloo North [5]
G. Brown, Oxford South [5,7]
L. Burwell, Elgin East [5,7]
F. H. Chambers, Brockville [5]
J. Cowan, Waterloo South [5]
J. Dickson, Huron & Bruce [5,7]
J. W. Dunsford, Victoria [5,7]
W. P. Howland, York West [2,5,7]
D. A. Macdonald, Glengarry [5,6,7]
J. Macdonald, Toronto West [5,6]
J. S. Macdonald, Cornwall [2,6,7]
R. Macfarlane, Perth [5]
A. MacKenzie, Lambton [5,7]
H. F. MacKenzie, Oxford North [5]
T. D. McConkey, Simcoe North [5]
W. McDougall, Ontario North [5,7]
W. McGiverin, Lincoln [5]
R. McIntyre, Renfrew [5]
A. McKellar, Kent [5,7]
O. Mowat, Ontario South [2,5,7]
H. Munro, Durham West [5,7]
W. Notman, Wentworth North [5,7]
T. S. Parker, Wellington North [5]
A. Rankin, Essex
(*A. N. Richards*, Leeds South) [2]
W. Ross, Prince Edward [5]
J. Rymal, Wentworth South [5,6,7]
T. Scatcherd, Middlesex West [5,6,7]
J. Scoble, Elgin West [5,7]
A. M. Smith, Toronto East [5]
J. S. Smith, Durham East [5]
D. Stirton, Wellington South [5,7]
D. Thompson, Haldimand [5]
T. C. Wallbridge, Hastings North [5,6]
J. P. Wells, York North [5]
J. White, Halton [5,7]
E. B. Wood, Brant West
Amos Wright, York East [5,7]

40

Moderate (Canada West); Passed from Liberals to Liberal-Conservatives in September 1863:
J. Y. Bown, Brant East [4,5]

1

Ex-Liberal Minister (Canada West); opposed Liberals Aug. 29, 1863; supported Liberals Sept. 18, 1863; supported Liberals Oct. 8, 1863; joined Liberal-Conservatives and became Cabinet Member Mar. 30, 1864; (C, Fig. VI):
(*M. H. Foley*, Waterloo North) [3,4]

Conservatives (Canada West):
R. Bell, Russell [7]
J. H. Cameron, Peel [7]
J. Carling, London [5,7]
R. J. Cartwright, Lennox & Addington [5]
J. Cockburn, Northumberland West [3,5,7]
W. S. Conger, Peterborough [5]
J. M. Currier, Ottawa City
W. Ferguson, Frontenac
T. R. Ferguson, Simcoe South [5,7]
T. Higginson, Prescott [5]
D. F. Jones, Leeds South
F. Jones, Leeds & Grenville North [7]
J. A. Macdonald, Kingston [3,7]
A. Morris, Lanark South [5,7]
W. F. Powell, Carleton [5,7]
J. S. Ross, Dundas [7]
W. Shanley, Grenville South
J. Simpson, Niagara [3,7]
T. C. Street, Welland [5,7]
A. Walsh, Norfolk [5,7]
C. Willson, Middlesex East [5]

21

Reformers (Canada West); (C, Fig. VI):
I. Buchanan, Hamilton [3,5]
G. Jackson, Grey [5,7]

2

Ex-Liberal Ministers (Canada East):
J. J. C. Abbott, Argenteuil [4]
F. Evanturel, Quebec County [4]
T. D. McGee, Montreal West [3,4]
L. V. Sicotte, St. Hyacinthe [4]

3

Rouges & Liberals (Canada East):
F. Bourassa, St. John's [6,7]
L. B. Caron, L'Islet [6,7]
S. Coupal dit LaReine, Napierville [6]
A. A. Dorion, Hochelaga [2,6,7]
J. B. E. Dorion, Drummond & Arthabaska [6,7]
A. Dufresne, Iberville [6,7]
M. Fortier, Yamaska [6,7]
A. Gagnon, Charlevoix [6,7]
F. Geoffrion, Verchères [6]
L. H. Holton, Châteauguay [6]
M. Houde, Maskinongé [6]
L. S. Huntington, Shefford [2,6,7]
P. G. Huot, Quebec City East [7]
H. G. Joly, Lotbinière [6,7]
L. Labrèche-Viger, Terrebonne [6,7]
M. Laframboise, Bagot [2,6,7]
C. Lajoie, St. Maurice [6]
J. O'Halloran, Missisquoi [6,7]
A. H. Pâquet, Berthier [6]
J. F. Perrault, Richelieu [6]
J. B. Pouliot, Temiscouata [6]
E. Rémillard, Bellechasse [7]
R. B. Somerville, Huntingdon [5,7]
I. Thibaudeau, Quebec City Centre [2,6]

24

Bleu (Canada East); voted with Liberals Aug. 29, 1863:
J. N. Poulin, Rouville

1

Moderate (Canada East); passed from Liberals to Liberal-Conservatives in April 1864:
G. Sylvain, Rimouski [4]

1

Moderate (Canada East): passed into opposition to Taché-Macdonald Ministry prior to June 14, 1864:
C. Dunkin, Brome [6]

1

Bleus (Canada East):
L. Archambault, L'Assomption
J. O. Beaubien, Montmagny [7]
J. H. Bellerose, Laval
J. G. Blanchet, Levis [7]
J. D. Brousseau, Portneuf [7]
G. E. Cartier, Montreal East [3,7]
J. Cauchon, Montmorency [7]
J. C. Chapais, Kamouraska [3,7]
H. Cornellier dit Grandchamp, Joliette
J. B. Daoust, Two Mountains [7]
C. B. DeBoucherville, Chambly [7]
P. Denis, Beauharnois [7]
J. Dufresne, Montcalm [7]
J. Gaudet, Nicolet [7]
H. L. Langevin, Dorchester [3,7]
J. LeBoutillier, Gaspé [7]
A. Pinsonneault, Laprairie [6,7]
J. Poupore, Pontiac [7]
R. Raymond, St. Hyacinthe
T. Robitaille, Bonaventure [7]
J. J. Ross, Champlain [7]
H. E. Taschereau, Beauce [6]
F. Z. Tassé, Jacques Cartier [7]
J. E. Turcotte, Three Rivers [7]

2

Speaker: L. Wallbridge (Liberal), Hastings South   1

Notes
[1] Names of members of the governments in italic.
[2] Member of the Macdonald-Dorion government.
[3] Member of the Taché-Macdonald government.
[4] Member who had supported Macdonald-Sicotte ministry in the seventh parliament, now voting with Liberal-Conservatives.
[5] Member who had divided at least once in favour of the principle of "representation by population" in the eighth parliament.
[6] Opposed Confederation Mar. 11, 1865.
[7] Member in the same alignment at the close of the seventh parliament.
Brackets are used to indicate the following: Waterloo North — Bowman vice Foley; Leeds South — Jones vice Richards; St. Hyacinthe — Raymond vice Sicotte. Members returned in by-elections after June 30, 1864, are not shown.

Conservatives (Canada East):
C. Alleyn, Quebec City West [7]
W. Duckett, Soulanges
A. T. Galt, Sherbrooke [3,7]
A. D. C. Harwood, Vaudreuil
G. Irvine, Megantic
A. Knight, Stanstead [7]
J. H. Pope, Compton [7]
D. E. Price, Chicoutimi & Saguenay [4]
J. Rose, Montreal Centre [7]
W. H. Webb, Richmond & Wolfe
Alonzo Wright, Ottawa County

11

TABLE 19
EIGHTH PARLIAMENT, 1864–6: COALITION AND LATER STAGES

OPPOSED TO CONFEDERATION | **SUPPORTERS OF THE COALITION GOVERNMENT** [1]

OPPOSED TO CONFEDERATION

Liberals (Canada West); opposed Confederation (A, Fig. VI):
J. L. Biggar, Northumberland East
D. A. Macdonald, Glengarry
J. Macdonald, Toronto West
J. S. Macdonald, Cornwall
J. Rymal, Wentworth South
T. Scatcherd, Middlesex West
T. C. Wallbridge, Hastings North
　　　　7

Conservative (Canada West); opposed Confederation:
M. C. Cameron, Ontario North [3]
　　　　1

Rouges and Liberals (Canada East); opposed Confederation and the Coalition Government:
F. Bourassa, St. John's
L. B. Caron, L'Islet
S. Coupal, Napierville
A. A. Dorion, Hochelaga
J. B. E. Dorion, Drummond & Arthabaska
A. Dufresne, Iberville
M. Fortier, Yamaska
A. Gagnon, Charlevoix
F. Geoffrion, Verchères
L. H. Holton, Châteauguay
M. Houde, Maskinongé
L. S. Huntington, Shefford
H. G. Loly, Lotbinière
L. Labrèche-Viger, Terrebonne
M. Laframboise, Bagot
C. Lajoie, St. Maurice
J. O'Halloran, Missisquoi
A. H. Pâquet, Berthier
J. F. Perrault, Richelieu
J. B. Pouliot, Temiscouata
I. Thibaudeau, Quebec City Centre
　　　　21

Conservatives (Canada East); opposed Confederation in 1865 but voted as Conservatives thereafter (D, Fig. VI):
C. Dunkin, Brome [2]
W. Duckett, Soulanges
　　　　2

Bleus (Canada East); opposed Confederation in 1865 (D, Fig. VI):
A. Pinsonneault, Laprairie
H. E. Taschereau, Beauce
　　　　2

Speaker: L. Wallbridge (Liberal), Hastings South
　　　　1

SUPPORTERS OF THE COALITION GOVERNMENT

Liberals (Canada West); supported the Coalition, 1864:
S. Ault, Stormont
I. E. Bowman, Waterloo North [3]
F. H. Chambers, Brockville
J. Cowan, Waterloo South
J. Dickson, Huron & Bruce
J. W. Dunsford, Victoria
W. P. Howland, York West
R. Macfarlane, Perth
H. F. Mackenzie, Oxford North [1]
T. D. McConkey, Simcoe North
W. McDougall, Lanark North
W. McGiverin, Lincoln
R. McIntyre, Renfrew
J. McMonies, Wentworth North [3,5]
A. Rankin, Essex
J. Scoble, Elgin West
A. M. Smith, Toronto East
J. S. Smith, Durham East
D. Stirton, Wellington South
D. Thompson, Haldimand
J. White, Halton
E. B. Wood, Brant West
Amos Wright, York East
　　　　22

Liberals (Canada West); supported the Coalition, 1864, but were returning to Opposition in 1866; (B, Fig. VI):
G. Brown, Oxford South
L. Burwell, Elgin East
A. Mackenzie, Lambton
A. McKellar, Kent
H. Munro, Durham West
T. Oliver, Oxford North [3,4]
T. S. Parker, Wellington North
W. Ross, Prince Edward
J. P. Wells, York North
　　　　9

Liberals (Canada East); supported Confederation and the Coalition Government:
F. Evanturel, Quebec County
P. G. Huot, Quebec City East
E. Rémillard, Bellechasse
P. A. Tremblay, Chicoutimi & Saguenay [3]
　　　　4

Bleu Independents (Canada East); though voting usually as Bleus, they did vote for some liberal motions:
H. Cornellier, Joliette
J. Gaudet, Nicolet
　　　　2

Liberal Independent (Canada East); absent much of 1865, 1866 Sessions (D, Fig. VI):
J. J. C. Abbott, Argenteuil [2]
　　　　1

(continued)

Conservatives (Canada West):
R. Bell, Russell
J. Y. Bown, Brant East
J. H. Cameron, Peel
J. Carling, London
R. J. Cartwright, Lennox & Addington
J. Cockburn, Northumberland West
J. M. Currier, Ottawa City
W. Ferguson, Frontenac
T. R. Ferguson, Simcoe South
T. N. Gibbs, Ontario South [3]
T. Higginson, Prescott
D. F. Jones, Leeds South
F. Jones, Leeds & Grenville North
J. A. Macdonald, Kingston
A. Morris, Lanark South
W. F. Powell, Carleton
J. S. Ross, Dundas
W. Shanley, Grenville South
T. C. Street, Welland
A. Walsh, Norfolk
C. Wilson, Middlesex East
　　　● 21

Reformers (Canada West); supported Confederation and Coalition of 1864, but supported more liberal motions than Conservatives. (C, Fig. VI):
F. W. Haultain, Peterborough [3]
G. Jackson, Grey
C. Magill, Hamilton [3]
A. Morrison, Niagara [3]
　　　　4

Bleus (Canada East):
L. Archambault, L'Assomption
J. O. Beaubien, Montmagny
J. H. Bellerose, Laval
J. G. Blanchet, Levis
J. D. Brousseau, Portneuf
G. E. Cartier, Montreal East
J. Cauchon, Montmorency
J. C. Chapais, Kamouraska
J. B. Daoust, Two Mountains
C. B. de Boucherville, Chambly
C. B. de Niverville, Three Rivers [3]
P. Denis, Beauharnois
J. Dufresne, Montcalm
G. G. Gaucher, Jacques Cartier [3]
H. L. Langevin, Dorchester
J. LeBoutillier, Gaspé
J. N. Poulin, Rouville
J. Poupore, Pontiac
R. Raymond, St. Hyacinthe
T. Robitaille, Bonaventure
J. J. Ross, Champlain
G. Sylvain, Rimouski
　　　　22

Conservatives (Canada East):
C. Alleyn, Quebec City West
A. T. Galt, Sherbrooke
A. D. C. Harwood, Vaudreuil
G. Irwine, Megantic
A. Knight, Stanstead
T. D. McGee, Montreal West
J. H. Pope, Compton
J. Rose, Montreal Centre
W. H. Webb, Richmond & Wolfe
Alonzo Wright, Ottawa County
　　　　10

Independent (Canada East); though liberal in view, supported Confederation. (D, Fig. VI):
R. B. Somerville, Huntingdon
　　　　1

Notes:
1 Names of members of Coalition government in italic.
2 Member absent from Confederation division Mar. 11, 1865.
3 Returned at by-elections since 1864.
4 Oxford North: H. F. Mackenzie voted for Confederation but died in June 1866. T. Oliver elected in his place.
5 Wentworth North: W. Notman was absent from the House in 1865, and died. J. McMonies elected in his place.

INDEX

(The names of all members of the Legislative Assembly appear in the appropriate tables and figures. Parliaments in which a member sat are indicated after his name in this Index, followed by page numbers if mentioned in the text, otherwise in parentheses. Separate page numbers indicate general text references.)